GENOCIDE AFTER EMOTION

The failure of the major Western superpowers to adequately respond to the genocide in the Balkan Wars constitutes a major moral and political scandal. *Genocide After Emotion* offers a new sociological concept, postemotionalism, as an explanation for this confused response of the West. Offered as an alternative to postmodernism, postemotionalism refers to the culture industry's manipulation of emotionally charged historical events and phenomena to create the puzzling international interplay of images and other "collective representations" pertaining to the current Balkan War.

Genocide After Emotion debunks and demystifies the postemotional perception of the current Balkan War. It documents:

- How and why the Croat–Serb war of 1991 really began.
- What a rational, *non*-postemotional solution to this Balkan crisis would be.
- The bias in the American media's presentation of the current Balkan War.
- Belgrade's psychological, financial and social preparation of war that began with the demise of communism.
- The irrationalities of the United States, British and French policies toward the Balkans.
- That Britain has learned from the Balkan Crises of 1876 to support the strongest force in any Balkan dispute regardless of whose position is just.
- How Italy has succeeded in glossing over is fascist past, being admitted into the community of civilized nations whilst Croatia has failed to overcome its Ustasha episode.
- Israeli media sympathy for Serbia in the context of the meaning of the Holocaust for Israeli society.

The book contains contributions by Philip J. Cohen, Norman Cigar, Slaven Letica, James J. Sadkovich, C. G. Schoenfeld, Thomas Cushman and Igor Primoratz.

Stjepan G. Meštrović is Professor of Sociology at Texas A&M University.

GENOCIDE AFTER EMOTION

The Postemotional Balkan War

Edited by Stjepan G. Meštrović

London and New York

First published 1996
by Routledge
11 New Fetter Lane, London EC4P 4EE

Simultaneously published in the USA and Canada
by Routledge
29 West 35th Street, New York, NY 10001

Typeset in Garamond by LaserScript, Mitcham, Surrey
Printed and bound in Great Britain by
Clays Ltd, St. Ives PLC

British Library Cataloguing in Publication Data
A catalogue record for this book is available from the British Library

Library of Congress Cataloging in Publication Data
A catalogue record for this book has been requested

ISBN 0–415–12293–7 (hbk)
ISBN 0–415–12294–5 (pbk)

To my mother

CONTENTS

CONTRIBUTORS

Stjepan G. Meštrović is Professor of Sociology at Texas A&M University. His other books on the current Balkan War are *Road From Paradise* (1993), *Habits of the Balkan Heart* (1993) and *The Balkanization of the West* (1994).

Philip J. Cohen, MD, was drawn toward the former Yugoslavia by the deeply disturbing rhetoric emanating from Belgrade that "all Serbs must live in one country," an idea reminiscent of Nazi rhetoric of 1938. His book, *Serbia at War With History* is being published by Texas A&M University (1996).

Norman Cigar was educated at Oxford University and is Professor of National Security Studies at the US Marine Corps School of Advanced Warfighting in Quantico, Virginia. His most recent book is *Genocide in Bosnia: The Policy of Ethnic Cleansing* (1995).

Slaven Letica is Professor and Head of the Department of Medical Sociology and Health Economics at the University of Zagreb Medical School. Author of numerous articles on the current Balkan War, his books include *The Fourth Yugoslavia* (1991) and *Intellectuals and Crisis* (1992).

James J. Sadkovich is Associate Professor of History at the American University in Bulgaria. He is widely published in scholarly journals on the topics of fascism and the history of World War II.

C. G. Schoenfeld has a BA from Yale University, an LLB from the Harvard Law School, and an LLM from New York University. He is the Book Section editor of the *Journal of Psychiatry and Law* and is a frequent contributor to various legal and psychiatric journals. He is the author of *Psychoanalysis and the Law* (1973) and of *Psychoanalysis Applied to the Law* (1984).

Thomas Cushman is Associate Professor and Chair of Sociology at Wellesley College and a Fellow of the Harvard Russian Research Center. He is the author, most recently, of *Notes From Underground: Rock Music Counterculture in Russia* (1995) and is currently at work on a book which explores the political involvement of physicians in postcommunist Croatia.

Igor Primoratz is Associate Professor of Philosophy at the Hebrew University in Jerusalem. In the 1970s and early 1980s he taught at the

University of Belgrade. His published work includes *Banquo's Geist. Hegels Theorie der Strafe* (1986) and *Justifying Legal Punishment* (1989).

PREFACE

In my *Balkanization of the West*, published by Routledge in 1994, I argued that ominous signs exist suggesting that despite the rhetoric of democracy and capitalism spreading to the former communist world, the rest of the world will become "Balkanized," e.g., it will splinter into ever-smaller units that are hostile to each other. The present volume may be read as an extension of this argument. Illustrative examples abound, from the Oklahoma City bombing in the United States of America on 20 April 1995, which uncovered widespread hatred of the federal government, to the divisions and fractures within the United Nations, the European Community, the North American Free Trade Agreement (NAFTA) countries, and many other units that were supposed to foster globalization and free markets. In the present volume, I introduce the theoretical concept, postemotionalism, in order to begin to remedy the failure of the most recent social theory, postmodernism, to account for these disturbing developments. Postmodernism promised tolerance and a "salad-bowl" model of multicultural diversity that was supposed to replace modernist assimilation, but ethnic strife, not tolerance, seems to be increasing in the 1990s. Postmodernism reduced the world to a cognitive text of rational media images, but failed to account for the power of emotions. Most important, postmodernism has vanquished Enlightenment-based rationalism and left democracy without secure philosophical foundations. The net result of these developments has been that since the end of the cold war, genocide in the former Yugoslavia has been continuing in full view of the enlightened, informed, democratic nation-states. These democracies and their many security arrangements seem impotent in the face of the genocide in the former Yugoslavia. As a result, a cultural climate has been established in which ethnic strife and genocide are becoming increasingly more likely world-wide, and especially in the former Soviet Union.

ACKNOWLEDGEMENTS

I would like to thank Joanne Trgovchich for organizing a conference in May of 1993 at the University of North Carolina at Chapel Hill in which several of the contributors to this volume – Cohen, Sadkovich, Letica, and Meštrović – presented papers and established contact with each other. Thanks also to Chris Rojek for his early support of this project.

Three of the contributing authors would like to acknowledge that various portions of their arguments in the present volume are found in previous journal articles: Norman Cigar in the *Journal of Strategic Studies*, vol. 16, no. 3, September 1993: 297–338; Philip J. Cohen in the *Pace International Law Review*, vol. 6, no. 1, Winter 1994: 19–40; and Stjepan G. Meštrović in *Society*, vol. 32, no. 2, January/February 1995: 69–77.

1

INTRODUCTION

Stjepan G. Meštrović

The current Balkan War is continuing in its fifth year as I write, and according to many of the world's respected fact-gathering organizations, it involves genocide. Yet, despite widespread media coverage – second in scope only to the media's coverage of the O. J. Simpson trial – many professionals as well as laypersons remain confused about the basics of this war: who started it and why, who is most culpable, whether it involves genocide, and how it can be stopped. For example, the acts that many regard as genocidal have been referred to typically with the euphemism, "ethnic cleansing." Even with this change of terminology, "the CIA has concluded that 90% of the acts of 'ethnic cleansing' were carried out by Serbs and that leading Serbian politicians almost certainly played a role in the crimes" (*The New York Times* 9 March 1995: A1). Despite this and similar findings, most Western diplomats continue, as of this writing, to negotiate with the suspected war criminals and the Serbian leaders Slobodan Milošević and Radovan Karadžić. Similarly, despite almost daily reports of Belgrade-sponsored crimes against humanity, the Serbian aim of establishing an ethnically pure Greater Serbia enjoys implicit sympathy from many Westerners who agree that even those Serbs who act as victimizers should be perceived primarily as victims.[1] The projected sense of victimization stems from quasi-historical arguments in which the Serbs are portrayed as victims of World War II Croatian Ustashe and further back in history, of the Ottoman Turks. Rarely if ever is the question raised by diplomats, journalists, or opinion-makers whether the rationalizations for a contemporary Belgrade-sponsored genocidal war of revenge for past wrongs should even be admitted into discourse concerning this Balkan War.

Thus, Anthony Lewis quotes Radovan Karadžić, leader of the Bosnian Serbs as saying: "If you continue to talk about the moral danger that Serbs are under in Bosnia, you will end up committing preemptive genocide."[2] Even Mr. Lewis, who is among the most outspoken critics of the Serbs, grants Mr. Karadžić a tiny benefit of the doubt by adding that "history – that is, the Nazi creation of a fascist Croatia during World War II – did make the

1

German role in 1991–2 a provocation to the Serbs, even a spark for paranoia."[3] The strange implication seems to be that Belgrade-sponsored crimes *in Bosnia* in the 1990s are somehow understandable because of Zagreb-sponsored crimes *in Croatia* from World War II.

Our aim in this book is to offer a scholarly analysis of this and related modes of apprehending and conceptualizing the current Balkan War. We shall introduce a new theoretical concept, postemotionalism, as an improvement on postmodernism in order to highlight how the central feature of perceiving the current Balkan War has been the obfuscation of facts through the use of displaced emotions from history. However, because this book – ostensibly about the current Balkan War and its attendant genocide – involves highly sensitive and emotional issues for many varieties of potential readers, it is necessary to include a number of disclaimers from the outset:

1   It is not a book about the "real" Balkan *War* but about perceptions, images, and collective representations concerning this war. Hence, it falls into the domain of cultural studies. Douglas Kellner's *The Persian Gulf TV War*[4] might serve as a point for comparison. The present study might also be compared with Noam Chomsky and Edward S. Herman's study of the Western media's role in propaganda concerning wars in Vietnam and Nicaragua.[5]

2   It is not a book about the current *Balkan* War because it involves the international coverage of this war as it has entered living rooms, via television, in Canada, the USA, Britain, France, and many other non-Balkan countries. Thanks to CNN, the Balkans are no longer confined to the Balkans, but are everywhere. And because so many nations, religions, cultural groups, and organizations hold expressed interests in the Balkans – from Britain and Russia to Malaysia, from Islam to Orthodoxy, from Europe to the USA, from NATO to the UN – the Balkans have become internationalized, symbolically speaking.

3   It is not really a book even about the "current Balkan War" because this particular war has not been named, and is sometimes referred to as a series of wars (Serbia against Slovenia; Serbia against Croatia; Serbia against Bosnia) and even wars within wars (Serbs, Croats, Muslims against each other within Bosnia; Bosnian Serbs, Croatian Serbs, and Serbian Serbs sometimes acting with the same plan for a Greater Serbia, and other times perceived to act at cross purposes). Complicating this already confusing state of affairs, the Pulitzer Prize winner and journalist, Roy Gutman, has paraphrased Dzemal Sokolović: "World War II began with a declaration of war and ended with genocide as a byproduct, but this genocide in Bosnia was the immediate aim, and the war was the consequence of the crime, not the cause."[6] Nor is it clear when this war began, in 1991 with Serbia's attack on Slovenia, or

earlier, in 1989, when Serbian President Slobodan Milošević ended the constitutional autonomy of Kosovo. For the sake of convenience, some of the authors use the term the "current Balkan War" to refer broadly to the conflict that began with the Serbian attack on Slovenia in June of 1991, and that continues, in one form or another, to the present. Other authors address different aspects of this war, such as the conflict between Croatia and Serbia. But the intent of the book is to explore the difficulties in finding conceptual boundaries to this/these war/wars, not to arrive at a neat, tidy, modernist set of distinctions.

4   It is not really a book even about the current *series* of Balkan Wars, because the ghosts of several past wars and past events are constantly invoked by the media and by politicians in discussions of these wars, including but not limited to the Ustasha regime in World War II, the Battle of Kosovo in 1389, Serbia's role in World War II, Nazism, and so-called German expansionism, among other historical events and phenomena. To these phenomena we should add historical traumas and irrational myths that affect the behavior of nations that claim to want to help in the Balkans: The USA is still suffering from its Vietnam syndrome; Great Britain still operates on the principle of upholding a regional power (in this case, Serbia),[7] as it did in the Balkan Crisis of the 1870s and many other European crises;[8] and France still refuses to come to terms with Vichy, which calls into question which France (Allied or pro-Nazi) was "allied" with which Serbia (the Partisans, the Chetniks or the pro-Nazi groups?). These historical *relics* are often treated in Western discourse as if they existed in the *present*, so that "this Balkan War" or "these Balkan Wars" seem to take on a seemingly postmodern dimension that invokes huge chunks of European, Islamic, and other histories. Thus, it is worth repeating that Serbian aggression against the newly recognized nations that used to be former Yugoslav republics is often rationalized by Belgrade as an act of fear on the part of Serbs based on the actions of Croatian Ustashe in World War II and Islamic domination of the Balkans from 1389. Yet the media as well as governments in the US, France, and Britain accept these rationalizations rather uncritically, and do not confront the ghosts from their pasts that continue to haunt them.

5   This is an academic book even though it seems to tackle a "war in progress" for reasons cited above, and also because Zygmunt Bauman has already set the precedent in his *Modernity and the Holocaust*[9] as well as other books[10] for studying genocide as an issue in cultural studies. In addition, there is no real "end-point" to this contemporary instance of Balkan genocide nor any other instance of genocide, past or present (Rwandan, Armenian, Cambodian, the Holocaust, etc.) nor to any other event, such as the Vietnam war and World War II, whose histories continue to be revised. First, genocide and other events from

history are still being written about and "revised," including but not limited to the role of Vichy France[11] in the Holocaust, for example.[12] Second, the Kantian framework which operates in the Western university system precludes any final assessment of any phenomenon. All phenomena are in constant flux at all times, so that this book shall concentrate on one central aspect of this flux pertaining to this topic, namely, postemotionalism. The concept of postemotionalism was first used in conversation by Slaven Letica[13] and in print by Meštrović.[14] It will be used primarily in this introductory chapter to orient the analyses that follow. But even though postemotionalism is not used explicitly by all the contributors to this volume, it is implied by all of them, as the rest of this chapter will demonstrate.

6 Those academics who wait for this metaphorical war "to be over" so it can be studied might be accused, 50 years from now of the same charges that Bauman levels at those academics who waited for the outcome of the Holocaust 50 years ago. Given the neo-Kantian premise that the thing-in-itself is out of reach anyway, it would seem to be an exercise in futile pedantry to wait for the impossible "end" to this war so that it can be studied "objectively." Moreover, the cultural representations pertaining to this as to any other phenomena *are* in place, *can* be studied, and provide an interesting focus for students of cultural studies and postmodernism. Thus, all of the contributing authors to this volume analyze the representations of this war in the information media as refracted through various cultural prisms. A final note is Bauman's finding that sociologists have largely failed to study the Holocaust sociologically even after it was allegedly "over."

Thus, the crucial factor is to study genocide as an issue in cultural studies – in general, and specifically the current genocide instigated by the Belgrade regime against Muslims and Croats in the former Yugoslavia – not to seek a pseudo-scientific beginning or end to any particular instance of genocide.

7 In his book, *Genocide in Bosnia: The Policy of "Ethnic Cleansing,"*[15] Norman Cigar has established that genocide has, in fact, occurred in the current Balkan War. The information media has also documented that the current Belgrade regime is sponsoring genocide against Croats and Bosnian Muslims.[16] Perhaps most importantly, respected institutions such as the International Court of Justice in the Hague demanded in April of 1993 that Serbia and Montenegro take preventative measures to prevent *genocide* from occurring in Bosnia. On 13 February 1995, the newly established International War Crimes Tribunal in the Hague charged a Serb with genocide and crimes against humanity. The US State Department has also adopted the term "genocide," when describing events in Bosnia-Herzegovina in its recent human rights overview. Commenting on these findings, Roger Cohen writes in *The New York*

Times that "the overwhelming majority of crimes were committed by Serbs in an orchestrated campaign to eliminate Muslims from Serb- held territory" (24 April 1994: A1). The conference of the Commission on Security and Cooperation in Europe issued a statement on 4 April 1995 which quotes Chairman Chris Smith, Republican Congressman from New Jersey, as noting that "the State Department human rights report refers to genocide in Bosnia." Ranking Minority member Steny Hoyer commented: "Let us be very clear about the subject of our discussion here today – it is genocide disguised as war."

Rather than discuss how the concept of genocide as a term used in international law can be interpreted and misinterpreted in various ways, we make the sociological observation that the fact that respected institutions have arrived at this assessment itself constitutes a "social fact" (in Durkheim's terminology).[17] The more interesting aspect of this determination, from our point of view, then becomes that the issue of genocide has been intertwined postemotionally and erroneously with the Holocaust and other sites of genocide, thereby obfuscating the emotional and pragmatic reaction that a finding of genocide demands according to the UN Charter.

Thus, the Belgrade regime has repeatedly sought to portray Serbs as contemporary as well as historical victims of genocide on a par with the Holocaust. For example, Dan Morgan wrote in the *Washington Post* (19 June 1994: A14):

> Like the Jews, Serbs are unified by the memory of a glorious defeat. The Serbian Massada is the Battle of the Blackbird Fields in 1389 . . . Serbs experienced their own World War II holocaust at the hands of the Croatian Ustashe. . . . The Jewish analogy is a recurring theme in Belgrade conversations.

Similarly, an opinion piece in the *Houston Chronicle* (16 March 1995: 33A) asserts that:

> During the time when the world is remembering the fiftieth anniversary of the end of the Holocaust, it seems appropriate to remind the American public of an often overlooked fact: After the Jews and the Russians, the next largest group to suffer the most from genocide in World War II were the Serbs. . . . Just like the Jews, the Serbs vowed, Never Again! . . . Croatia is today involved in a repugnant historical revisionism and rehabilitation of its Nazi past.

In response to conceptual linkages such as the ones above, the editor and contributing authors to this book take the position that there have been and continue to be many sites of genocide, but that there was only one Holocaust. We agree with Horowitz that any other position on this connection invites each victimized group to be able to claim the status of Holocaust as a badge of honor.[18] We disagree with those who use the refrain "Never Again!" with regard to either Serbs, as quoted above, or Serbia's victims, or any other sites of genocide.[19] Furthermore, there is no need to invoke the Holocaust in discussions of genocide concerning the current Balkan War, because no other instance of genocide can be reasonably compared with it.[20] The Holocaust is invoked in this book only to illustrate how the emotional energy of this event is misused by those who wish to make any number of postemotional points.

One such postemotional point is that since the genocide in Bosnia cannot compare quantitatively with the Holocaust, it does not need to be taken seriously. But the UN convention which outlawed genocide speaks of destroying or committing conspiracy to destroy, in whole or in part, a national, ethnic, racial, or religious group. The size of the group or the amount of destruction is not specified in the convention: what matters is the intentional and systematic attempt to destroy a group of people. Another issue has to do with the claims that since the Serbs were also the victims of genocide in the past, their contemporary genocidal actions are at least understandable. And, as Igor Primoratz demonstrates in his essay in the present volume, these postemotional arguments have hit their intended mark in Israel.[21] Against these interpretations, our position is that the crime of genocide needs to be determined solely on its merits and in its present context.

8 Despite the finding by the CIA and other organizations that the Serbs have committed the overwhelming amount of crime in the current Balkan War, some apologists have claimed that Croats and Muslims have committed similar crimes *qualitatively*. This is an illustration of the often-repeated argument that all sides are somehow equally guilty in the current Balkan War. In fact, Serbian atrocities in this war are qualitatively different from Croatian and Muslim atrocities. Writing on the previously cited CIA report, Roger Cohen notes in *The New York Times* (9 March 1995: A1):

> While war crimes were by no means committed exclusively by Serbs, they were the only party involved in a systematic attempt to eliminate all traces of other ethnic groups from their territory. . . . The report makes nonsense of the view – now consistently put forward by Western European governments and intermittently by the Clinton Administration – that the Bosnian conflict is a civil war for which guilt should be divided between Serbs, Croats and Muslims rather than a case of Serbian aggression. . . . "To those who think the parties are equally guilty, this report is pretty devastating," one official said. "The scale of what the Serbs did is so different. But more than that, it makes clear, with concrete evidence, that there

was a conscious, coherent, and systematic Serbian policy to get rid of Muslims, through murders, torture and imprisonment. Muslim and Croat actions lack the intensity, sustained orchestration and scale of what the Bosnian Serbs did."

Other respected fact-gathering organizations have arrived at similar assessments concerning both the quantity and quality of the war crimes ascribed to Serbs. Thus, the *Dallas Morning News* (22 March 1995: A12) reported that a United Nations study of rape in the current Balkan War found:

Patterns of Serb atrocities strongly suggest a systematic rape and sexual policy against Muslim women. . . . The commission confirmed previous reports that all sides have committed grave war crimes, including rape. But it explicitly rejected Serb contentions that all sides are comparably guilty. The vast majority of victims were Muslims, and only Serb nationalists committed rape as part of a comprehensive, countrywide scheme of terrorism known as ethnic cleansing. "It is clear," the panel wrote, "that there is no factual basis for arguing that there is a moral equivalence among the warring factions."

Similarly, in his book, *Serbia at War With History*, Philip J. Cohen reports that

As of June, 1993, the U.S. Department of State had submitted to the United Nations eight reports on atrocities and war crimes in former Yugoslavia . . . [and] 88% were attributable to Serbs, 7% to Bosnian Muslims, and 5% to Croats. . . . The most significant asymmetry, however, is that 100% of the *genocidal acts* in this war have been committed by Serbs, in accordance with Serbian policy. It is noteworthy that the Nuremberg trials distinguished between war crimes (something the Allies also did) and crimes against humanity and genocide (something which only the Nazis did).[22]

Thus, the reader should not misconstrue as polemical the position taken by this editor and the contributing authors that the Belgrade-sponsored regime is most responsible, quantitatively as well as qualitatively, for the crimes committed in the current Balkan War. This is a position based on data gathered by respected fact-gathering organizations. Moreover, I would point out that the determination by many to hold the position that all sides are somehow equally guilty is absurd even when applied to other wars. Thus, historians have documented that the Allies committed many and qualitatively horrendous war crimes during World War II, among them the British bombing of Dresden, the Allied fire-bombing of civilian targets such as Cologne, the fire-bombing of Japanese cities, and the dropping of the Atomic bomb on Hiroshima and Nagasaki, among others.[23] But no respectable historian or observer has concluded that because of these Allied war crimes, the Allies and the fascists are in any way morally equivalent.

9 During the 4 April 1995 CSCE hearing on genocide in Bosnia-Herzegovina, chairman Christopher Smith made the following statement:

> A recently released CIA report confirmed that Serb militants have been responsible for nearly 90% of the atrocities committed during Yugoslavia's violent break-up. Their crimes also were most likely to have been orchestrated, in order to carry out a policy directed from above. This does not translate into the popular notion that the Serbs are an evil people. . . . The deeds of Serbian political and military leaders, as carried out by their military minions, do not make Serbs collectively guilty.

We concur. The editor and contributing authors to this volume all regard themselves as children of the Enlightenment and do not subscribe to the doctrine of collective guilt with regard to Serbs or any other peoples. Where we refer to "Serbs" in discussions of atrocities we always mean specific individuals even when a precise designation such as "individual Serbs under orders from the Belgrade regime" would be cumbersome stylistically, although it is the designation that we intend.

At the same time, it is worth noting that this care not to ascribe collective guilt to the Serbs has never, to the best of my knowledge, been declared publicly with regard to either Croats or Bosnian Muslims.

10 This book is provocative and touches on emotionally charged issues, but does so in a standard, academic way: documentation, argumentation, and the use of established theory as context, all in the context of the newly proposed concept of postemotionalism. The issues of collective guilt, neo-Orwellian manipulation of emotional components of history, and failures to respond to documented genocide are important aspects of all the contributions to this volume. The authors recognize that many academicians shy away from writing about or otherwise addressing ongoing wars in general and the current Balkan War in particular in the interest of remaining value-free, neutral, and objective. Yet, nearly half a century of post-Holocaust consciousness raising has established that so-called neutrality with regard to genocide is not a true neutrality, but constitutes an implicit identification with the victimizer. Moreover, if academicians shun these topics for reasons stated above, then these issues will be addressed by nonacademic politicians, journalists, and opinion-makers anyway, and most likely in a less scientific and otherwise less satisfactory manner. In sum, high-caliber academic scholarship and emotionally charged, timely issues should not be necessarily incompatible.

A closely related paradox needs to be addressed: The twentieth century is the most positivistic and empirically oriented century in the history of humanity, yet this verifiable increase in positivism has been accompanied by a verifiable increase in historical revisionism in general, and Holocaust revisionism in particular. One might characterize revisionism as the leukemia of positivism,[24] the refusal by many to recognize the horrors of genocide in the twentieth century unless these horrors are perceived sensually. Eyewitness accounts from the Holocaust were treated by suspicion, but so were eyewitness accounts of genocide in Bosnia, and elsewhere, as argued by Pulitzer Prize winning journalist Roy Gutman in his book, *A Witness to Genocide*.[25] Clearly, in addition to empirical documentation, what is needed to make sense of genocide in the current *fin de siècle* is insight and theoretical astuteness in addition to positivistically oriented documentation.

11 Some might fear that the current Balkan war might soon be "over" and therefore this book will be obsolete. Again, several points above suggest that this and other genocidal wars are never "over" as phenomena: even in the 1990s, books are published on World War II, and often these books challenge received views and understandings. For example, French President François Mitterrand's Nazi collaboration during the Vichy regime has only recently been exposed, while the Nazi collaboration of Britain's Channel Islands is still awaiting in-depth analysis. Discussions of this sort question the neat and tidy division between "the Allies" and the Nazis that is still the staple of most academic as well as popular understandings of what happened in World War II. Indeed, the present volume will be relevant for many years to come precisely because it focusses on *postemotional* and *cultural* issues that often go back to World War II (and further back, to the Balkan Crisis of the 1870s, Italy's conquest of Ethiopia in 1935, the Spanish Civil War that began in 1936, and others) and that are refracted in the current Balkan War. Thus, in many ways, the quest for Greater Serbia might be regarded as a piece of unfinished business left over from World War II, World War I, and before that, the Balkan Wars of 1912 and 1913 and developments in Serbia in the nineteenth century, as argued by both Norman Cigar and Philip J. Cohen. Serbian-sponsored "ethnic cleansing" was an important aspect of all these wars. The many references in the media to France, Britain, and Serbia as former "allies" really call into question both historical accuracy and the role of France and Britain in this contemporary Balkan War.[26]

12 There is a need to address the *philosophical* issue concerning the claim, now repeated, that this is not a partisan book for placing most of the blame for the current war onto the Belgrade regime[27] because this is the general finding of the world's respected fact-gathering organizations.[28] Even if circumstances change and Belgrade's victims turn out

to be blamed as much or more in the future than Belgrade, the fact that most blame has been attributed to Belgrade from 1991 to 1995 at the same time that many Western nations are sympathetic to Belgrade's rationalizations for waging a war of aggression against its neighbors (that it fears Muslims and Croats based on what happened in history), will hold because it has been documented scrupulously by the media as well as respected international fact-gathering organizations. The findings by such organizations as Helsinki Watch, the CIA and the US State Department, among others, can be challenged, as all neo-Kantian facts can be, and we do not mean to imply that the Belgrade regime can be studied as a thing-in-itself. Thus, some future revisionists might challenge the objectivity of the Helsinki Commission, the US State Department, the International Red Cross, or some other respected fact-gathering organization, perhaps even with good reason. Nevertheless, given Kantian and neo-Kantian caveats, the current findings that lay most of the blame for the current genocide in the former Yugoslavia on the Belgrade regime do exist, can be cited, and are generally respected in the Western world as being "objective." If one chooses not to rely on facts gathered by Helsinki Watch and other such reputable organizations, then one cannot enter into a discussion of this sort with even the slightest pretense of objectivity. To wait for some magical, pure moment of objectivity is to preclude the possibility of meaningful discourse.

13 Given that the information media as well as most respected fact-gathering organizations have placed most of the blame on the Serbs as the primary "bad guys" – to borrow an American colloquialism – in this Balkan War, some readers may wonder why so many of the contributors to this volume seem to be preoccupied with the demonization of Croatia and the Bosnian Muslims. In fact, these phenomena are not mutually exclusive. At the same time that Belgrade-sponsored terror and ethnic cleansing had been documented by Western journalists and governments, Croatia was demonized as an essentially Nazi nation while the Bosnian Muslims were consistently portrayed as harboring Islamic fundamentalist aims and as masochists who fired upon their own people in order to gain the world's sympathy.[29] Thus, the appropriate response to the frame of analysis, "Belgrade is the aggressor," was consistently muted by at least two other, major, competing frames of analysis, that the current Croatian regime is an extension of the Nazi Ustashe regime from World War II,[30] and that the Bosnian Muslims are desperate fundamentalists playing on the world's sympathy.[31] The existence of these competing frames, among others, is analyzed thoroughly by all the contributors to this volume, and helps to explain the world's paralysis and failure to respond to Belgrade-sponsored genocide.

THE THEORETICAL FRAMEWORK

The present book aims to introduce a new sociological concept – post-emotionalism – to help explain the puzzling international interplay of images and other "collective representations" pertaining to the current Balkan War *and* the response of the West to this war. *Postemotionalism* shall be treated as a concept somewhat related to *postmodernism*, with the difference that it refers to the manipulation of *emotionally* charged collective representations of "reality" on the part of the culture industry. Thus, a working definition of postemotionalism might be that it is a neo-Orwellian mechanism found in Western societies in which the culture industry markets and manipulates dead *emotions* from history that are selectively and synthetically attached to current events. This process complements the culture industry's manipulation of cognitive categories already described by Theodor Adorno[32] and the other critical theorists. Postemotionalism is related to a number of existing theoretical perspectives, including but not limited to the following: David Riesman's other-directed "inside dopester" portrayed in *The Lonely Crowd*;[33] as a posttherapeutic development of Philip Rieff's "therapeutic society;" the nostalgic return to an imaginary community of bygone days popularized by Robert N. Bellah in *Habits of the Heart*;[34] and as an elaboration of Jean Baudrillard's idea that postmodernists are living "after the orgy" of the 1960s;[35] and among many other related concepts. With regard to classical social theory, postemotionalism draws on Georg Simmel's blasé urbanite, Durkheim's exasperated anomic type, Veblen's member of the leisure class for whom emotions are a luxury item, and even Freud's writings. C. G. Schoenfeld's contribution to this volume is an excellent exposition of how psychoanalysis may be used to understand the strange emotional reactions by Balkan as well as Western protagonists in the drama of the current Balkan War.

It is beyond the scope of the present discussion to explore post-emotionalism as it pertains to phenomena not related to the current Balkan War. I will conduct such an analysis in a future sociological treatise on postemotionalism is general. But it is important to note here, albeit in passing, that the postemotionalism surrounding the current Balkan War would not be possible without a general climate of postemotionalism in the Western world. For example, the current controversies surrounding "affirmative action" in the United States center on the postemotional issue whether the majority population is collectively guilty to some extent for oppression committed by its ancestors against minorities, and should therefore try to redress past wrongs in the present. The famous O. J. Simpson trial has deflected attention away from the issue of Mr. Simpson's guilt or innocence to racism such that, somewhat ironically, the Los Angeles Police Department has been put on trial alongside Mr. Simpson. Even the bombing of Oklahoma City on 20 April 1995 became a postemotional issue

11

almost immediately by means of media investigations into the historical significance of this date for various militias, ranging from the burning of Lexington on 20 April 1775 to the attack on the Branch Davidians on 20 April 1993 (*The New York Times* 22 April 1995: A1). It is uncanny how 20 April has taken on the postemotional significance for many American militias comparable to the meaning of 26 June for many Serbian militias (the date of the Battle of Kosovo). These and many other examples illustrate the fluidity with which historical instances of perceived victimization are used to justify contemporary victimizing.

We shall leave open the question of whether this emotional manipulation is more the result of some kind of conspiracy among the Western media and Western governments or whether what the critical theorists called "mass society" has turned journalists, government officials, as well as the bulk of citizens, into conformist inside-dopesters (from Riesman) and passive consumers of events. One finds this debate in the works of Jean Baudrillard, Umberto Eco, David Riesman, Douglas Kellner, and other writers concerned with the role of the information media. In the second explanation, guilt at not acting to halt genocide might be construed as leading to self-justification and then to the media reporting to a public which does not want to get involved.[36] To repeat, this dilemma of interpretation is not peculiar to the present volume, but haunts the works of all the critical theorists as well as some so-called postmodernist writers. Perhaps the most reasonable explanation combines elements of both interpretations: there may exist a small core of prejudiced journalists and government officials who act as "shepherds" to a mass society of docile sheep that includes other journalists, government officials, and ordinary citizens. It seems as unreasonable to suppose that there is absolutely no prejudice among journalists in a social climate which treats many of them as celebrities and opinion-makers[37] as it is to assume that everyone is a conformist member of mass society (for in that case, where is the origin of the distorted images that are consumed?). We reserve a fuller explication of this important issue for future theory and research, because it is not central to our aims here. However, James Sadkovitch offers an important analysis of this issue in the present volume as it pertains to the current Balkan War.

More important, for the purposes of the present discussion, is the fact that the miracle of information technology – what US Vice-President Al Gore has dubbed the "information highway" – has made sure that nearly everyone in the contemporary world knows "what is going on." The new characterization to which we point is that postemotional society *knows* more information than it ever did before, but is not able to react quickly enough with the appropriate emotions. We shall decline to offer a "how to" solution to postemotionalism. This is not a cookbook. Our aim is to expose the problem, and to point to a unified rational-emotional alternative that is consistent with the West's Enlightenment tradition. How or whether this alternative can be attained is beyond the scope of our study.

As applied to the current Balkan War, the postemotional aspect stems from Serbian rationalizations that their genocidal actions arise from fear[38] based on what the Croats did to the Serbs in World War II, and what the Muslims did to them in 1389. Moreover, there is hardly any contemporary discussion of Serbian atrocities against Croats and Muslims in World War II – Serbs portray themselves strictly as victims.[39] These are historical events. Cynically, one might say that is a long time for some Serbs to hold a grudge. There are many other factors here that are equally postemotional. The USA, France, and Britain blame Germany for this war even though Branka Magas[40] has argued convincingly that the war actually began in 1989 when Slobodan Milošević declared Kosovo to be sacred Serbian soil. Germany came in very late into the conflict, in 1992, by pushing for the recognition of Croatia and Bosnia, but Germany has gotten all the blame from Secretary of State Warren Christopher,[41] and others. Contrary to Mr. Christopher, one could argue that the Belgrade regime had its own carefully planned goals pertaining to territorial aggrandizement and so-called ethnic cleansing unrelated to the issue of German diplomatic recognition of Croatia and Bosnia (see the contribution by Slaven Letica in this volume). The more important point is that the structuring or frame used for blaming Germany for this Balkan War bespeaks a historically grounded anti-German attitude found in Paris, London, and Washington, the very powers that kept Serbia's victims outgunned with a questionable weapons embargo. (Anti-German sentiment in the West was betrayed also during the recent D-Day fest which President Clinton attended, and from which Germany was excluded, despite all the talk of a united Europe.)[42]

There are even postemotional rationalizations for why the West would not stop the slaughter in the Balkans. The United States of America invokes the Vietnam syndrome, that its involvement would lead to another Vietnam "quagmire."[43] That is an interesting rationalization, *because it focusses sentiment on the past rather than the present*. Following the fall of communism, American foreign policy is consistently refracted through the collective memory of the humiliating loss in Vietnam,[44] the loss of meaning because of Vietnam, and the need now for short, winnable wars that do not involve many US casualties, symbolized by the Gulf War and the more recent invasion of Haiti in the Fall of 1994. Using the postemotional concept, one could argue that the Gulf War was not really a war for oil and not even a war for image:[45] It was a neat and tidy war, at least by American standards, designed to help Americans get over emotions left over from the Vietnam War. There are many other postemotions that are involved here. Anytime one attempts to grasp the meaning of this Balkan War, a historical phenomenon is invoked by journalists and agents of various governments.

A very important postemotional syndrome involves the British penchant for regional stability. In the Balkan Crisis of the 1870s, in which peasants rose up against the Ottomans, first in Bosnia and later in Bulgaria, Britain supported the brutal suppression of civilians by Turkey in the name of stability. Brendan Simms notes the parallel that, in the current Balkan War, Britain seems to be supporting Serbia's brutal suppression of Bosnian Muslims for the same reason. But, Simms adds, Britain took similar positions that supported the victimizer and hurt the victim in the Abyssinian War of 1935–7, the Spanish Civil War that began in 1936 (by imposing an arms embargo on all sides), and the infamous appeasement of Hitler in 1938. Is the British government still living, postemotionally, in the 1870s? In 1938? Moreover, Britain and France both seem to fear the contagion effect of Croatian and Bosnian secession from the former Yugoslavia for their internal colonies (Scotland, Northern Ireland, Corsica). Any number of other postemotional motives might have played a role in British and French politics toward the Balkans: the fear of how "bad" an example Croatia and Bosnia could set for African states, and in the British case, there was the anti-European card of ensuring that a Europe set for unification failed in its first major internal crisis.

US, British, French and other nations' postemotional reactions to Serbian genocidal aggression have synchronized with Serbia's own postemotional obsession with the past, especially *postemotional* fears of the World War II Croatian Ustashe[46] and the 1389 defeat to the Muslims at the Battle of Kosovo. Despite the unanimous assessment reached by Helsinki Watch, the US State Department, and other respected fact-gathering organizations that the Belgrade regime is overwhelmingly responsible for setting into motion the current genocidal aggression, public opinion in the West tends to be sympathetic to Serbian rationalizations that Belgrade acted out of fear based on historical events, and has tended to demonize Croatia primarily on the basis of the World War II Ustashe. But, it should be noted, America, France, Britain and other Western nations have been reluctant to confront their own postemotional obsessions. A latent form of anti-Islamic prejudice seems to be present in the West, such that the Bosnian Muslims are referred to as innocent victims, but are consistently accused of harboring fundamentalist aims, and are denied the right to self-defense.

The fact that the current Balkan War has received extensive media coverage while genocide in Cambodia, Angola, and elsewhere in the world has not received such coverage points to an implicit *Eurocentrism* in the media which is of concern to those engaged in the postmodernism discourse. This Eurocentrism might be explained with reference to a *postemotional*, albeit unconscious, assumption that Europe is "superior" to other continents – and to the Balkans – *vis-à-vis* civilization, and therefore genocide should not be occurring in Europe in the 1990s – yet it is. It might also be a variation of a more blatant white prejudice in the sense that the allegedly "tribal" Balkans are being equated with "tribal" Africa in the Euro-American collective consciousness. The term "tribalism" seems to be the most frequently used term by Western journalists, diplomats, and politicians who engage in discourse concerning the current Balkan War.

Postemotionalism holds more explanatory power than the now fashionable concept of postmodernism with regard to the enigma of how this Balkan War has paralyzed the UN, NATO, and a host of other security arrangements in Europe. Postmodernism refers to that broad intellectual movement that centers on nostalgia, the blurring of the distinction between fiction and reality, and other anti-modern tendencies.[47] But postmodernism, like modernism, reduces the world to a semiotic text that is apprehended cognitively.[48] By contrast, postemotionalism assumes that the world is a cognitive text as well as an emotional structure. Harking back to Schopenhauer,[49] one might paraphrase this difference between postmodernism and postemotionalism with the claim that the world is will (emotion) and idea (text). Thus, the phenomena described above are more than nostalgia; rather, they involve the transference of "dead emotions" from the past into the living present. Instead of the circulation of fictions described by postmodernists, it is more accurate to point to the coexistence of reality with emotionally charged "fictions." For example, Helsinki Watch reports that condemn Serbian aggression exist alongside sympathy for Serb fears of the Muslims and Croats. Thus, there appears to be a need to move beyond the parameters of postmodernism in cultural studies.

Most newsworthy events pertaining to this Balkan War hark back in a postemotional manner to the past. Thus, the best-selling diary by 13-year-old Zlatka Filipović (translated into 22 languages), which describes the hell of living during the Serbian siege of Sarajevo, has been compared to Anne Frank's diary:

> In a world numbed by television images of daily atrocities in Sarajevo, in a Western Europe racked by guilt over its failure to halt the 21 month old conflict in Bosnia, the voice of an innocent child still carries special weight. Her publisher has predictably proclaimed Miss Filipovic to be the Bosnian War's version of Anne Frank.
>
> (*The New York Times* 6 January 1994: A1)

Compare this reaction with the fact that Diždarević's *Sarajevo: A War Journal*[50] also received publicity, but not as much as this post-Anne Frank book. Such widespread collective displacement of emotions deserves sociological analysis.

A POSTEMOTIONAL WORLD

Let us return to Jean Baudrillard – frequently cited as the foremost postmodernist writer – and his observations that the Gulf War and Vietnam

War did not happen, that these and other postmodern wars are just fictions played out on the television screen.[51] This assessment will be used as a springboard for further discussion, but an attempt shall be made to supersede it: It is not enough to dismiss cruel wars as fictions, because, after all, *real* people continue to suffer and die in recent wars. The postmodern discourse, broadly speaking, fails to address this obvious point. Thus, the more interesting question becomes: why is it that the world's postmodern audience treats wars – current as well as past – *as if* they were fictions, but – and this is the gist of our new interpretation – fictions charged with emotionalism borrowed from the past? Thus, to summarize portions of the discussion thus far: the current Balkan War becomes, for the Americans, a potential "Vietnam Quagmire;" for the Serbs, revenge against "the Turks" for 1389 and a mythical quest for *Greater Serbia*; for the French and British, a revival of *German expansionism*; and for the Russians, another instance of the West maltreating their "little Slavic brothers," the Serbs.

Closely related issues include the following: are all wars equally fictitious in Baudrillard's sense, or is postmodern fictitiousness a function of television and virtual reality? Prior to television, were the Crusades or the plague also "fictions" in the sense of myths? Furthermore, how does one distinguish fiction from reality when it comes to the conceptualization of the current Balkan War? How has its "reality" been transformed into various metaphors, euphemisms, and fictions? Are these euphemisms really just "circulating fictions," as argued by Baudrillard, or do they make a kind of sense? Some of these metaphors, euphemisms, and fictions (all of which are emotionally laden) will be listed briefly – for the sake of illustration – including the following neo-Orwellian characterizations of the current Balkan War:

- the Bosnian Muslims as the new Palestinians;
- the Bosnian Muslims as Native Americans on reservations or "safe havens";
- "safe havens" overrun by Serbs;
- making "peace" in war zones merely by sending in unarmed "peace-keepers";
- the social construction of "humanitarian aid": sending the Bosnians war rations left over from the Gulf War and other specific foods, but not cigarettes (which they request), and not psychiatric help for their rape victims;
- "peace negotiations" versus terms of surrender;
- "all sides are equally guilty";
- Germany is largely responsible for the current Balkan War because of its "premature recognition" of the sovereignties of Slovenia and Croatia;
- the West is not "involved," despite the weapons embargo imposed by the West on Serbia's victims;

- "tribes" in Europe;
- this Balkan War is like a natural disaster that requires bureaucratic (UN) assistance, but there is no question of putting an end to the suffering once and for all;
- ethnic division as a problem in mathematics, proposed by the European Community. That is, the EC told the "warring parties" to divide Bosnia into certain percentages of Croats (17 percent), Muslims (30 percent) and Serbs (53 percent). But what about mixed marriages and mixed parents? What about the millions of people who do not fit this neat, mathematical formula?
- when the Serbs take UN peacekeepers as hostages, the UN explains that these are not real hostages, but persons whose "liberty to move is taken away;"[52]
- former Secretary of State Lawrence Eagleburger's statement that the conflict will end when all the parties exhaust themselves. A wrestling match? A brawl?

Given that the above characterizations read like a laundry list of class projects from a course on Marketing 101, yet are apparently treated very seriously by the culture industry, one arrives at the following crucial issue: *Are we living in an age in which emotionalism and marketing have merged in a distinctive neo-Orwellian form?* A "social construction of reality"[53] is occurring on the levels of the phenomenon in question as well as the sociological tools that are used to assess it.

More precisely, the centerpiece of our alternative explanation to postmodernism, the concept of *postemotionalism*, points to a common pattern in all these euphemisms and metaphors: in an ideal-typical rational social universe that ran according to principles derived from the Enlightenment, a finding of genocide by respected fact-finding organizations demands action by the world community to stop the genocide. This principle is enshrined in the UN Charter. (A cynical counter might be – "So what?" The UN Charter, like so many other Western documents, often enshrines principles that the West refuses to enforce. Even if this cynicism is well founded to some extent, one needs a point of departure for discussion.) Instead of reacting in this way to the situation in the Balkans, Western politicians, diplomats, media, and laypersons react on the basis of *past* emotionally charged events that obfuscate the present. A significant aspect of this reaction is that it does involve emotion, only the emotion is displaced. Hence, Baudrillard and the postmodernists who follow his lead are wrong to claim that there is no pity in the dawning postmodern world, no compassion[54] among postmodern mass societies. On the contrary, plenty of emotion is shown in the postmodern 1990s, and the term "compassion fatigue" is used, but the emotion always involves history, and fails to address the situation at hand. As Roger Cohen puts the matter: "The world is tired of Sarajevo. There has been too much killing, too many stories of suffering over more than 1,000 days" (*The New York Times* 17 April 1995: A3).

Thus, German Nazism is invoked from World War II to "explain" Serbian fears of Croats, as an allegedly pro-Nazi "genocidal people." Yet the Nazi collaboration of the rest of Europe is *not* invoked; Serbia's World War II Nazi collaboration, in particular, is ignored; Croatia's large anti-fascist movement during World War II is overlooked; the horrors committed by communists are left out of the discourse completely; and no effort is made to contrast contemporary Germany with the prevalent image of Germany – left over from World War II – as an "expansionist" power. Discussions of Croatian Ustashe typically fail to mention that Croatia also had one of the largest anti-fascist movements in Europe in proportion to its population. In the words of C. Michael McAdams, "the Partisan war of liberation began in Croatia, was led by a Croat (Tito), and 39 of the Partisans' 80 brigades were Croatian" (*The New York Times* 29 April 1994: A14). And, one should note that the Croatian Ustashe were trained in fascist Italy, not Nazi Germany, and that World War II Croatia was split evenly between Nazis and Italian fascists. But Italian fascism fails to draw Western indignation, postemotional or otherwise, a topic pursued by Thomas Cushman. In this regard, it is important to raise the question: what are the economical and ideological reasons for selective political memory?

This touches on a truly intricate and sensitive issue: Why is Croatia demonized in the media while Vichy France is swept under the Allied rug, relatively and figuratively speaking?[55] The very countries that claim to be negotiating and claim to be engaged in making peace in the Balkans (including France, Britain, and Norway) are also engaging in a very subtle, but real revisionism of their own historical pasts and the history of World War II.

Thus, the President of France, François Mitterrand – a key player among Western nations who claim to seek a "peaceful" solution to this Balkan War – refuses to apologize for or discuss Vichy France (*The New York Times* 13 June 1993: E4). Moreover, Mitterrand was apparently a Nazi collaborator during Vichy:

> The young Mitterrand was an ardent follower of collaborationist leader Philippe Petain and believed in the 'national revolution' that begat the strict, anti-Jewish laws of 1940–41. As early as 1935, Mitterrand participated in an anti-foreigner rally in Paris. . . . At 26, Mitterrand also received the "francisque," Vichy's highest award, from Petain. He published articles in Petainist magazines that also carried rabidly anti-Semitic diatribes.
>
> (*San Francisco Chronicle* 3 September 1994: A11)

Yet the Western media accepts Mitterrand's claim that despite all this, he never personally witnessed anti-Semitism and was not an anti-Semite.[56]

Mitterrand basically took the position that he was young and foolish when he was a Nazi collaborator, and his impropriety seems to have been largely forgiven by France as well as the world. It is interesting to contrast the Western media's attacks on the President of Croatia, Franjo Tudjman, with its relatively mild treatment of Mitterrand's Nazi collaboration. Tudjman was a partisan general who fought the Nazis, while Mitterrand collaborated with them. Tudjman apologized formally and officially for Croatia's Ustasha regime, while Mitterrand refuses to even acknowledge Vichy for what it really was. Yet Mitterrand continues to hold the image of a "Western" (pro-democratic, liberal) political leader while Tudjman is demonized.

In May of 1994, I was in Oslo to observe the presentation of an award to the Norwegian people, donated by the Jimmy Carter Center, for their role of bringing together the Israelis and PLO. But the setting for presenting this award of peace was a castle, first built in the 1300s, which was used by Vidkun Quisling for his Nazi headquarters. Quisling's name is so notorious that the phrase "Quisling regime" has come down to us because of him. Nevertheless, the Norwegian people hold a collective reputation for peace, despite Norway's World War II Nazi collaboration. A great deal of historical revisionism is involved in the fact that Jimmy Carter could make this presentation and call Norwegians peacemakers on these formerly Nazi grounds without the slightest protest from the information media. Similarly, one should note that most Western governments as well as media supported Jimmy Carter's "peace mission" to Serb-occupied Bosnia on 18 December 1994, made at the invitation of the suspected war criminal and leader of the Bosnian Serbs, Radovan Karadžić.

Contemporary Italy's contemporary neo-fascism is similarly glossed over by the Western media. Many other European countries enjoy a similar immunity from Western indignation concerning Nazism. One has to consider why some Europeans countries have been absolved of the guilt for the evil of Nazism in their collective pasts while others have not.

Moreover, the assumption that Croatia is collectively guilty because of the Ustasha while France, Norway, Italy, and other Western nations are not leads to the following question: is it just to allow the Croatian people to be overrun by Belgrade-sponsored genocidal aggression based on alleged collective guilt from the past? The modern answer is an immediate, "No." As children of the Enlightenment, we cannot imagine that a Croatian baby born in the 1990s should have its limbs blown off by Serbian grenades based on something someone in its ethnic group might have done in World War II. There is something monstrous about such a doctrine. On the other hand, the fact is that this argument is being made and being said in very high places, namely, that Croats deserve what they are getting based on the crimes of the Ustasha in World War II. I might add that the United States Ambassador to Croatia, Mr. Peter Galbraith, told me that many of his friends think that Croatia is getting what she deserves, and I have heard American journalists say something similar. This doctrine of collective guilt is a fact, a reality. It is an aspect of traditional collective consciousness that Durkheim was concerned with, and it does not seem to be going away despite modernism. It is a very difficult issue to deal with on a purely cerebral level because it does in fact involve emotion.

These and other examples seem to point to a new and distinctive Orwellian *double-speak* that has been perfected by the culture industry according to the rules of Marketing 101 with the aim of postemotional displacement. In a sense, what is called postmodernism seems to confound the action, "I feel," with the action, "I think." But this tendency is not adequately treated by writers engaged in the postmodernist discourse, and seems to require the sort of elaboration captured by the concept of postemotionalism.

In sum, the postmodernists seem to imply an abstract world of rootless fictions devoid of emotions, while we are implying a concrete world of rooted fictions saturated with emotions that are *displaced*, even misplaced. Durkheim's notion of "collective effervescence" serves as an excellent basis for this elaboration. Durkheim[57] argued that there exist times of rapid social change in which collective representations seem to explode as if they had been contained under tremendous pressure. The key difference between Durkheim's and the postmodernists' versions of "fictions" is that, for Durkheim, these representations can be traced to a cultural point of origin and involve *emotion*. They seem haphazard and misplaced only because of the tremendous release of pressure. The end of communism constitutes one such instance of a "release of pressure," and it has given rise to representations that have been repressed up to now, pertaining to the Holocaust, the Yugoslav civil war in the midst of World War II, the Vietnam syndrome, the quest for a Greater Serbia, and Europe's Nazi collaboration. All of these suddenly-released collective representations are colliding into one another and are producing the seeming chaos in perceptions. But far from these representations colliding into one another spontaneously, they seem to be manipulated by modernist centers of the culture industry emanating from Belgrade, London, Paris, Washington, and Moscow. The other important difference between Durkheim's understanding of collective representations and the postmodern understanding of circulating fictions is that Durkheim claimed consistently that representations involve the dualism of human nature or what he called "*homo duplex*." Thus, for Durkheim, every representation involves a cognitive conceptual as well as a perceptual *emotional* component.[58]

POSTEMOTIONAL POLITICS

If this Balkan War is the penultimate postemotional war, then President Clinton might be termed the postemotional president. Consider the coverage given to his notorious love affair; his famous, "I feel your pain" line; his inability (as indicated by polls) to lead, etc. For example, opinion-makers on both sides of the political spectrum in the USA have labeled President Clinton's recent NATO Summit and "Partnership for Peace" as all smoke and no substance. (More surprisingly, the post-summit opinion polls show that President Clinton's public approval ratings *increased* in the USA.) President Franklin Roosevelt also referred to a "Partnership for Peace," and it was equally insubstantial. Mr. Clinton "fits" the postemotional times in which he lives (in a Durkheimian sense) in that he "plays" on the old emotional images of the 1960s, of John F. Kennedy (with whom he has been compared frequently), and in general, on the needs of the aging baby-boomers who are looking back at their collective youth in the 1960s with considerable nostalgia, and transferring some of that emotional energy onto the present.

The counter might be that President Clinton's ideological barricade is easier to puncture than President Kennedy's because the news media in the 1990s is not restrained by the earlier "gentleman's agreement" not to cover a president's love affairs. Insiders "knew" of JFK's love life, but it was kept secret. But this would not explain why Americans elected Mr. Clinton even after his moral character was attacked, nor why his approval ratings would increase even after he consistently refused to take steps to stop genocide in Europe.

One could argue that despite all this soothing talk from President Clinton, he and other Western leaders (primarily British and French) have kept the victims of the Balkan slaughter outgunned and unable to defend themselves. One could argue that these leaders pretend to condemn "ethnic cleansing," but propose to keep the "peace" between a gulag of disarmed Muslim ghettos and the armed ethnic cleansers themselves. The post-emotionalism concept enables one to *expose* the emotional and other discrepancies in how the West arrived at this point, pushing ethnic partition and division when its own cultural principles point to pluralism.

We review the situation: from 1991 to 1995, the President of Serbia, Slobodan Milošević, used the Yugoslav People's Army directly to arm the suspected war criminal, Radovan Karadžić, and directly to help seize and "cleanse" one-third of Croatia, and then 70 percent of Bosnia.[59] He succeeded by convincing the West that the Serbian minority in Croatia was right to fear the Croats as an allegedly "genocidal people" because of the atrocities committed by the World War II Ustashe. To repeat, the Serbian line makes skillful use of the emotionally charged and traditional pheno-menon of collective guilt, which runs contrary to principles derived from the Enlightenment, principles which hold only individuals responsible for crimes. But the more important point, for the purposes of the present discussion, is that this *postemotional* argument worked on the West which is involved in its own postemotional traumas stemming from Vietnam,

Vichy, Hitler, and beyond. And another important point is that collective guilt is an integral aspect of Euro-Christian culture even though it is denied, and despite the smokescreen of the Enlightenment. Euro-American politicians routinely punish whole peoples for the actions of a few: witness the trade sanctions against Iraq and Haiti, the British bombing of Dresden, the weapons embargo against Israel in 1947, etc. Very few sociological and anthropological treatises have explored this ambiguity in the West regarding collective guilt.

One might be tempted to conclude that much of the preceding discussion sounds like scapegoating, so that there is no need to invoke the new term, postemotionalism. But the bulk of the present discussion thus far has exposed the postemotional mixing of emotional *memories* with *mythical* historical events such that history and the present become rough equivalents, whereas scapegoating keeps history and the present distinct. Thus, a better term must be "scapememories," such that selective memories are used politically and culturally to punish some groups and to allow others to escape the wrath of moral outrage. For example, when Serbian propagandists claim that Bosnian Muslims are really just Islamicized Serbs, they evoke strong emotions of loathing against Islam as well as nationalist pride in being a Serb. In fact, the phrase "Islamicized Serb" is as absurd as the claim that the French people are only Catholicized Tartars.[60] But Britain engages in "scapememories" when it repeatedly uses the line "peace with honor" from 1876 to 1938 to 1995.

A side-effect of this misplaced emotionalism is treated by Norman Cigar, namely, the in-fighting between the former allies, Croats and Bosnian Muslims. Western politicians cite this fighting between Serbia's victims as evidence that this really is a war of all against all, tribalism, and a potential Vietnam quagmire. The ex-Yugoslavia is thereby portrayed as a tortured land unworthy of the West's compassion, impossible to save from itself. An alternative explanation might be that the West had made it clear that it would not try to stop genocide, ethnic partition, or territorial aggrandizement attained by Belgrade-sponsored aggression, and thereby gave a green light to criminal elements among Croatians and Bosnian Muslims. Thus, the situation on the ground in the Balkans became at one point something of a self-fulfilling prophecy: a three-way war of all against all that made it increasingly difficult for politicians to affix blame on Serbian aggression. William A. Gamson captures this seeming confusion well: "Genocide is one framing of the events in Bosnia but there is a powerful competitive frame: feuding neighbors. The Bosnian conflict, in this view, is a dirty little ethnic war, a re-emergence of ancient tribal feuds."[61] The question to which our analysis points is the following: was the West "right" to characterize itself as a completely innocent bystander, and to characterize the unruly Balkans as it did, or, did the West contribute (even if unconsciously) to this tragic outcome? Again, one must deconstruct here the presupposition in Western ideology that the West is unequivocally "civilized" and all "tribalists" are bad. We suggest that the West's efforts to partition Bosnia-Herzegovina – an effort that runs against its principle of upholding ethnic pluralism – coupled with its advertisement of the fact that it would not stop Belgrade-sponsored aggression, contributed to the in-fighting between Serbia's victims, the Muslims and the Croats. One might characterize this in-fighting as a riot among prisoners, with Belgrade as the jailer who holds the keys.

An important aspect of our analysis is the suggestion that Western military intervention is insufficient without Western moral intervention – where morality is referred to in a Durkheimian sense, a set of collective represen-tations pertaining to fair play, justice, individualism, and responding effectively to the evil of genocide. The West's moral principles derived from the Enlightenment are really at stake in the Balkans. But this immediately raises the issue: whose moral principles are these? One option would be that the West will invoke "its" principles, in which case Serbian aggression could be readily defeated, and this would also be a defeat of apartheid (ethnic partition), naked aggression, and the evil of genocide. Democracy and pluralism in postcommunist Europe would be the victors, and the emotionalism surround-ing the "New World Order" might become credible. (But again, even this concept, invoked by Mr. Bush, is highly ambiguous and charged with postemotionalism, for it was also invoked by the Nazis and by H. G. Wells to promote a socialist Utopia in the 1930s.) The other option involves Balkan-ization continuing unabated, crimes against humanity going unpunished, and a green light being given to would-be dictators and extremists in the former Soviet Union. The sudden rise of Zhirinovsky's influence in Russia as well as Boris Yeltsin's dictatorial tendencies as exhibited against Chechnya seem to make this a credible fear. But again, the West's actions with regard to Bosnian genocide are not really that different from its actions in the past regarding other sites of genocide or other crises, only its hypocrisy seems easier to deconstruct this time around.

In deflecting their share of the guilt for Nazi collaboration onto the Croats, the Belgrade regime has perfected Nazi propaganda techniques to the ultimate level of refinement. The West fell for it completely, not just because of the skill of the propagandists or the lack of skill by the Croats in purchasing the services of a good public relations firm, but also because of the collective state of postemotionalism in Western societies which made them conducive to such anti-Enlightenment arguments. Ultimately, the Belgrade regime has succeeded in Balkanizing the West: it is France and Britain against Germany, again – not militarily or economically, but politically and *emotionally*. Thus, France and Britain blocked all German efforts to help the Slovenes, Croats, and Bosnians on the basis of the historical argument of stopping German expansionism. This is a pre-cold war strategy that confuses matters even further because it involves cold war institutions, such as NATO and the UN. Additionally, Britain distanced itself from the USA over Bosnia. Brendan Simms writes:

> The most succinct summary of the British government's absurd position on Bosnia runs like this: the Bosnians cannot be allowed to protect themselves, because this would endanger the troops sent there to protect them, but who failed to do so [and] we should do all in our power to prevent the Americans from coming to its [Bosnia's] aid, even at the price of a catastrophic transatlantic rift. We are left with the truly bizarre fact that while there is no political will in Britain to save the Bosnians from aggression and ethnic cleansing, there are great hidden reserves of political will and invective to prevent the Americans from doing so.[62]

Thus, ordinary people are led to believe that the peoples of the former Yugoslavia have succumbed to "tribal" hatred, and that the West should not get involved. This is an interesting, seemingly postmodern mixing of metaphors, Nazism and primitive tribes. Yet the West *is* involved. Instead of standing up for a pluralistic society, which is a key Western ideal and especially a key component of American civil religion, it is the West that is promoting a quasi-apartheid system of ethnic partition in Bosnia-Herzegovina. And the West is doing this ostensibly on the basis of a *postemotional* humanitarianism. It is ironic that the Bosnian government is trying to stand up for pluralism derived from an Islamic tradition dating back to the Ottoman Empire,[63] whereas President Clinton seems to be supporting the ethnic partition proposed by Lord Owen and the Europeans that is the central component of the so-called peace plan that has been on the table in Geneva. President Clinton rebuffed President Izetbegović's plea for military help, and instructed him to cut the best deal that he could with those seeking to dismember his country along ethnic lines.

Instead of standing up for the Western principle of national and territorial sovereignty with regard to both Croatia and Bosnia-Herzegovina, the West is trying to rationalize away its diplomatic recognition of these countries. Even after the international community recognized the sovereignties of Croatia and Bosnia-Herzegovina, it continued to deprive these nations of their inviolable right to self-defense, as set forth in Article 51 of the UN Charter. Certain emotionally charged aspects of Western political culture seem to be violated here, most notably the principle of "fair play." It is important to observe that the United States and other democracies can act relative to the inherent right to self-defense without permission or even endorsement by the UN Secretary-General. The UN Charter acknowledges the right of individual and collective self-defense as inherent. That is, this right existed before there was a Charter or a UN. Yet, the rationalization for withholding weapons from Serbia's victims that has been made by Western heads of state has been that more weapons would only prolong the "fighting." Again, this explanation can be characterized as emotional, even compassionate (albeit paternalistic), but postemotional in that it fails to address the slaughter – as it is called by Bosnian Muslims – occurring in the present.

We need to guard against reifying the West here according to the ideals it sometimes espouses. We use these ideals in order to expose the inconsistency of Western actions relative to its postemotional rhetoric of concern and sympathy. But the real intent is to deconstruct this rhetoric, and expose the Western penchant for ethnic partition, collective guilt, and acquiescence to genocide that is so very evident from a glance at European history.

If it is true that the Gulf War was a memorable major war fought under the "illusion" (in the postmodern sense) of the West standing up to aggression, then the current Balkan War is a watershed event in that it is a "major" war (symbolically) in the sense of the West appeasing aggression under the guise of humanitarian and compassionate concern. Even here, the concept of postemotionalism adds a new dimension to discourses of this sort. But this postemotional complex has now blocked intelligent responses to Belgrade-sponsored aggression, and is causing new problems on the world's political scene: Would-be dictators and extremist parties in the former Soviet Union are watching eagerly as the West fails to live up to its ideals. The West is fantasizing that Boris Yeltsin will succeed in a post-cold war, Disneyworld process of magical, instant democratization and "free-market reform" even though it is giving the green light to anti-democratic forces. On the threshold of the next century – a time that promises to be one of ethnic and religious violence dominated by pro-paganda images on the television screen – the West has apparently learned little from a bloody twentieth century. Is all this leading to a major European War for the third time in this century?

CONCLUSIONS

The keystone of the present volume is the new concept, postemotionalism. The authors use this concept to capture the confusion, hypocrisies, hysteria, nostalgia, ironies, paradoxes and other emotional excesses that surround Western politics toward the postcommunist Balkans as well as the inability of Western cultural analysts and intellectuals to make the Balkan War intelligible to the masses. Postemotionalism holds greater explanatory power than postmodernism, because postmodernism holds that one should revel or feel comfortable in the face of the ironies, inconsistencies, and contradictions such as the ones that we have uncovered. But we hold that genocide and crimes against humanity are neither an occasion for revelry nor situations that make one feel comfortable. Thus, like the post-modernists, we debunk, demystify, and criticize the explanations given by the media and governments involved. Unlike the postmodernists, we go beyond the argument that social life consists of a mental text of circulating fictions that are not supposed to make sense to include the emotions. And we point out that the postmodern goal of tolerance is not being achieved: extreme intolerance seems to be the rule, not the exception, in the postcommunist world, as we head for the end of the century.

Far from being an instance of Eurocentrism, the current Balkan War seems to be a watershed event in our *fin de siècle* that involves Islamic, European, and American cultural interests. It seems to be foreshadowing ethnic violence that has already increased, and will probably increase in the coming century: in Rwanda, Angola, the southern fringes of the former Soviet Union, and so on.[64] If critical theory was largely a response to the horrors of modernism exemplified by Stalin and Hitler; if postmodernism was largely a foreshadowing of the collapse of the modernist system in Communism and a reaction to the last stages of modernist capitalism; I propose that postemotionalism ought to be regarded as a new theoretical construct to capture the fission, Balkanization, ethnic violence and other highly *emotional* phenomena of the late 1990s.

NOTES

1 See, for example, Elizabeth Neuffer, "Sense of Victimization Bolsters Bosnia Serbs," *Boston Globe*, 10 August 1994: A2; Roger Cohen, "Balkan Moral Order Upset As Victim Becomes Victor," *The New York Times*, 6 November 1994: E1.

2 Anthony Lewis, review of *Slaughterhouse* by David Rieff, *New Republic*, 20 March 1995: 29.

3 Lewis (see note 2).

4 Douglas Kellner, *The Persian Gulf TV War* (Boulder, Colo.: Westview Press, 1992).

5 Edward S. Herman and Noam Chomsky, *Manufacturing Consent: The Political Economy of the Mass Media* (New York: Pantheon Books, 1988).

6 Statement made to the Commission on Security and Cooperation in Europe, 4 April 1995.

7 Mark Almond, *Europe's Backyard War* (London: Heinemann, 1993).

8 Brendan Simms, "Bosnia: The Lesson of History?" paper presented at the conference on "Weighing Up the Century," Zagreb, Croatia, 17 December 1994.

9 Zygmunt Bauman, *Modernity and the Holocaust* (Ithaca, N.Y.: Cornell University Press, 1989).

10 Zygmunt Bauman, *Modernity and Ambivalence* (Ithaca, N.Y.: Cornell University Press, 1991); *Intimations of Postmodernity* (London: Routledge, 1992).

11 See, in particular, Robert O. Paxton, *Parades and Politics at Vichy* (Princeton, N.J.: Princeton University Press, 1966); *Vichy France: Old Guard and New Order, 1940–1944* (London: Barrie & Jenkins, 1972).

12 Many such books question the standard historical rationalization that the Western Allies stood up to Nazism, and seek to expose Western collaboration with the Nazis. Noteworthy examples include the following: Pierre Pean, *Une jeunesse française: François Mitterrand, 1934–1947* (Paris: Fayard, 1994);

Michael Marrus and Robert O. Paxton, *Vichy France and the Jews* (New York: Basic Books, 1981); Daniel Patrick Moynihan, *Pandaemonium: Ethnicity in International Politics* (New York: Oxford University Press, 1993); L. C. Gardner, *Spheres of Influence: The Great Powers Partition Europe, From Munich to Malta* (Chicago: Ivan R. Dee, 1993).

13 Specifically, Letica introduced it over a meal with Meštrović and Barry Glassner in a Thai restaurant in Miami in August of 1993. These three sociologists were attending the annual meeting of the American Sociological Association.

14 See S. G. Meštrović, "Postemotional Politics in the Balkans," *Society*, 1994 (January): 69–77.

15 Norman Cigar, *Genocide in Bosnia: The Policy of "Ethnic Cleansing"* (College Station, Tex.: Texas A&M University Press, 1995).

16 See "Ethnic Cleansing – And a Cry for Help from Bosnia," *Newsweek*, 17 August 1992: 16–27; Tom Post, "A Pattern of Rape," *Newsweek*, 11 January 1993: 32–6; John F. Burns, "Bosnian Survivors Tell of Mass Ethnic Killings: Comparisons With Nazis Are Drawn as Attacks Rage in the Republic," *The New York Times*, 21 May 1992: A28; John F. Burns, "Bosnian Strife Cuts Old Bridges of Trust: Ancient Ties of Coexistence Are Broken by 'Ethnic Purification'," *The New York Times*, 22 May 1992: A1; Laura Silber, "The Street Was a River of Blood," *The Washington Post*, 28 May 1992: A1; Roy Gutman, "Ethnic Cleansing: Yugoslavs Try to Deport 1,800 Muslims to Hungary," *Newsday*, 3 July 1992: 5; Roy Gutman, "Prisoners of Serbia's War. Tales of Hunger, Torture at Camp in North Bosnia," *Newsday*, 19 July 1992: 7; Roy Gutman, "Croats Deported in Freight Cars," *Newsday*, 21 July 1992: 4; Roy Gutman, "If Only They Could Flee. Muslims, Croats Held in City," *Newsday*, 26 July 1992: 4; Roy Gutman, "Death Camps: Serbs Imprison Thousands for Slaughter, Starvation," *Newsday*, 3 August 1992: 4; Roy Gutman, "Bosnia Rape Horror," *Newsday*, 9 August 1992: 4; Roy Gutman, "Deadly Transfer," *Newsday*, 26 August 1992: 3; Roger Cohen, "Ex-Guard for Serbs Tells of Grisly 'Cleansing' Camp," *The New York Times*, 1 August 1994: A1; Roger Cohen, "Bosnian Camp Survivors Describe Random Death," *The New York Times*, 2 August 1994: A1 – among many other articles.

17 Emile Durkheim, *The Rules of Sociological Method* (Glencoe, Ill.: The Free Press, [1895] 1938).

18 Irving Louis Horowitz, "Counting Bodies: The Dismal Science of Authorized Terror," *Patterns of Prejudice*, vol. 23, no. 2: 4–15, 1989.

19 See, for example, Anthony Lewis, "Never Again," *The New York Times*, 3 April 1995: A11; Zbigniew Brzezinski, "Never Again – Except for Bosnia," *The New York Times*, 22 April 1993: A21.

20 See, for instance, George Kenney, "The Bosnia Calculation" (*New York Times Magazine*, 23 April 1995: 42–3), in which Kenney refers to the genocide in Bosnia as genocide with "a little g" compared to Genocide with "a capital G" as in the Holocaust "and, perhaps, Cambodia or Rwanda."

21 See also Elizabeth Rubin, "In War-Torn Yugoslavia, Jews Are All the Rage," *Jewish Forward*, 5 August 1994: 3.

22 Philip J. Cohen, *Serbia at War With History* (College Station, Tex.: Texas A&M University Press, 1995: 174).

23 See, for example, John W. Dower, *War Without Mercy: Race and Power in the Pacific War* (New York: Pantheon, 1986). Dower notes on p. 301 that General Henry H. Arnold bombed Tokyo the night of 14 August 1945 with 828 bombers and 186 fighter escorts. They suffered no losses and had not yet all returned to base when President Truman announced Japan's unconditional surrender. Also, on pp. 39–40, Dower exposes the hypocrisy of the Allies, who condemned German raids on Rotterdam, but used 334 aircraft against Tokyo on 9 May 1945,

burning 16 square miles of the city, leaving a million people homeless, and killing 80,000 to 100,000 civilians. Dresden, of course, was similar.

24 A phrase introduced to me by Rabbi Peter Tarlow of the Texas A&M University Hillel Foundation.

25 Roy Gutman, *A Witness to Genocide* (New York: Basic Books, 1993).

26 Historian Vivian R. Gruder observes in a letter to the editor published in *The New York Times* (8 December 1994: A18) "that while it is true that in the First World War Serbia was an ally of Britain and France, it should also be remembered that the act that precipitated the outbreak of war – the assassination of the Austrian Archduke in Sarajevo – was committed by a Serbian nationalist to advance the cause of Greater Serbia. That goal again brought about the war first against Croatia [in 1991], and which continues now [1994] against Bosnia. . . . As to the so-called alliance between Serbia and France, during World War II, which France? Vichy? De Gaulle? How could De Gaulle, in London, ally with the Serbian Chetniks when Churchill allied with Tito's Partisans? Sympathy with former allies is another fig leaf to conceal the absence of will of the British and French to honor the commitments they made in the UN and in NATO to protect the 'safe areas' in Bosnia."

27 The editors of *The New York Times* (4 January 1994: A14) wrote: "Responsibility for the crimes [in Bosnia] is not evenly shared on all sides of the conflict, as some UN members suggest. As the Clinton Administration notes, the term 'ethnic cleansing' was developed precisely to describe the Bosnian Serbs' explicit method, backed by Belgrade, of creating an ethnically 'pure' Greater Serbia. In contrast, the Bosnian government supports a multi-ethnic state, and where there have been violations by its local commanders, it has denounced them."

28 These findings seem to constitute generally accepted knowledge, as illustrated by this claim in the *Wall Street Journal*: "UN investigators blame Serbs for the worst atrocities" (23 February 1993: A1), and in *The New York Times*, "The Serbs are the aggressors. None of the ethnic groups in the conflict is above reproach. But it is the Serbs who have grabbed pieces of territory in Croatia and Bosnia" (26 February 1993: A15).

29 For example, an article in *The New York Times* (27 September 1994: A7) quotes a United Nations major in Sarajevo as claiming that a particular instance of shelling "appeared to be part of a continuing attempt by the [Bosnian] government to ensure that the situation in Sarajevo remains critical, thus drawing world attention to its plight."

30 See, for example, Ivo Banac, "Croatianism: Franjo Tudjman's brutal opportunism," *The New Republic*, 25 October 1993: 20; Stephen Kinzer, "Croatia's Founding Chief is Seen as a Mixed Story,' *The New York Times*, 5 August 1993: A10; David Binder, "In Croatia, Ruling Party Reflects a House Divided," *The New York Times*, 21 December 1993: A16; Stephen Kinzer, "Pro-Nazi Rulers' Legacy Still Lingers for Croatia," *The New York Times*, 31 October 1993: A10; Robert D. Kaplan, "Croatianism," *The New Republic*, 25 November 1991: 16; Roger Cohen, "Croatia's Currency Name Protested," *The New York Times*, 28 May 1994: A3.

31 Chuck Sudetic, "Bosnian Army Said to Shell Own Territory," *The New York Times*, 11 November 1994: A4.

32 Theodor Adorno, *The Culture Industry* (London: Routledge, 1991).

33 David Riesman, *The Lonely Crowd* (New Haven, Conn.: Yale University Press, 1950).

34 Robert N. Bellah, Richard Madsen, William M. Sullivan, Anne Swidler, and Stephen M. Tipton, *Habits of the Heart* (Berkeley, Calif.: University of California Press, 1985).

35 Jean Baudrillard, *America* (London: Verso, 1986).
36 As argued by David Riesman in a letter to Meštrović dated 7 December 1994.
37 For an interesting discussion of this point, see William Glaberson, "The New Press Criticism: News as the Enemy of Hope" (*The New York Times*, 9 October 1994: E1), in which he writes that "under the guise of analysis, the critique continues, journalists have begun to supply judgments."
38 Chuck Sudetic quotes Radovan Karadžić in *The New York Times* (14 July 1994: A5) as follows: "This war grew out of the Serbs' fear of Muslim and Croatian domination and because of our refusal to accept an independent state of Bosnia and Herzegovina."
39 See Steven A. Holmes, "Photographs of Balkans Draw Fire: Serb Groups Fault Holocaust Museum," *The New York Times*, 24 September 1994: A6. Holmes writes: "A new photography exhibit on the war in the Balkans that opened on Thursday at the US Holocaust Museum is drawing criticisms from Serbian-American and some Jewish organizations. . . . While the exhibit depicts all sides in the war in the former Yugoslavia as victims, the bulk of the pictures show results of atrocities committed by Bosnian Serbs against Muslims and Croats in Bosnia. Serbian-American groups, angered by the symbolic linking of the Bosnian Serb activities with those of the Nazis, have protested. Joined by some Jewish groups, they have also objected to the use of the Holocaust Museum for an exhibit depicting Croats as victims, noting the persecution of Jews by the fascist puppet government set up under Nazi control in Croatia."
40 Branka Magas, *The Destruction of Yugoslavia: Tracking the Break-up 1980–92* (London: Verso, 1993).
41 In *USA Today* (17 June 1993: 11A), Mr. Christopher is quoted as stating: "There were serious mistakes made in the whole process of recognition, quick recognition, and the Germans bear a particular responsibility in persuading their colleagues and the European community. We were not in office at the time, but many serious students of the matter think the beginning of the problems we face here today stem from the recognition of Croatia and thereafter of Bosnia."
42 Peter Schneider, "Invasion and Evasions," *The New York Times*, 7 June 1994: A15.
43 See, for example, A. M. Rosenthal, "Dole on Bosnia," *The New York Times*, 18 April 1995: A15.
44 Consider, for example, former US Defense Secretary Robert McNamara's belated confession that he was wrong to support the Vietnam War, made in a book published in 1995.
45 As argued by Stephen Graubaurd, *Mr. Bush's War: Adventures in the Politics of Illusion* (New York: Hill & Wang, 1992).
46 Mark Heprin writes: "What do the Serbs want? The Serbs say they want to protect themselves. . . . When Yugoslavia broke up, the Serbs' memories of the second World War made them rush to the premature rescue of Serbs left outside the fold" (*Wall Street Journal*, 6 May 1993: A14).
47 See Keith Tester, *The Life and Times of Post-Modernity* (London and New York: Routledge, 1992).
48 John O'Neill, *The Poverty of Postmodernism* (London and New York: Routledge, 1994).
49 Arthur Schopenhauer, *The World as Will and Idea* (New York: Dover Press, [1818] 1965).
50 Zlatko Diždarević, *Sarajevo: A War Journal* (New York: Fromm International, 1993).

51 Baudrillard's critic, Douglas Kellner, actually elaborates on these themes in his *Television and the Crisis of Democracy* (Boulder, Colo.: Westview Press, 1990) and *The Persian Gulf TV War*.

52 John Darnton, "Hope is Seen for Captive UN Troops," *The New York Times*, 3 December 1994: A1. Darnton quotes a spokesman for the British Ministry of Defence: "I wouldn't regard these people as hostages in a way. They're being prevented from carrying out their task."

53 Peter Berger and Thomas Luckmann, *The Social Construction of Reality* (New York: Doubleday, 1967).

54 The term "compassion" requires much deconstruction and elaboration. What Baudrillard and others call compassion might more properly be termed pity, because pity is tinged with contempt for the object of one's charitable emotions. In this sense, the West shows *pity* for the Bosnians, but not compassion, in Arthur Schopenhauer's sense of co-suffering, which demands *action* to put an end to the suffering which makes pity seem necessary.

55 See Alan Riding, "Long Live French Illusions," *The New York Times*, 25 September 1994: E3. Riding writes: "Charles de Gaulle and François Mitterrand agreed on one thing – that it served no purpose to look too closely at France's behavior during its occupation by Nazi Germany. From the moment of the Liberation 50 years ago, De Gaulle set about restoring French honor by creating the myth that most French resisted the occupiers. . . . Mr. Mitterrand is a metaphor for postwar France, which also felt the need to rewrite its resume, in order to be recognized as a victorious ally in 1945 and a major power today. Thus when the President's defenders argue that 100 percent of the French supported Marshall Petain when he took over a humiliated nation in 1940, they are inevitably undermining De Gaulle's romanticized lie about the extent of French resistance."

56 Pierre Pean, *Une jeunesse française* (Paris: Fayard, 1994).

57 Emile Durkheim, *The Elementary Forms of the Religious Life* (New York: Free Press, [1912] 1965).

58 This aspect of Durkheim's sociology of knowledge is elaborated by Stjepan Meštrović, *Emile Durkheim and the Reformation of Sociology* (Totowa, N.J.: Rowman & Littlefield, 1988).

59 See especially Roger Cohen, "Serb Defector Offers Evidence on War Crimes," *The New York Times*, 13 April 1995: A1.

60 An example given by Paul Garde at a conference on the end of the century held in Zagreb, Croatia, on 16 December 1994.

61 William A. Gamson, "Hiroshima, the Holocaust, and the Politics of Exclusion," paper presented to the American Sociological Association, Los Angeles, 6 August 1994, p. 10.

62 Brendan Simms, "Why America is Right About Bosnia," *The Independent* 2 December 1994: A10.

63 Noel Malcolm, *Bosnia: A Short History* (New York: New York University Press, 1994).

64 See Akbar Ahmed, "Ethnic Cleansing: A Metaphor for Our Time?", *Ethnic and Racial Studies*, vol. 18, no. 1: 2–25, 1995.

2

ENDING THE WAR AND SECURING PEACE IN FORMER YUGOSLAVIA

Philip J. Cohen

INTRODUCTION

The current war in the former Yugoslavia has been driven from its outset by Serbia's extremist nationalism and quest for territorial expansion.[1] As this tragedy has unfolded, the United States, European Community, Helsinki Commission, and United Nations have all concluded that Serbia bears the overwhelming responsibility for the war and its consequences.[2] However, no policy has been crafted or implemented by any of these entities that would effectively restrain the aggressive behavior of Serbia against her neighbors. Serbia's aggression has introduced a potentially dangerous destabilization of post-cold war Europe, in a region in which Western Slavic, Eastern Slavic, and Turkish cultures, Catholicism, Eastern Orthodoxy, and Islam all converge in a delicate balance. Failure to contain Serbian aggression endangers regional stability and threatens a wider regional conflict.

FORMER YUGOSLAVIA AS A PRECEDENT FOR REGIONAL INSTABILITY

In the land-grab by which Serbia is attempting to create an ill-conceived, ethnically pure Greater Serbia, Serbs constitute less than 40 percent of the population of this envisaged territory.[3] In pursuit of Greater Serbia, Serbs predictably would continue their brutal policy of "ethnic cleansing" of the non-Serb population, the only measure they have historically used to establish control over newly conquered territories. "Ethnic cleansing," a term introduced by the Serbs themselves, is a sanitized euphemism for genocide and ethnic-based expulsion, and should be read as such. Ironically, the UN has criticized Croatia, with its war-shattered economy and over 750,000 refugees (about 500,000 from Bosnia), for not accepting more Bosnian refugees.[4] By demanding that Croatia accept more refugees rather than making sure that Serbia stops creating them, it places the international community in tacit complicity with the principal Serbian war aim – territorial expansion by the expulsion of non-Serbs.[5] No European country has done more for the Bosnian refugees than Croatia, and Croatia is among those least able to cope with this burden economically.

If Serbia is not stopped in Bosnia, the aggression predictably will extend to Kosovo and Macedonia, where ominous signs point to the possibility of wider regional conflict.[6] It is clearly Serbia's intent to "ethnically cleanse" Kosovo, home to nearly two million ethnic Albanians.[7] This has been a Serbian aspiration for well over 50 years.[8] In opposing the recognition of Macedonia, Greece had expressed its "fear" that ex-Yugoslav Macedonia (although disarmed and with 20 percent the population of Greece) intended to invade the northern Greek province called Macedonia. Greek troops are deployed on the ex-Yugoslav Macedonian border, and Greek military aircraft regularly fly over ex-Yugoslav Macedonia. If Serbia and Greece finally execute their agreement to divide ex-Yugoslav Macedonia, which Serbia calls "southern Serbia" and which Greece calls "the stolen jewels of Greece," other countries may no longer feel constrained from intervention. Albania, Bulgaria, Hungary, and Turkey each have ethnic minorities threatened directly by designs to create a "Greater Serbia." Turkey, a traditional enemy of both Greece and Serbia, has resisted unilateral military intervention primarily because of Turkey's sensitivity toward integration with the rest of Europe. Nevertheless, Turkey has grave concerns for the endangered Muslim populations of Bosnia, Sandjak, Kosovo, and Macedonia, where ethnic Turks also reside. Bulgaria, a traditional enemy of Serbia, also has a significant ethnic minority in Serbia as well as in Macedonia. The persecution of over 350,000 Hungarians in the Vojvodina province of Serbia has received relatively little attention, but evokes considerable concern in Hungary.

The UN's recognition for the sovereignty of Croatia and Bosnia-Herzegovina, coupled with the continuation of an arms embargo on these states, has proven an incompetent exercise of United Nations authority. The net effect has been to encourage one-sided Serbian aggression by obstructing the self-defense of Muslims and Croats, even as they are victims of genocide. Since September 1991, the USA, EC, and later the UN, have interfered in the Balkans by imposing an arms embargo that extended to the victims of genocide, but have not intervened on the victims' behalf. With no serious help ever offered to stop Serbian aggression, a power vacuum has been created in the Balkans, with the opportunity for terrorist states to extend their influence to the region.[9] The recent attempted shipment of arms from Iran is evidence of the failure of USA, EC, and UN to stop Serbian aggression. This policy failure has led to opportunistic involvement of other countries in the Balkan conflict and potentiates further destabilization of the region. Further, the betrayal of these small countries has sent "a very clear message to other small nations that they cannot count on principles. They should forget democracy and the free market, and arm themselves first.'[10] The USA and Europe are losing an historic opportunity to strengthen the bridge of trust between the Muslim world and the West.[11] The contrast between the willingness of the USA to use force in Iraq but not in former Yugoslavia is straining alliances with Turkey, Egypt, and other Middle East allies.[12] The Islamic world, with one billion followers, will long remember, as a seminal event of their modern history, the relative indifference of Europeans and Americans toward the genocide against the Bosnian Muslims.

In the former Soviet Union, in which over 160 ethnicities reside and where four republics possess nuclear weapons, there remains significant potential for multiple armed conflicts over borders. Russia has keenly noted the non-response of the West to Serbia's program of "ethnic cleansing," in flagrant violation of the Geneva Conventions. Despite Yeltsin's recognition of the independence of the Baltic republics, many Russian factions retain aspirations to control the strategic Baltic ports. To leave Serbian expansionism unchallenged would encourage those Russian elements.[13] The economic and political situation in Russia is volatile, and there is the risk that Yeltsin's fragile democracy may be replaced by ultra-nationalistic elements, which may attempt to re-establish Russia's influence in the Balkans by support of Serbian war efforts.

A RATIONAL STRATEGY FOR ATTAINING PEACE

A meaningful political solution to the war in the former Yugoslavia will first require the military defeat of Serbian aggression and the end of Serbia's unchallenged military superiority. The first step should be to lift the arms embargo on Croatia and Bosnia-Herzegovina and permit those republics to defend themselves, in accordance with international law and the UN Charter. This step would obviate the need for any foreign ground troops and should terminate the debate on which foreign country should send troops to former Yugoslavia. If they were to possess adequate weaponry, ground forces under the command of the legitimate governments of Croatia and Bosnia-Herzegovina could successfully reverse Serbia's land-grab. It should be noted that Serbian fighting forces have prevailed on the basis of superior arms. However, the wide swathes of territory they hold are thinly defended by irregular forces motivated primarily by the thrills of looting, raping, and torture. They are characteristically undisciplined and nearly always drunk. By undertaking strategic air strikes, a relatively low-risk operation, as enunciated by Margaret Thatcher,[14] Jeane Kirkpatrick,[15] and others,[16] the international community could greatly shorten the conflict. Air strikes would accomplish several well circumscribed, but vital goals:

1   the grounding of Serbia's air power by the bombardment of radar stations and airfields, a total of approximately one dozen targets;

2   the severing of military supply lines from Serbia to proxies in Bosnia-Herzegovina and Croatia by the bombardment of bridges over the Drina River, across which personnel and supplies currently flow to Serbian forces;

3   the destruction of munitions plants within Serbia.

In addition, the steady flow of oil and strategic supplies to Serbia from Russia, Ukraine, and Romania via the Danube must be firmly blockaded.

The current practice of forcing the victims of Serbian aggression to negotiate with their tormentors, while keeping the victims weak through an arms embargo, is morally reprehensible and politically unwise, serving only to reward Serbia's aggression by legitimizing ill-gotten war gains. Predictably, it will also have the effect of creating the context for continued fighting, as the dispossessed struggle to recover their territories. Serb-occupied territories must be returned to the control of their legitimate governments, *before* negotiations are undertaken. Following the restoration of the territorial integrity of Croatia and Bosnia-Herzegovina, internationally-sponsored peace negotiations can address several problems:

1   the rights and security of all ethnicities and minorities must be guaranteed;

2   refugees must be permitted and assisted to return safely to their rightful homes, where many dwellings need to be rebuilt;

3   war crimes trials for violators on all sides must be undertaken, to underscore the seriousness of the world community's commitment to human rights.

BACKGROUND

Initially, Slovenia and Croatia did not seek their constitutionally guaranteed right to secession,[17] but rather a greater degree of cultural, political, and economic autonomy within a Yugoslav confederation, permitting democracy and a free-market economy. Serbia and its ally Montenegro instead demanded the preservation of centralized communist authority. The confederal proposal was rejected by Serbian president Slobodan Milošević, who controlled four of the eight votes in the federal presidency.[18] Plebiscites were subsequently held, and in democratic open elections 94 percent of Croatian and 88 percent of Slovenian voters chose independence.[19] In June 1991, the Yugoslav Army attacked Slovenia, but met a humiliating defeat by the armed and prepared Slovenian Territorial Defenses.[20] Slovenia, the most economically productive republic, with its homogeneous population of two million (96 percent Slovenian), contained virtually no Serb minority and shared no common border with Serbia. The Serbian leadership in the Yugoslav government later conceded Slovenia's secession from Yugoslavia,[21] which would have left Serbia with four of seven votes in the federal presidency.

Croatia, a republic of 4.5 million, including 600,000 ethnic Serbs (11.5 percent), was of fundamental strategic interest to Belgrade. Croatia contains the most productive oil-fields of Yugoslavia (in eastern Slavonia, especially in the vicinity of Vukovar). Croatia, occupying most of the Adriatic coast of Yugoslavia, possessed valuable commercial seaports, with rail links to Central and Eastern Europe. Croatia's tourist industry alone generated 50 percent of Yugoslavia's hard currency, which was routed to the Belgrade-controlled Yugoslav bank. Serbia, by contrast, was oil-poor, land-locked, and economically dependent on Croatia and Slovenia, especially on Croatia.

Preparations for war against Croatia began long before 1991. As early as 1986, the "Memorandum" of the Serbian Academy of Arts and Sciences delineated the rationale for joining all lands with Serbian minorities into one large Serbian state, with the sole concern being the "minority rights" of Serbs. Overt military preparations for war began in 1989. Under pressure from the Yugoslav Army, the disarmament of the Croatian Territorial Defense Force, which had begun in the fall of 1989, was mostly completed by May 1990, when Croatia held elections.[22] Croatia's preparedness against military attack was further reduced when Croatia demobilized its police in January 1991 in response to threats of attack by the Yugoslav Army if weapons were not surrendered.[23] The Yugoslav Army, historically the main institution of the Serbian warrior class, aligned itself with Serbia against Croatia.[24] Concurrently, Serbian irregular forces covertly supported by Serbia escalated their armed attacks on Croatian civilians. The Serbian-dominated Yugoslav Army "intervened" in the conflicts on the pretext of separating warring sides, but systematically assured a series of victories for the Serbian irregular forces.[25] Serbian leaders calculated that Croatia's resistance would quickly be crushed in a battle that might cause thousands of deaths and that international censure, a small price to pay, would be a temporary inconvenience.[26] Without declaring war, Serbia launched a massive military assault and seized over 35 percent of Croatian territory. Parts of eastern Slavonia (specifically, Baranja) and the provinces which Serbs call Krajina[27] became "Kroatenfrei.'[28] The pretext for such a brutal military invasion was to protect the "endangered" Serb minority in Croatia, but in truth, three-quarters of Croatia's 600,000 ethnic Serbs lived outside of the lands which Serb forces seized.[29] The beginning of the war against Croatia was the end of Yugoslavia's constitutionally legitimate central government. The multirepublic federal presidency, with constitutional authority over the Yugoslav Army, proved impotent to constrain the Serbian offensive and soon collapsed.[30] Subsequently, the machinery of the Yugoslav government was usurped by Serbia and Montenegro, under the leadership of Serbian president Slobodan Milošević, the dictator who largely controlled military policy.[31]

For several months, however, the USA and EC continued to support the integrity of Yugoslavia.[32] An ill-conceived arms embargo imposed by the

EC, USA, and UN on all the republics of former Yugoslavia [33] froze the military imbalance in favor of Serbia, which already effectively controlled the entire arsenal of the Yugoslav Army (tanks, ships, fighter planes, and heavy artillery).[34] The former Yugoslav government itself, dominated by Serbs, petitioned for this embargo.[35] Predictably, the lack of international involvement to stop initial Serbian advances provided time for Serbia to conquer more Croatian territory,[36] severely damage the Croatian economy,[37] and inflict great human losses.

Bosnia-Herzegovina at first pursued a cautious path, trying to avoid a confrontation with Belgrade.[38] Encouraged by the EC, Bosnia-Herzegovina, a republic of 4.3 million, conducted a plebiscite on independence on 29 February and 1 March 1992. Most of the Serbs of Bosnia-Herzegovina boycotted this vote under the direction of Belgrade,[39] although Serbs there had no legitimate claim of discrimination or persecution.[40] Despite attempts of armed Serbs to block the voting,[41] 65 percent of citizens participated, and more than 99 percent of those voting chose independence.[42] Shortly after, in April 1992, both the EC and USA recognized the sovereignty of Bosnia-Herzegovina, which, along with Slovenia and Croatia, became a full member of the UN in May 1992. Despite Bosnia's warm international welcome, however, the European Community took no action to prevent or halt the subsequent Serbian attack on Bosnia. Only after Serbia's aggression had produced 600,000 Bosnian refugees did the EC follow the USA initiative to impose economic sanctions on Serbia.[43] However, the hesitation of the EC and its unwillingness to sanction force against Serbia emboldened Serbian attacks. Bosnia itself remained under an arms embargo (inherited from an earlier arms embargo on the whole territory of Yugoslavia). In this way, the USA and EC disregarded Article 51 of the UN Charter by denying the Bosnians the right to defend themselves against aggression. Article 51 is quoted:

> Nothing in the present Charter shall impair the inherent right of individual and collective self-defense if an armed attack occurs against a member of the United Nations, until the Security Council has taken measures necessary to maintain international peace and security. Measures taken by members in the exercise of the right of self-defense shall be immediately reported to the Security Council and shall not in any way affect the authority and responsibility of the Security Council under the present Charter to take at any time such action as it deems necessary in order to maintain or restore international peace and security.

Although Serbs constituted 31 percent of the population of Bosnia-Herzegovina, Serbian forces engaged in "ethnic cleansing" against Muslims and Croats and soon controlled 70 percent of Bosnian territory.[44]

Macedonia is a republic of 2.1 million people, consisting of 64 percent Slavic Macedonians and several other ethnicities, including ethnic Albanians, Bulgarians, Gypsies, Serbs, and Turks. Macedonia's plebiscite overwhelmingly affirmed the republic's determination for independence,[45] and Macedonia fulfilled the same criteria for recognition by the European Community as Bosnia-Herzegovina.[46] However, international recognition was blocked by Greece, on the pretext that Macedonia, by retaining its centuries-old name, was signaling its aspirations to the northern province of Greece of the same name.[47] The Serbian-controlled Yugoslav Army withdrew from Macedonia to fight in Bosnia and left Macedonia essentially disarmed.[48] Although Serbia has been under international sanctions and diplomatic isolation, Greece cultivated warmer diplomatic ties to Serbia and was the first country to be caught in a large violation of the UN sanctions against Serbia.[49] Greece remains a major violator of the economic embargo against Serbia and Montenegro.[50] Both Greece and Serbia have made extensive use of embargoes against Macedonia, blocking oil, food, and medicine.[51] It seems just a matter of time before Serbia and Greece execute their plan to divide Macedonia, which Serbia calls "southern Serbia" and which Greece calls "the stolen jewels of Greece."

In the former autonomous region of Kosovo, the nearly two million ethnic Albanians, comprising 93 percent of the population, are in grave and imminent danger. In 1989, Serbian authorities dissolved the legitimate parliament of Kosovo, an unprecedented act in recent European history. Under Serbian pressure, Yugoslav authorities imposed military occupation and a system of apartheid characterized by expropriations of Albanian property, forced expulsions, mass firings of ethnic Albanians, political imprisonment, and political murders. Serbian authorities have also encouraged the routine harassment (including looting, rape, and murder) of Albanian civilians by Serbian irregular forces in Kosovo. Serbia has clearly stated the intention to "ethnically cleanse" Albanians from Kosovo. A small Croatian minority of Kosovo suffers from the same repression as the Albanian majority.

The former autonomous region of Vojvodina, consisting of lands that traditionally were part of Hungary and Croatia, is the most ethnically heterogeneous region of former Yugoslavia, with dozens of ethnicities. Among its two million inhabitants, more than 350,000 ethnic Hungarians and some 200,000 Croats are subject to severe persecution and expulsions. As occurred in Kosovo, the parliament of Vojvodina was dissolved and replaced by Serbian authority in 1989.

In summary, the essential cause of the war in former Yugoslavia has been extremist Serbian nationalism, with an agenda of territorial expansion. Serbs usurped the political machinery and military hardware of the former Yugoslav federal government for their plan to create Greater Serbia, a centuries-old Serbian aspiration.

PHILIP J. COHEN

THE UNITED STATES ROLE IN CATALYZING AND SUSTAINING SERBIAN AGGRESSION

One-sided US support for a centralized communist Yugoslavia encouraged this war from the outset. Secretary of State James Baker chastised both Slovenia and Croatia for their moves towards independence and flatly stated that a "cold welcome" awaited these republics if they left Yugoslavia. Just days before the invasion of Slovenia, in June 1991, Baker visited Belgrade and assured its government that the USA was committed to the "territorial integrity of Yugoslavia."[52] The Belgrade government dominated by Serbian nationalists interpreted this message as a "green light" for the military invasion of the democracy-seeking secessionist republics. Immediately after this invasion, the US administration expressed concern that Hungary, Romania, Greece, or Albania could be drawn into the conflict, but that the US role in this explosive crisis would be only to advise and advocate the preservation of the unity of Yugoslavia.[53]

From the outset, the USA ceded leadership of the resolution of the Yugoslav crisis to the EC.[54] Having done so, the USA shaped the framework in which the EC was to operate

1   rejection of independent, democratically elected governments;
2   an arms embargo on both the heavily armed aggressor as well as the disarmed victims of aggression;
3   no US support for military intervention.

The intrinsic flaw of placing this crisis under EC guidance could have been anticipated from the beginning, since EC decisions required unanimous consensus, rendering the formulation of policy slow, inefficient, and ineffective. Despite the self-congratulations of the Europeans over their initial mediation efforts,[55] Serbian aggression steadily escalated. Even when the USA denounced Serbia as the aggressor in September 1991,[56] the accompanying message was that the USA, finding no strategic interest, would not militarily intervene to stop the killing. At the same time, the EC also announced that it was not prepared for military intervention.[57] Encouraged by announcements of no military intervention, Serbia further escalated attacks on civilians in Croatia.[58] When, in November 1991, the USA joined the EC in economic sanctions against Serbia, President Bush expressed doubt that sanctions, including a proposed oil embargo, would end the war.[59] The US, however, offered no further alternatives.

Larger geopolitical considerations may explain why the US from the outset favored the *status quo* of the communist regime in former Yugoslavia in preference to the support of the democratic aspirations of the majority of its people. At that time, three Baltic republics of the Soviet Union were also seeking independence. Gorbachev, seeing the dissolution of Yugoslavia as a precedent for the dissolution of the Soviet Union, vigorously opposed the secession of Slovenia and Croatia. Since *détente* with the Soviet Union was then an overriding concern of American policy, it was not surprising that the USA supported Gorbachev in opposing independence bids in both the Soviet Union and Yugoslavia. However, justification for discouraging the democracy- and independence-seeking Yugoslav republics came to an end with the break-up of the Soviet Union late in 1991. The world changed quickly, but US policy remained unchanged, even as Serbia's indiscriminate attacks upon civilians escalated.[60] Moreover, when the EC finally did achieve the delicate consensus to recognize the independence of Slovenia and Croatia, the USA actively campaigned against recognition, undermining the European initiative. In November 1991, the EC imposed economic sanctions on Yugoslavia, but, in early December, these were lifted on all republics except Serbia and Montenegro.[61] Only days after the Europeans made their sanctions selective against the aggressors and removed sanctions from the victims, the US imposed sanctions against all of Yugoslavia, in an action uncoordinated with the EC.[62]

Despite reluctantly recognizing Slovenia, Croatia, and Bosnia-Herzegovina in early April 1992,[63] and despite clearly labeling Serbia as the aggressor,[64] the USA did not significantly reformulate its Balkan policy. For a brief period thereafter, the USA assumed a more active role, threatening to suspend Yugoslav membership in the Commission on Cooperation and Security in Europe (CSCE) and to suspend future US aid to Serbia.[65] Serbia responded by launching a major offensive.[66] Three weeks later, however, the USA announced it was withdrawing "in anger and frustration" with "no policy . . . other than to follow the lead of the European Community."[67] As Serbian forces achieved major advances in "ethnically cleansing" Bosnian territory during the succeeding weeks, this US non-policy drew criticism from a wide political spectrum, including Jeane Kirkpatrick, Anthony Lewis, and William Safire.[68] The administration soon announced limited diplomatic, political, and economic sanctions against Belgrade.[69] Much stronger rhetoric came days later, as Mr. Baker implied that "cleansing operations" by Serbs forces were reminiscent of Nazism. Invoking Chapter VII of the UN Charter, previously used as a framework for the Persian Gulf War, Baker pointedly suggested the possibility of US participation in a multinational military force. Furthermore, he assailed the EC for "looking for reasons not to act, or arguing somehow that action in the face of this kind of nightmare is not warranted at this time."[70] Although Mr. Baker appeared to have enunciated a cogent policy, the administration remained divided on the question of military involvement.[71]

The test of the seriousness of Mr. Baker's rhetoric came less than two months later. At the July 1992 CSCE meeting in Helsinki, when several Western countries indicated willingness to intervene militarily, President Bush declined to support this initiative. Moreover, when the Bosnian president pleaded directly with Bush for military intervention to stop the slaughter of civilians, Bush refused.[72] Rather, he characterized the murder of tens of thousands of civilians and expulsion of over two million people from their homes as a "hiccough" in the New World Order, and concluded that the USA cannot respond to every such situation. This stance betrayed a paucity of insight into the kind of principled leadership required to create the climate in which international aggression finds no opportunity.

A heightened moral and political imperative for intervention came in early August 1992, when the existence of Serbian concentration camps was revealed. The State Department, although condemning atrocities, again ruled out military intervention.[73] When an outraged public and bipartisan group of senators demanded a forceful response to these atrocities, which appeared to be taking on the characteristics of the Nazi extermination of Jews,[74] the administration responded by reversing its position from the previous day and questioning the existence of the concentration camps,[75] even as video footage of the camps was shown on national television that very day. However, after a public outcry which followed the media presentation of thousands of men, women, and children in concentration camps, President Bush denounced ethnic cleansing and suggested a shift towards the use of force limited to the delivery of humanitarian aid.[76] By narrowly defining US goals, however, President Bush was apparently seeking to limit any US military role.[77] By "hiding behind disaster relief,"[78] President Bush avoided the issue of the USA helping to disarm the Serbian aggressor. He also refused to lift the arms embargo on Bosnia-Herzegovina.

One plausible explanation for the failure of the USA to form an effective policy against Serbian aggression is the pro-Serbian orientation of Lawrence Eagleburger and Brent Scowcroft, President Bush's principal advisers on Yugoslavia. Eagleburger, a former Yugoslav ambassador, and Scowcroft, also formerly connected with the US embassy in Belgrade, have long-standing diplomatic, personal, and business ties with Belgrade and reportedly describe themselves as part of the "Belgrade Mafia," a government apparatus that includes Foreign Service officers, experts, and intelligence analysts.[79] It has been suggested that President Bush's prolonged silence on the reports of concentration camps in Bosnia reflected the influence of these advisers. In fact, both Lawrence Eagleburger and Brent Scowcroft have seriously misrepresented the situation in the Balkans to the American public. Mr. Eagleburger, treating the victims and victimizer as equal, has suggested all along that "we should wait until they exhaust themselves and then move in,"[80] by which time Bosnia would exist only in history. Only days after the revelation of Serbian concentration and death camps, when the administration found itself under great pressure to intervene militarily, both Eagleburger and Scowcroft appeared on network television (Sunday 9 August). Scowcroft portrayed Serbia's invasion of Croatia and Bosnia as a "civil war," despite US recognition of both republics as sovereign states.[81] Eagleburger suggested that it was unnecessary to lift the arms embargo, since "there are already enough arms there." Margaret Thatcher, appearing the same day on network television, directly addressed this obfuscation, agreeing that there are indeed plenty of arms in Bosnia, but adding that "they are in the hands of the aggressor."[82] George Bush and Margaret Thatcher, with their policies in opposition, have been respectively compared with Neville Chamberlain and Winston Churchill.[83]

In addition to the administration's steadfast commitment to minimize direct involvement in the Balkans, perhaps the most consistent feature of the US policy toward former Yugoslavia has been its inconsistency. The administration has alternated between flurries of activity and virtual disengagement.[84] On each occasion that the White House or State Department has hinted at the possibility of military intervention, it has quickly backtracked, undoubtedly to the relief of the Serbian leadership. Even while the USA was publicly condemning the Serbian invasion and supporting international sanctions against Serbia, the USA continued to train the military personnel of the Serbian aggressor.[85]

By continuous misassessment of the problem of former Yugoslavia and Eastern Europe, the USA has forfeited an historic opportunity to foster European stability and security in the post-cold war era. In August 1992, George D. Kenney resigned from the State Department, prompted by frustration over a policy primarily consisting of rhetoric, but practically "ineffective" and "counterproductive." Mr. Kenney further charged that US reliance on repeated cycles of fruitless EC-mediated negotiations was a "charade" whose outcome was known in advance.[86]

THE INEFFECTIVENESS OF THE UNITED NATIONS AND EUROPEAN COMMUNITY

The EC and UN role in mediating the conflict in former Yugoslavia offers an example of how, by analogy, a physician can worsen the course of a disease by inappropriate intervention. This conflict could have been prevented, but instead was exacerbated by incompetent international meddling.[87] In the first months, Serbian attacks were more limited and cautious. Possibly, Serbia was constrained by the perception that the post-Gulf War world community possessed an efficient mechanism to stop naked aggression, as was shown in Iraq. However, a chorus of subsequent announcements that the EC, the Western European Union, UN, and USA were proposing only negotiations, but not military intervention, emboldened Serbian aggression. The hesitancy of foreign powers to intervene would not have been so problematic, if there were not an arms embargo freezing the military imbalance in favor of Serbia. Although the EC did recognize Slovenia, Croatia, and Bosnia-Herzegovina in early 1992, the arms embargo on these countries was maintained in clear violation of their inalienable right to self-defense. As Serbian aggression escalated, the EC continued to negotiate dozens of meaningless cease-fires, equally blaming the aggressors and victims. Through 39 toothless cease-fires brokered by Lord Peter Carrington (a former business partner of Serbian president Slobodan Milošević), Serbia predictably expanded the war front, using each cease-fire to reposition troops and artillery for subsequent attack. Lord Carrington's ultimate resignation from the leadership of these sham EC "peace conferences" was long overdue,[88] but certainly too late to reverse the tragedy, which insightful diplomacy could have prevented.[89]

A further demonstration of international ineffectualness has been the unconstructive presence of the UN "peacekeeping" force, UNPROFOR, which has functioned as Serbia's silent partner, aiding in the achievement of Serbian war aims. UN forces became *de facto* "caretakers" of Serbian-controlled Croatian territories, maintaining the *status quo* and preventing Croatian forces from re-establishing control over their own land. This arrangement freed Serbian irregulars to move to the war front in Bosnia. Indeed, UNPROFOR soldiers have been observed to unprofessionally fraternize with Serbian forces *behind Serbian lines*.[90] In addition, UNPROFOR soldiers are reportedly engaged in bribery and illegal black market activities.[91] Moreover, UN forces have been successfully coerced to assist in "ethnic cleansing," conducting expelled civilians to "safety," because Serbian forces had threatened to otherwise kill them. In the parts of Slavonia under Serbian control, ethnic cleansing has virtually eliminated all non-Serbs, including Hungarians, Ukrainians, and Slovaks.[92] In violation of Serbia's agreement with the UN, Serbia has never complied in disarming the Serbian irregulars in Croatia. Even with UNPROFOR stationed in Croatia, Serbian forces have never ceased their daily shelling of Croatian cities from Serbian-occupied regions. According to UN Under-Secretary Marrack Goulding, UNPROFOR observers "are not there to physically prevent the shells from being fired." Rather, their purpose is to take notes and file reports when the weapon are used.[93] In a revealing statement, the military commander of UNPROFOR in Sarajevo "hinted broadly . . . that the reason he and other UN officials do not publicly point the finger at the Serb side for shelling civilians is fear of retaliatory attack on his troops."[94] Since the UN mandate has forbidden UNPROFOR to employ force to defend the civilian victims of Serbian aggression, continued expulsions of civilians by the Serbs have proceeded under direct UN observation.[95]

CONCLUSION

It is abundantly clear that Serbia and Serbian forces bear the overwhelming responsibility for the violence and atrocities which have characterized this one-sided aggression. This war could have been prevented if, from the outset, the international community had given clear support to the aspiring democracies, rather than favoring the communist regime, which sought to repress them. Instead, incompetent international maneuvering by the EC and the USA has had the net effect of encouraging Serbian aggression and weakening Serbia's victims. By freezing the military imbalance in favor of the aggressor, the ill-conceived arms embargo, imposed on all of what was once Yugoslavia, undoubtedly has had its greatest impact on Serbia's victims, Croatia and Bosnia-Herzegovina. Most incomprehensibly, the embargo has been retained on the victims, in mockery of the UN Charter, even after their independence and sovereignty was internationally recognized. The slow and ineffectual response to Serbia's aggression, coming only months after the highly coordinated international response to Iraq's aggression, has mocked the concept of a New World Order in which "aggression will not stand" (as George Bush emphatically stated in response to Saddam Hussein's invasion of Kuwait). Thus, the Islamic world, horrified by the systematic extermination and expulsion of Muslims under the watch of the USA, EC, and UN, is skeptical of Western principles of justice. In light of the West's failure, Muslim countries are now re-evaluating their own option and obligation to stop the slaughter and brutality in Bosnia.

The challenge remains to stop Serbia's aggression to prevent a larger international conflict and to affirm the West's commitment to the rule of international law. Former Yugoslavia is not Vietnam, not Lebanon, not Northern Ireland. The more appropriate analogy is Adolf Hitler and, more recently, Saddam Hussein, that is, a ruthless aggressor seeking territorial aggrandizement and employing genocide to accomplish its end. The crisis in former Yugoslavia has epitomized the choice between the paths of Neville Chamberlain and Winston Churchill. The Churchillian path has thus far been avoided, to the disgrace and shame of those who have presumed to lead.

NOTES

1 V. P. Gagnon, Jr., "Yugoslavia: Prospects for Stability," *Foreign Affairs*, vol. 70, no. 3, Summer 1991: 17–35.
2 Blaine Harden, "EC Withdraws Ambassadors From Belgrade: Serbia Rebuked Again on Bosnian War," *Washington Post*, 12 May 1992: A14; "US Joins EC in Recalling Envoy From Belgrade. Serbian Aggression in Bosnia Cited as International Countermeasures Take Shape," *Washington Post*, 13 May 1992: A25; Jeri Laber and Ivana Nizich (op-ed), "Milosevic's Land Grab," *Washington Post*, 25 May 1992: A25; Chuck Sudetic, "Observers Blame Serb-Led Army for Escalating War in Croatia," *The New York Times*, 3 December 1991: A8.
3 Christopher Cviic, "Looking for Hope Beneath the Ashes," *The Tablet*, London, 15 August 1992: 1004.
4 Chuck Sudetic, "UN Asks Croatia to Admit Bosnians," *The New York Times*, 4 November 1992: A18.
5 "The U.N.'s Bad Example on Bosnians" (editorial), *The New York Times*, 11 November 1992.

6 Stephen Kinzer, "Ethnic Conflict is Threatening in Yet Another Region of Yugoslavia: Kosovo," *The New York Times*, 9 November 1992: A8; John F. Burns, "Winds of Yugoslavia's War Threaten To Engulf Ethnic Enclave in Serbia," *The New York Times*, 26 May 1992: A6; John Burns, "'Free' Macedonia Faces Hostile World," *The New York Times*, 1 April 1992: A15; Robert L. Keatley, "Kosovo Could Trigger a Balkan War," *Wall Street Journal*, 29 June 1992: A14.

7 Robert L. Keatley (see note 6); Peter Maass, "Serbians Pressing Ethnic Albanians In Uneasy Kosovo," *Washington Post*, 15 July 1991: A13; Ken Danforth, "Serbs can't wait to get at the Albanians," Philadelphia *Inquirer*, 3 June 1992: A15:

> in the last three years, tear gas, indiscriminate beatings and killings, arrests of wounded people in hospitals, 85,000 ethnic Albanians kicked out of their jobs and total control of schools, the press and food distribution have become a way of life . . . Many Serbs, including Belgrade intellectuals, attach monstrous crimes to the Albanians whom they consider subhumans, simians, citing in detail their lascivious overbreeding.

Michael T. Kaufman, "A Different Kind of War in Kosovo: Serbian Repression vs. Quiet Resistance," *The New York Times*, 23 June 1992: A10.

8 Vaša Čubrilović [1897–1990], "Iseljavanje Arnauta" [The Expulsion of Albanians] in Bože Čović (ed.), *Izvori velikosrpske agresije* [Roots of Great Serbian Aggression] (Zagreb: August Cesarec & Školska knjiga, 1991: 106–24). The author, a political adviser for the royalist Yugoslav government, originally presented "The Expulsion of Albanians" as a lecture to the Serbian Cultural Club on 7 March 1937 and subsequently as a memorandum to the Yugoslav government. It is a blueprint for rendering the lives of Albanians so intolerable and terror-filled that they will emigrate to Albania and Turkish lands. Under the subtitle "The International Problem of Colonization," Čubrilović writes:

> At a time when Germany can expel tens of thousands of Jews and Russia can shift millions of people from one part of the continent to another, the expulsion of a few hundred thousand Albanians will not lead to the outbreak of a world war. However, those who decide should know what they want and persist in achieving this, regardless of the possible international obstacles.

Under the subtitle "The Ways of Expulsion," Čubrilović writes:

> As we have already said, the mass removal of Albanians from their [geographic] triangle [Debar–Rogozna–Niš] is the only effective way for us. To bring about the mass relocation, the first prerequisite is the creation of a suitable psychosis. It can be created in many ways. As it is known, the Muslim masses, in general, are readily influenced, especially by religion and are superstitious and fanatical. Therefore, first of all, we must win over their clergy and men of influence, either by money or threats, to support the relocation of the Albanians. Agitators to advocate this removal must be found, as quickly as possible, especially from Turkey, if it would provide them for us. They must describe the beauties in the new territories in Turkey, the easy and pleasant life there, kindle religious fanaticism and awaken pride in the Turkish state among them. Our press can be of colossal help by describing the gentle removal of Turks from Dobrudja [a region in southeastern Romania, previously populated by a significant Turkish minority] and their fair settlement in the new regions. By this description, a favorable mood would be created among our Albanian masses as well. Another means would be coercion by the state apparatus. The law must be

enforced to the extreme, to make staying intolerable for the Albanians: fines, imprisonments, the ruthless application of all police dispositions – such as the prohibition on smuggling, cutting forests, damaging agriculture, leaving dogs unchained – compulsory labor, and any other measure that an experienced police can contrive. From the economic aspect: the refusal to recognize old land deeds, the work with the land register in all regions should immediately include the ruthless collection of taxes and the payment of all private and public debts, annul grazing rights on state and municipal lands, the withdrawal of permits to operate a business, cancellation of permits of monopoly, dismissal from state, private, and civic offices, etc., will hasten the process of their removal. Health measures: the forceful application of all regulations, even in the homes, the pulling down of encircling walls and high hedges around the houses, the rigorous application of veterinary measures which will result in impeding the sale of livestock on the market, etc., also can be applied in a practical and effective way. In matters of religion, the Albanians are very touchy, and therefore they must be harassed in this area, too. This can be achieved through the ill-treatment of their clergy, the destruction of their cemeteries . . . Private initiative, too, can greatly assist in this direction. We should distribute weapons to our colonists, as need be. The old forms of Chetnik action should be organized and secretly assisted. In particular, a tide of Montenegrins should be launched from the hills, in order to create the large-scale conflict with the Albanians . . . [T]he whole affair should be presented with peace in our hearts as a conflict between clans and tribes and, if need be, ascribed to economic reasons. In an extreme necessity, local riots can be incited. These will be bloodily suppressed with the most effective means, but by colonists, the Montenegrin tribes, and the Chetniks, rather than by means of the army. There is one more means that Serbia very effectively used after 1878, secretly burning down Albanian villages and quarters in the cities.

(pp. 113–14)

The original document is deposited in the Military-Historical Institute of the Yugoslav People's Army in Belgrade: Archive of the Royal Yugoslav Army, 2/4, Box 69. After World War II, Čubrilović held several posts in the Federal Yugoslav government.

9 Douglas Jehl, "Iran Reported Trying to Send Arms to Bosnia," *Los Angeles Times*, 10 September 1992: A1.
10 Barbara Crossette, "Bosnia, Fearing Ethnic Partition, Will Propose 4 Local Authorities," *The New York Times*, 20 August 1992: A1, quoting Bosnian Foreign Minister Haris Silajdžić.
11 Kim Murphy, "Islamic World Galvanized by Reported Killing of Bosnia's Muslims, Deplores Inaction by UN," *Los Angeles Times*, 14 August 1992: A5; Gerald F. Seib, "Split Between Islam and West Widens Because of Crisis in Bosnia-Herzegovina," *The Wall Street Journal*, 17 August 1992: A4.
12 Jackson Diehl, "Contrast in US Policies Is Straining Alliances: "Double Standard" Seen in Bosnia, Iraq," *Washington Post*, 19 September 1991: A17.
13 Paul Goble (op-ed), "Serbians' Success Echoes in Russia," *The New York Times*, 13 August 1992: A23. The author is a former State Department specialist on Soviet nationalities and is currently a senior associate at the Carnegie Endowment for International Peace.
14 Margaret Thatcher (op-ed), "Stop the Excuses. Help Bosnia Now," *The New York Times*, 6 August 1992: A23.

15 Jeane Kirkpatrick (op-ed), "The Only Way to Stop Aggression," *Washington Post*, 3 August 1992: A19.
16 Leslie H. Gelb (op-ed), "The West's Scam In Bosnia," *The New York Times*, 9 August 1992: E17; "George Kenney's Message" (editorial), *The New York Times*, 27 August 1992: A22; George D. Kenney (op-ed), "Bosnia – Appeasement in Our Time," *Washington Post*, 30 August 1992: C7.
17 V. P. Gagnon, Jr. (see note 1).
18 V. P. Gagnon, Jr. (see note 1). The eight votes within the federal presidency of Yugoslavia were derived from six republics (Bosnia-Herzegovina, Croatia, Macedonia, Montenegro, Serbia, and Slovenia) and two autonomous regions (Kosovo and Vojvodina) within Serbia. In 1989, Serbian authorities dissolved the legislatures of both autonomous regions, but retained their votes in the federal presidency. Thus, Serbia directly controlled three of eight votes. Montenegro and Serbia, voting in a block, effectively controlled four of eight votes, frequently deadlocking the federal presidency.
19 Chuck Sudetic, "Croatia Votes for Sovereignty and Confederation," *The New York Times*, 20 May 1991: A3. More than 86 percent of eligible voters participated. Republic of Slovenia, [*Republic of Slovenia – 1990. Chronicle of Slovenian Year of Secession in Words and Pictures*], Ljubljana: Zaloznistvo Slovenske Knjige, 1991: 175. According to these data, 93.2 percent of all eligible voters participated; 88.2 percent supported independence; 4 percent opposed independence; and 7.8 percent of votes were not valid.
20 Jim Fish, "Yugoslav Army Upended in Slovenia. Takeover Begun Leisurely Becomes Albatross for Privileged Force," *Washington Post*, 2 July 1991: A1:

> The overconfident army generals, thinking they would subdue Slovenia's Territorial Defense Force within hours, sent fewer than 100 tanks to seize Slovenia's 27 major border crossing points . . . The tanks were crewed mainly by young draftees whose supplies of food and fuel soon ran out.

Blaine Harden, "Slovenia Nears Independence as Croatia Faces Civil War: Slovenes See Army Pullout as Key Step to Freedom," *Washington Post*, 20 July 1991: A1. Robert Marquand, "Yugoslav Accords Bring Calm to Slovenia's Capital," *Christian Science Monitor*, Boston, 2 July 1991, p. 3.
21 Blaine Harden (see note 20).
22 Croatia and Slovenia, both attacked by the Yugoslav Army, fared very differently. Slovenia, with no significant Serb minority, had retained control over 50–70 percent of the military *materiél* of its Territorial Defense Force. Slovenia faced no Serb insurgency, and the Yugoslav Army was unprepared. In contrast, Croatia had a significant Serb minority, which mobilized quickly as an insurgency, with the support of the Yugoslav Army and Serbian leadership. Eighty percent of the *materiél* of the Croatian Territorial Defense Force was appropriated by the Yugoslav Army, which, in turn, supplied weapons to Serbian insurgents.
23 Blaine Harden, "Croatia Charges Army Shadows its Officials. Police Arming for Showdown with Serbia," *Washington Post*, 19 January 1991: A10:

> In early December [1990], the federal minister of defense threatened to use force to take weapons away from police and local militia in Croatia and Slovenia.

Blaine Harden, "Croatia Agrees to Demobilize Police: Showdown with Yugoslav Army Averted by Compromise," *Washington Post*, 27 January 1991: A14.

24 Ian Traynor, "Army is Calling the Shots in Belgrade," *The Guardian*, London, 29 January 1991.

25 Jim Fish, "Yugoslavia Sends Troops to Croatia. Local Police Clash With Demonstrators," *Washington Post*, 3 March 1991: A20; Mary Battiata, "Serbian Guerrilla Camps Operate Inside Croatia . . . Serbs Train inside Croatia for Civil War," *Washington Post*, 22 July 1991: A1:

> There is ample evidence that Serbian fighters [in Croatia] are receiving clandestine support and equipment from Serbian officers in the Yugoslav Federal Army. The officers corps in the Yugoslav Federal Army are dominated by Serbs. At camp headquarters, the commander reads positions from detailed, Yugoslav Army topographical maps. Soldiers wear crisp, new camouflage uniforms . . . identical to those worn by the special forces of the federal army. Local officials say they were provided by federal army officers.

Stephen Engelberg, "Serbia Sending Supplies to Compatriots in Croatia," *The New York Times*, 27 July 1991: A3: "Officials of Serbia say their republic has been directly aiding rebellions by Serbs in Croatia."

26 Andrew Borowiec, "General Wants to Punish Croats," *Washington Times*, 27 July 1991: A1. General Blogoje Adžič, Chief of Yugoslavia's general staff was quoted:

> Even if there has to be a thousand deaths, the outside world will not intervene to back the two secessionist republics against the federal army led mainly by Serbian officers.

Jian Paolo Rossetti, Gigi Zazzeri, "[Here Are The New Warlords]," *Europeo* (Italy), 19 July 1991, no. 29: 22. Following the invasion of Slovenia, Yugoslav General Adzic, a key military strategist, stated, "This rebellion must be terminated, even if it is going to generate a thousand deaths. The international community will be agitated a bit, but three days later everything will be forgotten and our objectives will be obtained."

27 *Leksikon*, Zagreb: Jugoslavensk leksikografski zavod, 1974: 1056. Krajina, meaning "border," refers to the Croatian military border. These Croatian lands, apposing territories of the Ottoman Empire, were administered from Graz, Austria. The military border was disarmed in 1873 and legally disbanded in 1881.

28 Christopher Cviic, "Looking for Hope Beneath the Ashes," *The Tablet*, London, 15 August 1992: 1003.

29 John Tagliabue, "Serbs in Croatian Cities are Quiet and Invisible," *The New York Times*, 6 September 1991: A14: "the largest concentrations of Serbs in the republic are in heartland cities like Zagreb." Figures quoted are from the official Yugoslav census of March 1991.

30 Jim Fish, "Serbia Keeps Croatian From Top Post. Deadlock of Collective Presidency Adds to Yugoslav Turmoil," *Washington Post*, 16 May 1991: A27; Celestine Bohlen, "Rotation of Yugoslav Leaders Blocked by Dominant Region," *The New York Times*, 17 May 1991: A1.

31 Ian Traynor (see note 24).

32 Chuck Sudetic, "Yugoslav Battles Rage on Eve of Talks," *The New York Times*, 5 November 1991: A3; "Unity and Stability Not the Same: Yugoslavia is a Challenge for the New Europe" (editorial), Montreal *Gazette*, 5 July 1991: B2; Laura Silber, "Serbs, Croats Press War of Words, Guns," *Washington Post*, 6 November 1991: A26; David Binder, "Unified Yugoslavia Goal of US Policy," *The New York Times*, 1 July 1991: A6. David Binder, "US Voices Regret on Yugoslav Crisis: Plans to Ignore the Secession Attempts by Croatian and Slovenian Republics," *The New York Times*, 27 June 1991: A10.

33 John M. Goshko, "UN Imposes Arms Embargo on Yugoslavia," *Washington Post*, 26 September 1991: A1.

34 Blaine Harden, "Yugoslav Army Attacks Slovenia, Meets Resistance at Border Posts," *Washington Post*, 28 June 1991: A1.

35 Marian Houk, "UN Backs Yugoslav Call for Embargo," *Christian Science Monitor*, 27 September 1991: 4.

36 "Europe: The sense of a senseless war" (editorial), *Economist*, 23 November 1991: 53.

37 Blaine Harden, "Yugoslavia's Tensions Kill Croatian Tourism: Serbs Accused of Sabotaging Travel Industry," *Washington Post*, 15 June 1991: A17; Eric Bourne, "Ethnic Violence Exacts Heavy Economic Toll in Yugoslavia," *The Christian Science Monitor*, 6 September 1991: 7.

38 Blaine Harden, "Bosnia-Herzegovina on the brink. Yugoslav Republic Seeks to Steer Clear of Ethnic Carnage by Showing Political Flexibility," *Washington Post*, 15 January 1992: A17; Laura Silber, "Bosnian Leaders Seek to Halt Serb-Croat Fighting," *Washington Post*, 28 March 1992: A18.

39 Staff of the Commission on Security and Cooperation in Europe [Helsinki Commission], *The Referendum on Independence in Bosnia-Herzegovina: February 29–March 1, 1992*, CSCE, 237 Ford House Office Building, Washington, DC 20515, 12 March 1992: 12 [hereafter Referendum on Independence].

40 John F. Burns, "Bosnian Strife Cuts Old Bridges of Trust . . . Ancient Ties of Coexistence Are Broken by 'Ethnic Purification'," *The New York Times*, 22 May 1992: A1.

41 Referendum on Independence, p. 18.

42 Laura Silber (see note 32).

43 Henry Kamm, "Yugoslav Refugee Crisis Europe's Worst Since '40's," *The New York Times*, 24 July 1992: A1.

44 Staff Report to the Committee on Foreign Relations, "The Ethnic Cleansing of Bosnia-Herzegovina," Washington, D.C., 15 August 1992.

45 John Tagliabue, "Yugoslav Republic Votes to Secede, The Third to Do So," *The New York Times*, 10 September 1991: A1. About 75 percent of the 1.3 million eligible voters participated, with about three-quarters choosing independence.

46 Blaine Harden, "Greece Blocks Recognition of Macedonia," *Washington Post*, 10 June 1992: A25. "It is not because Macedonia . . . fails to meet modern tests of statehood. Among the six former republics of collapsed Yugoslavia, it has the highest scores. It respects human rights and tolerates dissent. It controls its own borders and its constitution forbids claims on its neighbors' land."

47 Alan Riding, "Europe Nods to Bosnia, Not Macedonia," *The New York Times*, 7 April 1992: A3.

48 Blaine Harden (see note 46).

49 Blaine Harden (see note 46).

50 Michael Wines, "US Says Greek Shipping Lines Are Violating Yugoslav Embargo," *The New York Times*, 18 November 1992: A14.

51 John Burns, "'Free' Macedonia," (see note 6).

52 David Hoffman, "Baker Urges Yugoslavs to Keep Unity: US Would Not Recognize Independent Republics, Secretary Says," *Washington Post*, 22 June 1991: A1.

53 John M. Goshko, "US Opposes Using Force To Keep Yugoslavia United," *Washington Post*, 27 June 1991: A36.

54 Lawrence Freedman, "Order and Disorder in the New World," *Foreign Affairs*, vol. 71, no. 1, 1992: 33.

55 William Drozdiak, "Europeans Laud Their Efforts in Yugoslavia," *Washington Post*, 30 June 1991: A20:

Leaders of the European Community today hailed their intervention in Yugoslavia's civil war as evidence of a new era in which they are prepared to launch bold initiatives to resolve troubles on their own continent and are less inclined to await guidance from the US.

56 Thomas L. Friedman, "Bush's Yugoslav Policy Shifts to Serbs," *The New York Times*, 27 September 1991: A6.
57 William Drozdiak, "Lack of an Armed Option Limits EC's Yugoslav Peace Initiative," *Washington Post*, 5 September 1991: A23.
58 Blaine Harden, "Yugoslav Tanks Roll Into Croatia. Army Launches Biggest Offensive," *Washington Post*, 21 September 1991: A1.
59 Ann Devroy, "Bush Backs Yugoslav Sanctions," *Washington Post*, 10 November 1991: A39.
60 "US Not Jumping on Bandwagon," *The New York Times*, 16 January 1992; Stephen Kinzer, "Europe, Backing Germans, Accepts Yugoslav Breakup," *The New York Times*, 16 January 1992: A10.
61 Laura Silber, "Serbia Excepted as EC Lifts Yugoslav Sanctions. Community Team Accuses Federal Army of Brutality; UN Envoy to Visit Osijek," *Washington Post*, 3 December 1991: A9.
62 [AP,] "US Imposes Sanctions Against All of Yugoslavia," *Washington Post*, 7 December 1991.
63 David Binder, "US Recognizes the Independence of 3 Breakaway Yugoslav Lands," *The New York Times*, 8 April 1992: A10.
64 Blaine Harden, "US Joins EC," (see note 2).
65 David Hoffman, "US Urges Europe To Protect Bosnia. Baker Maps Protest to Serb Leaders," *Washington Post*, 15 April 1992: A1.
66 Blaine Harden, "Serbia Seems Unmoved By Western Warnings. Belgrade Presses Offensive in Bosnia," *Washington Post*, 17 April 1992: A25.
67 David Binder, "US, Frustrated, Backs Off From the Crisis in Yugoslavia," *The New York Times*, 5 May 1992: A10.
68 Anthony Lewis (op-ed), "The New World Order," *The New York Times*, 17 May 1992: E17; Jeane Kirkpatrick (op-ed), "Folding in the Face of Violence. This isn't a Comic-opera War, so Hold the Talk of a New World Order," *Washington Post*, 18 May 1992: A21; William Safire (op-ed), "Punish the Serbs," *The New York Times*, 21 May 1992: A29.
69 Barbara Crossette, "After Weeks of Seeming Inaction, US Decides to Punish Belgrade," *The New York Times*, 23 May 1992: A1.
70 Don Oberdorfer, "Baker Urges UN To Sanction Serbs. Armed US Role Not Ruled Out," *Washington Post*, 25 May 1992: A1.
71 Barton Gellman, "Administration is Sharply Divided On Whether to Expand Balkan Role," *Washington Post*, 9 July 1991: A19.
72 Don Oberdorfer and Mark Fisher, "Bush Turns Aside Bosnian Plea for Military Intervention. Western Allies at Helsinki Summit Favor More Action," *Washington Post*, 10 July 1992: A13.
73 David Binder, "No US Action Seen on Prison Camps. State Dept. Confirms Reports of Abuses but Cites Policy Avoiding Intervention," *The New York Times*, 4 August 1992: A6.
74 Don Oberdorfer and Helen Dewar, "Clinton, Senators Urge Bush to Act on Balkans. Forceful Response to Atrocity Reports Is Sought," *Washington Post*, 6 August 1992: A1.
75 Krauss, Clifford, "US Retreats From Taking Atrocities in Bosnia Camps as Fact," *The New York Times*, 5 August 1992: A12.

76 Don Oberdorfer, "Bush Shifts Toward Force to Aid Bosnia," *Washington Post*, 7 August 1992: A1.

77 Gordon Michael R., "Limits of U.S. Role. White House Is Seeking to Minimize Any Use of Military in Balkan Conflict," *The New York Times*, 11 August 1992: A6.

78 "Margaret Thatcher as Churchill" (editorial), *The New York Times*, 11 August 1992: A18.

79 Saul Friedman, "'Belgrade Mafia' Seen Influencing U.S. Policy. Slow Response tied to Scowcroft, Eagleburger," New York *Newsday*, 9 August 1992: 4.

80 "George Kenney's Message" (see note 16).

81 Don Oberdorfer, "State Dept. Backtracks on Atrocity Reports: Calls for Action on Serb Camps Rise," *Washington Post*, 5 August 1992: A1; Andrew Rosenthal, "Allies Inch Closer to Bosnia Aid Pact. Agree on Strong Words, but Differ on Strong Actions," *The New York Times*, 10 August 1992: A8. "Mr. Scowcroft and Mr. Eagleburger . . . said the fighting in the remnants of Yugoslavia was really a civil war, even though Mr. Bush announced last week that he would open diplomatic relations with Bosnia and Herzegovina, Croatia, and Slovenia."

82 Margaret Thatcher, interviewed by David Brinkley, WABC-TV, 9 August 1992.

83 "Margaret Thatcher as Churchill" (see note 78); Anthony Lewis (op-ed), "Yesterday's Man," *The New York Times*, 3 August 1992: A19.

84 David Binder, "Administration Policy: Bush Policy on Yugoslavia Has Fluctuated," *The New York Times*, 28 July 1992: A10.

85 Slobodan Lekić, "Yugoslav military readies for West," Huntsville *Times*, 8 August 1992: A6. Late in 1991, during the height of the Yugoslav Army assault on the Croatian city of Vukovar (which was ultimately reduced to rubble), Yugoslav Army Major Petrović was received at the US Air Force Command and Staff College at Maxwell Air Force Base in Montgomery, Alabama. Following 10 months of training, he returned to Serbia, where he described plans to counterattack US forces, in the event of foreign military intervention in Bosnia-Herzegovina.

86 Oberdorfer and Dewar (see note 74).

87 Mark Almond, "Blundering in the Balkans: The European Community and the Yugoslav Crisis," second edition (School of European Studies, London, 1991).

88 Barbara Crossette, "Europe's Envoy in Yugoslav Crisis Quits," *The New York Times*, 26 August 1992: A8.

89 Norman Stone, "Blame the Somnolent Man of Europe for the Yugoslav Horror Show," *The Sunday Times*, 31 May 1992, at Features section.

90 Eyewitness testimony of Judy Darnell, RN, an American nurse who volunteered in the medical corps on the Croatian front lines. Her written statement is available from the author upon request.

91 *Corriere Della Sera*, Milan, 26 August 1992.

92 Cviic (see note 3).

93 Blaine Harden, "Relief Plane Crashes Approaching Sarajevo: US Search Copters Report Hostile Fire," *Washington Post*, 4 September 1992: A27.

94 Blaine Harden (see note 93).

95 Documentation of the expulsion of thousands of Croats from UN protected zones within Croatia is available from the Office of UNPROFOR, Zagreb, Croatia.

3

THE SERBO-CROATIAN WAR, 1991

Norman Cigar

The Serbo-Croatian War fought in 1991 is only one of a series of wars in which Serbia has been involved or may yet become involved in the wake of Yugoslavia's break-up. This war has already had significant regional implications but, as Clausewitz posited, the end-state of a war in the real world is seldom, if ever, definitive.[1] Like a receding horizon, the result desired by one belligerent may be elusive if the other party believes the outcome to be unjust and reversible. While it is still too early to tell what the ultimate situation will look like in this case, this chapter will maintain that the cease-fire agreement signed on 3 January 1992, in whose adoption Western pressure played a considerable part, is inherently unstable, particularly in so far as its implementation, arguably, has favored one belligerent – Serbia – to the detriment of the other.

In seeking to identify the causes of the war, conventional wisdom has stressed either the hatreds dating over the past millennium or the immediate decision by Croatia to seek independence in May 1991, as a result of which the Serbian minority, fearing for its fate and wishing to remain part of Yugoslavia, rebelled. I will argue that the key catalyst for the Serbo-Croatian War, is to be found, rather, in the decision taken in the mid-1980s to seek the establishment of a Greater Serbia (that is, claiming for Serbia any lands where Serbs have settled, even if only constituting a minority of the population) and in the subsequent attempts to implement that goal. Moreover, corollary theses will be that without the direct active involvement in Croatia by Serbia and by the Serbian-dominated Yugoslav People's Army (Jugoslavenska Narodna Armija – JNA) there very likely would not have been a war, and that secession by the Serbs was well on its way already while Croatia was still ruled by a communist government.

Further, it will be argued that this was very much in the Clausewitzian tradition of inter-state wars, with Slobodan Milošević's government in Belgrade the strategic center of gravity of the Serbian war effort; that heavy regular units were the operational center of gravity (that is, the key variable in implementing strategy on the battlefield); that the JNA was a far less

51

formidable fighting force than most had expected it to be; that Serbian national will has been relatively weak; and that Milošević agreed to a cease-fire only after Serbia had reached its culminating point, at which time the cost of continuing to prosecute the war exceeded the likely benefits.[2]

THE ROAD TO WAR

The historical context

History, of course, has helped to shape the confrontation and can help us understand it. However, it was not the deterministic factor that some have suggested. History does not doom one to a repetition of the past or to immobilism and, in the case of Yugoslavia, such blanket evaluations are often misleading, because inter-ethnic relations have been far from frozen over time, with fluid communal alliances common. Blaming today's conflicts in the former Yugoslavia solely on atavistic ethnic hatreds, while superficially attractive, is often only a convenient rationalization for shrugging one's shoulders and doing nothing. Most wars are fought to achieve political objectives, and both Croatia and Serbia have developed national strategies based on concrete present-day national interests which have guided their policies.

The vision of a Greater Serbia

However, if there has been one overriding historical factor whose legacy has had a continuing impact on the modern political development of all the ethnic groups in what eventually came to constitute Yugoslavia, it has been that of the quest for a Greater Serbia. Since the emergence of Serbian nationalism in the early nineteenth century, territorial expansion has been a pivotal force, due to the central place in the formulation of Serbian nationalism of having all Serbs, wherever they might be, live within a single state.

The 400 years of Ottoman rule were far from the uniformly bleak period of popular lore and, for the Serbs, marked a time of expansion, with the start of a long-term migration into present-day Croatia (as well as Bosnia and Vojvodina), whether as Ottoman or Habsburg mercenaries, official settlers, or refugees. The descendants of these settlers, and those of other Orthodox settlers who eventually assimilated with the Serbs, today are known as the *Prečani* Serbs ("those Serbs who live on the other side"). A policy of official settlement continued after the formation of Yugoslavia in 1918, with large-scale transfers of Serbs to Croatia (as well as to Vojvodina, Macedonia, and Kosovo). At present, these Serbs living outside of Serbia number over two million, and those in Croatia account for 12.2 percent of the population.

After achieving autonomy in 1830, Serbia gained its formal independence from the Ottoman Empire after the war of 1878 and, at the same time, added parts of present-day Southern Serbia. In the Balkan Wars of 1912–13, Serbia annexed Kosovo, the Sandžak, and Macedonia from the Ottoman Empire. After World War I, it gained parts of Bulgaria. Finally, in 1945, with the reconstitution of Yugoslavia under the aegis of Tito's communist movement, Serbia added for the first time or reaffirmed its control over minority-Serb areas such as Vojvodina, Kosovo, the Sandžak, and Srijem (the latter at the expense of Croatia), as well as part of Kosovo which neighboring Montenegro had conquered in 1913. Montenegro, many of whose inhabitants also view themselves as Serbs, has followed a similar pattern, sharing in the partition of Albanian-inhabited territory and the Sandžak in 1912–13, and annexing the Boka Kotorska coastline from Croatia and the Herceg-Novi coastline from Bosnia-Herzegovina in 1945.

Since the nineteenth century, however, Serbian nationalists have envisioned an even larger Greater Serbia. Although all Serbs were united in a single state with the establishment of Yugoslavia after the collapse of the Habsburg Empire in 1918, the subsequent hegemony by the Serbs and the resulting alienation among the other ethnic groups led to chronic instability, which was instrumental in Yugoslavia's rapid disintegration under the German onslaught of April 1941.

World War II

The quest for a Greater Serbia perhaps took its most violent form when it was revived during World War II, a watershed for inter-ethnic strife in Yugoslavia. Croatia (Pavelić) and Serbia both established fascist states allied to Germany. In addition to the Serbian state under Ljotić and Nedić allied to Germany, more extreme Serbian nationalists organized the Chetnik resistance movement, whose focus was to establish a Greater Serbia. Led by Draža Mihailović, a royalist officer who had gone underground after Yugoslavia's defeat by the Germans, the Chetnik leadership had drafted by June 1941 a formal policy document for a "Homogeneous Serbia." The plan called for a "Greater Serbia" extending over present-day Bosnia-Herzegovina, Montenegro, Macedonia, Kosovo, Vojvodina, much of Croatia, northern Albania, and parts of Rumania, Hungary, and Bulgaria. Recognizing that Serbs were usually in the minority in these areas, the strategy envisaged "the cleansing of the lands of all non-Serb elements."[3] Their extremist counterparts on the Croatian side, the Ustaše, had a similar exclusivist ethnic program, and established a Croatian state extending over Croatia and Bosnia-Herzegovina, arguing that most Slavic Muslims until 1945 identified themselves as "Muslim Croatians."

The parallel Chetnik and Ustaše movements, along with Tito's communist partisans (in which both Serbs and Croatians participated), accounted for most of the mass killings, expulsions, torture, and destruction which marked the period. The most reliable estimates place the number of deaths from all causes in Yugoslavia during and immediately after World War II at a million, about equally split between Serbs and non-Serbs. Apart from the obvious human tragedy, this massive population loss was to remain also a powerful political symbol for all national communities in Yugoslavia.

Postwar Yugoslavia

Although the defeat of the Chetniks in World War II by Tito's communists prevented the fulfillment of their program, as a compromise intended to buttress his new government, Croatian-born Tito granted Serbia the areas of Kosovo, Vojvodina, and the Sandžak, even though non-Serbs were a majority in each case. In addition, the Serbs were given a disproportionate share of positions in the federal bureaucracy, military, diplomatic corps, economic infrastructure, judicial system, and the Communist Party, a situation which continued until the break-up of Yugoslavia. On a regional level, the postwar system also led to an uneven distribution of power between Serbia and Croatia, to the latter's detriment.[4]

This imbalance was also institutionalized within Croatia itself. According to the 1981 census, Serbs accounted for 11.5 percent of Croatia's population of 4.6 million but, in 1989, they held 24.8 percent of the republic-level and 21.4 percent of the local political posts, as well as having significant influence in the ruling Croatian League of Communists, as the party was known, with over 20 percent of its membership in the mid-1980s, and a lopsided presence in Croatia's Ministry of Defense (32 percent), police force (70 percent), judiciary, and state-run media.[5]

The discontent and suspicion among the other ethnic groups in Yugoslavia which resulted from what they perceived as Serbian attempts to dominate caused much of the political gridlock into which the country had fallen by the 1980s. At the same time, the passing away of Tito's generation of leaders, committed to a vision of a communist Yugoslavia, removed a significant element of coercion and opened the way toward democracy and change. However, the withering of authoritarianism inevitably would have meant calls to redress this unequal situation and, potentially, the dissolution of Yugoslavia. This deeply concerned many Serbs who saw a potential loss of status and privilege on an individual and communal basis, as well as the end of the opportunity to create Greater Serbia. These concerns provided the backdrop for the resurgence of Serbian nationalism in the mid-1980s and underlay the road to war.

The Serbian Memorandum

If one is to look for a definable and traceable catalyst to the Serbo-Croatian War, it is most likely to be found in the form of the *Serbian Memorandum*. Drafted by Serbia's leading intellectuals – many of whom subsequently have become key political figures – and released by the Serbian Academy of Arts and Sciences in 1986, the *Memorandum* proclaimed in no uncertain terms that the traditional goal of a Greater Serbia retained its validity. The manifesto maintained that the "national question" of the Serbs had been thwarted by the communists at the end of World War II, since the Serbian people "did not get its own state like other peoples." Therefore, the only solution, according to the *Memorandum*, was "the territorial unity of the Serbian people," to be achieved by uniting all the Serbs in a single Serbian national state or, in its words, "the establishment of the full national integrity of the Serbian people, regardless of which republic or province it inhabits is its historic and democratic right."[6]

Coming at a time of impending change and uncertainty, the *Memorandum* seemed to answer the need for a national strategy blueprint for Serbia. However, it also set the stage for the outbreak of war, since implementing its objectives was bound to clash with the interests of Yugoslavia's other national communities. Unless the latter accepted the *Memorandum*'s implications passively – an unlikely scenario – it could only be put into effect through the use of force.

Predictably, most of the Communists then in power in Belgrade reacted to this agenda of creating a Greater Serbia with hostility, since they viewed it as a point of no return toward communal violence. In an address at Belgrade University on 30 October 1986, Ivan Stambolić, Serbia's President and a reformist communist, for example, assessed that:

> The so-called Memorandum is not new. It is the old chauvinist concern for the fate of the Serbian cause with the well-known formula that the Serbs win the wars but lose the peace . . . In short, the so-called Memorandum, more precisely and with an easy conscience, could be entitled "In Memoriam" for Yugoslavia, Serbia, Socialism, self-management, equality, brotherhood, and unity . . . Essentially, it is diametrically opposed to the interests of the Serbs throughout Yugoslavia.[7]

The *Memorandum* might have languished had it not been for a rising strongman in the ruling Serbian League of Communists, Slobodan Milošević, who saw nationalism as a potential vehicle to power in place of the decaying communist legitimacy. It was thanks to Milošević that Serbia's communists were to forge a symbiosis with the non-communist nationalists and to provide the organization necessary to implement the program.[8]

Moreover, the JNA could be counted upon, at least in the short run, to provide the necessary muscle to deal with any resistance, thanks to parallel interests with Milošević and the nationalists. Serbian militants were soon busy lobbying the Serb officers within the JNA openly to back their program. Lobbying tactics included the use of pamphlets playing on Serb solidarity.[9] The JNA's officer corps was heavily Serbian and some high-ranking officers were early supporters of nationalism, such as General Colonel Života Panić, who was motivated by what he saw as the need to fulfill the "legitimate goal of all Serbs to live in a single state."[10] However, the JNA's senior leadership – dominated by hardline communists – for the most part was less moved by the vision of a Greater Serbia than by that of a highly centralized communist Yugoslavia, and what alarmed it most in the late 1980s was the drift toward democracy in Croatia and the other republics. Above all, a shift to democracy was likely to end the JNA's significant privileges as an independent political player. For example, the JNA had its own representation equal to that of an autonomous province in all national-level government and party bodies and equivalent representation at republic- and local-level government, as well as control over an extensive network of economic enterprises, and significant individual perks.

Reflecting its concern, in December 1990 the JNA created its own hardline Communist Party, judging that the parent League of Yugoslav Communists was becoming too liberal. At the very least, the shared interests included the scrapping of the more liberal 1974 Constitution and the decentralized federal structure it enshrined, that is, the sweeping away of the *status quo* which also obstructed the *Memorandum*'s goals. That the JNA foresaw that violence would be necessary in order to restructure the country is suggested by a meeting of its leadership in mid-1990, at which time some of the JNA's Croatian generals expressed their opposition to taking such a course of action.[11]

Milošević and his hardline faction were able to gain power within the Serbian League of Communists over more moderate rivals by December 1987 by playing the nationalist card. His most effective method was to intimidate rivals using violent street rallies, which were sustained initially by the Serbian nationalist backlash in Kosovo, where Serbian influence had eroded *vis-à-vis* the Albanian majority during the last decade. Once secure in Serbia, he proceeded throughout 1988 and 1989 to finance and organize more street violence to consolidate Serbia's hold over the autonomous provinces of Vojvodina and Kosovo – as well as his personal power base. His supporters succeeded in overthrowing the moderate communist leadership in Vojvodina and the pliant Albanian leadership in Kosovo and, for all intents and purposes, when Serbia ratified a new constitution in July 1990, the two provinces' traditional autonomy was completely quashed. In Montenegro, mob pressure was also successful in bringing hardline pro-Milošević nationalists to power. Moreover, in a charged speech at

Gazimestan, on 28 June 1989, on the 600th anniversary of the Battle of Kosovo (in which the Ottomans had defeated medieval Serbia) Milošević had signaled his government's intention to extend the nationalist agenda beyond Serbia's borders. When coupled with active measures being undertaken in neighboring republics, his emphasis that "The Serbs have always liberated themselves and, when they had the chance, also helped others to liberate themselves," seemed to commit Serbia to a forcible redrawing of Yugoslavia's long-established internal borders. The fact that the Serbian Orthodox bishop from Croatia's Dalmatia region, who was invited as a keynote speaker at the event, compared Dalmatia to Kosovo and concluded that both had made the same vow to Milošević also suggested greater interest by Milošević beyond Serbia.[12]

However, despite the friction between Serbs and non-Serbs in the political and economic spheres in the postwar period, ethnic groups in Yugoslavia had managed to coexist without overt violence for over a generation (with the exception of the periodic crackdowns against Serbia's Albanian minority). The sea-change in inter-ethnic relations needed for the mass mobilization of the Serbs in support of the *Memorandum* therefore required an intensive and methodical political and media campaign in the 1980s. As part of his mobilization strategy, Milošević encouraged the Serbs to focus their wrath against other ethnic groups who stood in the way of fulfilling the *Memorandum*'s goals. Serbia's state-controlled media, as well as many intellectuals, began a sustained campaign in support of the nationalist agenda, emphasizing such themes as the World War II deaths of Serbs and the alleged present-day danger of renewed genocide, and accusing virtually every other ethnic and religious community of threatening the Serbs. The attacks against Islam, which often bordered on overt racism, were particularly vicious.

At rallies in Serbia and Montenegro in 1988 and 1989, such slogans as "Slobodan [Milošević] send us lettuce; we will already have meat [since] we will slaughter the Croatians," "Oh Muslims, you black crows, Tito is not around to protect you," "We love you Slobodan because you hate the Muslims," and "I'll be first, who'll be second to drink some Turkish [i.e., Muslim] blood?" were common. Perhaps most ominous were the "spontaneous" demands voiced at such staged rallies of "we want arms."[13] Milošević, moreover, cast a benign eye over the reemergence of various Chetnik organizations, banned since 1945, most of which set up their own armed militias and soon became the mainstream of the nationalist movement.

Serbia's officials, media, and nationalist leaders have continued to whip up popular sentiments, explaining the threat not only in domestic terms, but also with such twists as Germany's drive toward "warm waters," the oil of the Balkans, and trade routes to the East; and Germany's desire to find a dump for nuclear waste materials. The obsession with raising the specter of the German threat extended even to allegations by the army journal that

German-Americans, including General H. Norman Schwarzkopf and the US Ambassadors to Belgrade and Moscow, were actually manipulating US foreign policy to Germany's benefit.[14] In addition, the Serbian media has claimed to see conspiracies to reconstitute the Habsburg and Ottoman Empires; the Vatican's desire to convert Orthodox Christians; the Islamic world's intention to invade Europe; and even a "Bonn–Vienna–Zagreb–Sofia–Tirana–Rome axis," with the reason for hostility toward the Serbs said to be that the latter allegedly stand in the way of these plans. At the very least, Belgrade's attitude probably spurred the growth of other nationalisms as a self-defensive reaction.

Milošević and Croatia's Serbs

Whatever tensions and confrontations were bound to emerge in the upheaval as the communist system gave way to a more democratic one in Croatia, it is doubtful that any of them were of such severity as to make war unavoidable. However, one of the most prominent themes of Belgrade's political program was that the Serbian minorities outside Serbia were being persecuted and were in danger of impending genocide, a threat which could be averted only if all Serbs rallied around Milošević and the *Serbian Memorandum*.

As far as Croatia was concerned, even while the latter was still under communist rule, according to the *Memorandum*

> At no time in their history, apart from the period of the NDH [Croatia's wartime Fascist state], have the Serbs in Croatia been so threatened as they are today. The solution of their national status imposes itself as a political issue of the first magnitude.[15]

In particular, Belgrade soon began to emphasize the potential resurrection of the wartime fascist system which, it warned the Serbs in Croatia incessantly, would implement a policy of genocide. Although inter-ethnic tensions had indeed risen in Croatia by the late 1980s, and the prospects for local Serbs retaining their disproportionate share of positions in the political and security structures of the republic were dim in a more democratized system, there does not appear to have been any realistic likelihood of anti-Serbian genocide. Even such an experienced observer as the veteran Serbian dissident and one-time Tito right-hand man, Milovan Djilas, concluded:

> Of course, that is a false, invented, motive; genocide did not occur . . . I do not believe there was even any danger that genocide would occur again in Croatia; the Croatian government was elected legally, it is a legitimate, multi-party, government with a parliamentary system.[16]

Rather than seeing the ensuing war as one needed to protect their community, many of Croatia's Serbs themselves apparently viewed it as little more than a vehicle for Belgrade's achievement of a Greater Serbia. As a Croatian Serb, who had fled to Belgrade rather than fight, told a returning Serbian veteran, "It was you who wanted a Greater Serbia, so you fight for it."[17]

The fear of a reemergence of fascism in Croatia proved overblown. Croatia quickly established a multiparty system, which included several Serbian political parties. Moreover, Franjo Tudjman, who was to be elected Croatia's first president, as a young man during the war had fought in the Partisan movement against the Ustaše, as had also many of the new Croatian government and opposition leaders of his age group. The only Croatian party inspired by the Ustaše, the Hrvatska stranka prava (HSP – Croatian Party of Rights) managed to get only marginal popular support despite the ensuing war, garnering a meager 5 percent of the vote. Moreover, the HSP was to have exceptionally strained relations with the Tudjman government, which harassed and sought to ban it, as well as with virtually all the opposition parties and media.

However, Milošević's actions, feeding on the Croatian Serbs' latent fears born of the experience under the Ustaše campaign of terror during World War II, undermined the prospects for coexistence and negotiated solutions. The long-term propaganda campaign emanating from Belgrade since 1988, in particular, was instrumental in intensifying the drift toward armed confrontation by setting the emotional stage early and by sharpening the ordinary Serb's mistrust of other ethnic groups in what was a period of change and uncertainty. The direction set in Belgrade also prepared the moral atmosphere which subsequently led to the worst war crimes in Europe since the end of World War II.

Despite the tensions and the propaganda campaign, without Serbia's direct involvement and agitation in Croatia, there probably would have been no war and a political accommodation with the Serbian community would have been found. However, political organizers from Serbia and personnel from Serbian nationalist militias, often with the direct support of the Milošević government, became active in Croatia well before the latter had opted for independence. Their thrust early on was for Croatia's partition and the promotion of a Greater Serbia. At mass rallies organized in Croatia in 1989 – in which Serbs from Serbia took a prominent part – to celebrate the anniversary of the Battle of Kosovo, for example, the flying of Serbian flags and slogans such as "This is Serbia" and "Slobo[dan] [Milošević], we are waiting for you" set the tone.[18]

At the same time, Serbian intellectuals reportedly were formulating a plan to detach a large portion of Croatia's territory in order to set up a separate Serbian republic with the city of Karlovac as its capital.[19] Nationalist incidents involving "tourists," arriving from Serbia in buses carrying Milošević's photo and armed guards, also became a common occurrence in Croatia's coastal areas throughout the summer of 1989. By February 1990 – while Croatia was still ruled by a communist government – rallies in Croatia by local Serbs had become overtly Chetnik in orientation, and were being accompanied by slogans such as "We will plow Zagreb under and bomb the Vatican." According to one of the early organizers, "the goal of our movement was to liberate Western Serbia [i.e., territory in Croatia] and to unite with Bosnia-Herzegovina, Montenegro, and Moravska Serbia [i.e. Serbia proper]." Moreover, at the same time, Serb dissidents were setting up their first military organizations in Croatia with the direct assistance of advisers from Serbia.[20]

The gathering storm

The process to secede from Croatia, with Serbia's encouragement, was already well advanced before the April–May 1990 multiparty elections, which saw the recently organized pro-independence Croatian Democratic Union (HDZ) emerge as the dominant political party in Croatia, much less Croatia's own decision to seek independence the following year. Tensions escalated notice-ably after the replacement of Croatia's communist government and, when the first session of the new Croatian parliament was held in July 1990, the Serbian delegates who had been elected refused to attend and held a counter Serbian parliament. However, the delegates limited their demands to autonomy for areas with large Serbian populations, rather than independence.

This contrasted with the call for secession by more hardline elements whom Belgrade supported and who eventually came to be dominant within Croatia's Serbian community.[21] The latter soon set about detaching the territories from Croatia and Milan Babić, at the time the pro-Milošević leader of the separatist wing in the Knin region, noted in an interview conducted in 1991 that "We have been functioning independently in fact from last summer . . . Croatia has no sovereignty. Croatia is not a sovereign state."[22] By August 1990, armed Serbian elements were also cutting road and rail traffic and, on 23 November 1990, they ambushed a police patrol (like most local police in predominantly Serb-populated areas, composed of Serbs). Despite the potential for spiralling violence, the JNA turned down requests from within its leadership to ensure freedom of passage through the affected areas.[23]

These developments notwithstanding, President Tudjman, as well as the Slovene and Bosnian leadership (probably in contrast to their consti-tuencies), continued to support a reconstituted Yugoslavia and, in October 1990, presented a project for a new confederal system. Milošević, however, adamantly rejected this option in favor either of a more centralized Yugoslavia – seconded in this by the JNA, and an option which the non-Serbs feared would be, as in the past, a vehicle for Serbian domination – or for Croatia's departure, minus significant parts of its territory. For many,

Serbia's disinterest in Yugoslavia's survival seemed to be confirmed at a particularly sensitive time when, in December 1990, the Milošević government syphoned from the national bank half of the country's planned investment funds to spend on benefits intended to attract potential voters in Serbia's upcoming local elections.[24]

Also, in May 1991, an opposition Serbian politician, Vuk Drašković, today leader of a moderate Chetnik party, the Serbian Renewal Movement, was to present to Yugoslavia's then-President, Croat Stipe Mešić, a map of a new Yugoslavia, in what Drašković has described subsequently as an attempt to come to an agreement "without bloodshed and unnecessary victims."[25] His map, however, envisioned the transfer of large tracts of territory from Croatia and Bosnia-Herzegovina to Serbian control. Although occurring before full-scale war had erupted, such a gesture probably only reinforced Croatian suspicions that Serbia intended to take as much land as possible, whether peacefully or otherwise.

Amid growing disarray at the top of the country's federal political structure as tension mounted, incidents between the JNA and Croatian civilians on the one hand, and armed Serbs and the Croatian police on the other, began to grow apace in the spring of 1991. This period was punctuated by numerous confrontations, including an attempt by Serb militants to take over the national park at Plitvice on 31 March. On 2 May the ambush and beheading of a dozen Croatian policemen, with the participation of Chetnik militia personnel from Serbia, in the village of Borovo Selo, near Vukovar, marked a further deterioration in the situation.[26] Rather than calming the tension, the JNA, along with the Serbian government and Serbian-based militias, provided arms and armed personnel to the Serbian community in Croatia, at times whether the latter wanted them or not.[27] The pattern was also being set by which the JNA would step in to prevent Croatian policemen from reasserting control over areas taken over by Serb militants, leading to increasingly larger areas being cut off from Croatian control and proclaiming their union with Serbia.

The May 1991 referendum on Croatia's independence, and the declarations of independence by Slovenia and Croatia in June, served as a signal for the JNA to transition to more active military operations. Significantly, the US Secretary of State James Baker, during his visit to Belgrade in early June 1991, had spoken of the "dangers of disintegration of this country," while the Bush administration had warned that the USA would not recognize the independence of Slovenia and Croatia. Although it is difficult to determine what role such policy statements played in their decision-making, the JNA and Milošević may have interpreted them as a "green light" by the international community to use any means, including force, against the emerging independence movements without fear of censure.

Despite the increasing number of incidents involving JNA personnel by June, full-scale war might still have been avoided had the JNA not launched its ground attacks against Slovenia and Croatia in July and August, respectively, igniting a conflict punctuated by fifteen cease-fires before winding down at the end of 1991.

CROATIA'S WAR FOR INDEPENDENCE

The nature and course of the war

The Serbo-Croatian War was very much in the tradition of modern-day inter-state wars, with the goal, in the case of Croatia, of setting up a new state and, in the case of Serbia, of enlarging its state. Although guerrilla-like operations and small-unit actions did take place, it was the regular army, often operating as brigades and corps, which proved decisive by providing the strike forces and firepower spearheading the JNA's seizure of areas in Croatia and making the consolidation of such control possible. Even Serbian militia forces sought to obtain whatever heavy conventional arms they could, including, in one case, an armored train in the Krajina area, the "Krajina Express."[28] Likewise, the Croatian side sought to field a regular army as soon as possible, its use of heavy weaponry and large units limited only by access to the necessary equipment.

Neither belligerent proclaimed a "people's war," despite the tradition and personal experience of many within the leadership, although Croatia's Minister of Defense, General Martin Špegelj, had favored doing so.[29] On the Croatian side, this was no doubt hampered by the fact that "ethnic cleansing" in areas occupied by the JNA removed the human pool needed for an insurgency. Yet, the potential loss of control over such movements was probably a more central concern for the JNA and in political circles in both Zagreb and Belgrade limiting irregular warfare.

The JNA, at least initially, visualized this as a total war in terms of its objectives – hoping to occupy all of Croatia and to overthrow its new government – and, in the ensuing operations, was to use virtually everything in its arsenal except chemical weapons. To achieve its objective, the JNA pursued a strategy of using its mobile forces to control the main transportation arteries and to isolate individual regions in Croatia to facilitate its drive toward Zagreb. The Yugoslav Navy played a significant supporting role in an attempt to seal off Croatia's long coastline, while also attacking port towns. Unable to sweep over Croatia, however, by October 1991 the JNA had to revise its objectives to more limited ones of controlling territory, with a focus on seizing large cities and relieving its garrisons after these were put under siege.

Milošević, on the other hand, apparently settled for an expanded Serbian state, rather than trying to put Yugoslavia together again under Serbia's aegis, after the JNA's defeat in Slovenia. He envisaged the war against Croatia as a limited one from the start, with an objective of having the JNA seize territory while Serbia maintained plausible denial of any direct involvement. Although constitutionally subordinate to the federal authorities, the JNA instead often acted on its own, with Serbia's and Montenegro's representatives neutralizing all attempts at federal-level meetings to rein in the JNA.[30] In addition, Serbia worked to prevent Croatia's recognition by the international community. As a way to further weaken Croatia, Serbia also tried to interest Italy in reviving its long-dormant claims to the Croatian littoral, but was only able to engage Italy's neo-fascist Italian Social Movement.[31]

Before the war broke out, the JNA claimed about 205,000 active duty personnel, of whom 70,000 were already in Croatia, and was mobilizing additional reserves in Serbia and Montenegro. Its order of battle included, 1,850 main battle tanks (of which 700 older models were in storage), 500 armored personnel carriers, over 2,000 pieces of towed and self-propelled artillery (including multiple rocket launchers), 489 fixed-wing combat aircraft, and 165 armed helicopters. On the other side, Croatia's Minister of Defense reported that the republic had 34,000 policemen and guardsmen under arms.[32] Although he also claimed to have enough light arms for an additional 85,000 personnel, other officials later acknowledged that this was largely bluff.[33]

When Croatia's HDZ won the elections in May 1990, but before it had set up a government, the JNA demanded that the arsenals belonging to Croatia's Territorial Defense Forces, the republic-based reserve organization set up in 1969 in the wake of the Soviet invasion of Czechoslovakia, be transferred to JNA control. The incoming government faced a dilemma according to Josip Manolić, Croatia's premier-elect: whether to refuse the JNA's order and thereby potentially spark an immediate confrontation, or to yield, but thereby also risk that Croatia would enter any confrontation subsequently at a great disadvantage in armaments.[34] In the event, Croatia's new officials decided to relinquish the weapons. The confiscated arsenal reportedly had included 200,000 rifles, 1,400 mortars, 500 anti-tank missiles, and 1000 artillery pieces.[35] In retrospect, this was a mistake, although at the time the Croatians may still have believed that a clash was avoidable and had still not set up a well-articulated political infrastructure. As a result, as Croatia edged closer to an open confrontation with the JNA, some informed Croatians were pessimistic about their republic's chances, with one observer who specialized in military affairs concluding in July 1991 that "we are not strong enough for war."[36]

Croatia, which faced the real possibility of losing its newly-proclaimed independence, nevertheless fought a limited war, in so far as both methods and objectives were concerned. For Croatia, the challenge was to respond everywhere with very limited forces. The Zagreb government adopted a static defense initially, trading space for time with the advancing JNA units deploying from Serbia and Bosnia-Herzegovina, despite the fact that the

Croatian Defense Minister had favored mass mobilization for defense and small, mobile, regular units going on the offensive against the JNA as soon as possible.[37] Subsequently, the siege and reduction of JNA garrisons became a key element of Croatian strategy, not least as the principal source of arms for the Croatian Army, which in many regions started out with little more than hunting rifles.[38]

The performance of the JNA in the Serbo-Croatian War was, if anything, lackluster, although initially the impression among JNA personnel at least was that the JNA would win the war quickly.[39] Long touted as one of the strongest armies in Europe, the JNA had a difficult time in Croatia handling what was initially a small, lightly-armed, police force. At first, the JNA benefited from the confusion accompanying the disintegration of Croatia's communist system and by what was at times a tentative and reactive strategy by Croatia's new government. In part, the lack of preparedness was the result of the view prevalent among the Croatian leadership that the crisis would be resolved peacefully or that the international community would step in to protect Croatia if war did erupt. General Martin Špegelj, for example, noted that "people believed that fighting would not occur," while Tudjman, for his part, announced naively that "he would not hesitate to call in Western troops to defend Croatia if the republic was attacked." And, even in August, Yugoslavia's President Mešić continued to believe that international pressure would force the JNA to stop its operations.[40]

Within this context, as late as May 1991, the Croatian Minister of Defense had still been recommending that Croatians respond to the national draft, while Croatian police struck a deal to relinquish control to the JNA of the bridges between Croatia and Serbia, and subsequently provided traffic management for JNA armor crossing into Croatia.[41] Another result of such assumptions was that local "crisis staffs" were left to their own devices to organize a defense. Also, this attitude led to a delay in the mobilization of reserves and, after his dismissal as Minister of Defense, General Špegelj complained bitterly that his calls for mobilization had been ignored for a long time.[42] The failure to coordinate defense strategies with other republics seeking to break away from Yugoslavia was also a major error. During the fighting in neighboring Slovenia, for example, Croatia had remained passive, despite the fact that General Špegelj wanted to block JNA units based in Croatia as they were deployed to attack Slovenia and to join with Slovenia against the JNA.[43] Zagreb no doubt hoped to avoid provoking the JNA. Yet it thereby lost a golden opportunity to gain the initiative and to mount a combined operation against a common enemy, thus allowing time to the JNA to reposition and refit its forces after the fiasco in Slovenia.

More directly, the JNA exploited its superior firepower and organization, as well as its ability to deny Croatia arms imports thanks to its control of the land and sea borders. The blanket international arms embargo on Yugoslavia, which the Conference for Security and Cooperation in Europe enacted on 4 September and the United Nations (UN) on 25 September, in particular, crippled Zagreb's efforts to acquire arms abroad, but affected the JNA little, since the latter had already accumulated large stocks and had access to Yugoslavia's considerable arms production capability. In the mistaken expectation that negotiations would end the war quickly, Croatia also waited until 7 September to cut off oil supplies to Serbia and until 13 September before initiating a full-scale siege of JNA garrisons – which up to then had continued to receive food, water, and power.

Nevertheless, eventually the Croatians were able to overcome many of their material and organizational shortcomings and to create an army numbering 200,000 personnel, according to the then Chief of Staff, General Anton Tus, while fighting in six distinct operational zones, in itself no mean achievement.[44] By late fall 1991, thanks to a stubborn defense, they succeeded in stalemating the JNA and even went on the counteroffensive in some areas to regain some of the lost territory. However, Croatian forces never sought to carry the fight beyond Croatia's borders, despite the fact that the JNA was staging and firing directly from Bosnia-Herzegovina, Montenegro, Vojvodina, and Serbia proper, and even though this might have improved Zagreb's military position and result in bargaining leverage.

The strategic center of gravity

That the government in Belgrade – and Milošević in particular – was the strategic center of gravity for the Serbian war effort has not always been self-evident. Milošević himself denied any involvement by Serbia in the war against Croatia until February 1992, when he admitted that Serbia had indeed helped the Serbs in Croatia "first economically and politically . . . but, finally, when all this proved insufficient, with arms."[45]

Serbia alone provided the sinews of war to the JNA, including all the funds and most of the personnel, since the break-up of Yugoslavia in 1991 and, in the absence of Serbia's active cooperation, especially in financing and recruiting, the JNA would not have been able to wage war. By mid-1991, draftees from non-Serbian communities were becoming rare, and non-Serb career officers, likewise, virtually disappeared as their home republics left Yugoslavia. Without the active involvement of the Serbian authorities in administering and enforcing the draft system and punishing draft-dodgers, the JNA would probably have been left irretrievably under-strength. As it was, a Member of the Serbian Parliament estimated that over 100,000 reserve personnel from Serbia saw service on the Croatian front.[46] The Serbian authorities have continued to enforce the draft, including the forcible return of reluctant refugees who had fled from the war zones in Croatia to Serbia for military service with the local forces the Krajina territories in Croatia. As of December 1992, Serbia also announced it would pay survivor benefits to the families of "fallen fighters" among the Serbs in Croatia.

In addition, the Serbian government actively supported both the militias raised on Croatian territory and those deploying from Serbia with funding, personnel, and arms, as well as providing an operational base. According to the minutes of meetings released in 1992, Serbia's Ministry of Defense was the main conduit for such activities.[47] As one Serbian militia leader in Croatia confirmed, moreover, "Arms were obtained from Serbia and from the Territorial Defense, first from that of Vojvodina and subsequently also from that of Šumadija [i.e., a region in Serbia]."[48] The ruling Socialist Party of Serbia itself fielded its own militia.[49] Throughout the fighting in Croatia, irregulars from Serbia were not only permitted to go to the front, but were treated as heros by Serbia's state-controlled media, were given time off from their state-sector jobs, and were provided with the same benefits as regular military personnel.

Similarly, Milošević has wielded more influence on the political outcome than he has taken credit for. Once he had concluded that Serbian forces had reached their culminating point and had opted for a UN presence along the newly established front lines, he was able to impose his view (albeit with the JNA's concurrence). The ability of Milošević to influence the course of events beyond Serbia's borders became evident when the Krajina leadership initially sought to oppose the UN-sponsored Vance Peace Plan, claiming that not all desired territory in Croatia had been taken yet nor had union with Serbia been achieved. In the end, he was able to brush aside bitter recriminations and charges of treason by the local Serb authorities in the occupied territories, as well as by many nationalists in Serbia, who wanted continued Serbian expansion. Milošević, arguing that this was the best that could be expected for the time being, and that all key Serbian interests would be protected, attempted to brow-beat a recalcitrant Krajina President, Milan Babić, whom he summoned to Belgrade. According to Babić, Milošević subsequently engineered his elimination from the Krajina government and set up a more pliant leadership in his place.[50]

The occupied territories in Croatia also have continued to be heavily dependent on Serbia for their existence, and are unlikely to adhere to any policy independent of Belgrade. According to a Krajina official, the Yugoslav Army and military intelligence have retained their presence within the Krajina's defense forces well after they had supposedly withdrawn.[51] Asked who controlled the Krajina's military and police, Babić admitted that "the military is under the control of the senior leadership and the General Staff [of the Yugoslav Army], while the police gets its pay and orders from Slobodan Milošević."[52] Moreover, not only does Serbia provide the territories' only outlet to the outside world, but Belgrade also finances the local budget' and provides vital food and oil supplies, as well as serving as the ultimate military guarantor. As Milan Martić, the Minister of the Interior of the Krajina, admitted, "Without a physical corridor to Serbia, we would be completely destroyed."[53]

As for Serbia's "national will," this has been problematic as an alternative center of gravity. Although some observers have attributed to the Serbs such overwhelming commitment to their cause that any outside involvement would meet with an open-ended and fanatical resistance that would not be amenable to even military pressure, the reality is more nuanced. While it is probably true that most Serbs are in favor of the general objective of a Greater Serbia in the abstract, what is less clear is how deep and widespread that commitment is in concrete terms and what cost average Serbs are willing to pay for its achievement. In contrast to the small nucleus of hard-core nationalists, the Serbian population at large appears less than willing to pay a heavy price for a Greater Serbia. A woman from Belgrade, for example, noted that she enjoys such things as scented soap, cosmetics, fine clothes, appliances, going out to dinner and the theater, and fretted, "I don't want them to stamp me as a traitor because I don't think that the Serbian people need war . . . Am I crazy, Comrade Milošević?"[54]

Neither was the atmosphere on the home front very receptive to returning veterans. A soldier, for example, upon his return to Belgrade, was disappointed by the fact that "many people . . . are not excited about a war in which, after all, I was wounded."[55] Many Serbs, in particular, have been reluctant to risk their lives for the nationalist cause as it has been cast up to now. The response to the JNA's mobilization efforts in Serbia, which represented its essential power base, for example, was tepid.

Draft-dodging and desertion were continuing concerns throughout the Serbo-Croatian War, and military sources routinely announced trials of draft dodgers. In one case, in the Serbian city of Valjevo, of 2,000–3000 "volunteers" expected after a call-up, only two showed up.[56] Those with connections or who could afford to do so often went abroad in order to avoid the draft. One report placed those who ignored the call-up in Serbia at 15,000, while another source put the number of those who had left Serbia to avoid the possibility of being drafted at 200,000, and a Montenegrin dissident estimated that 12,000 in Montenegro had avoided the draft call-up for the war in Croatia.[57] In Belgrade, a drafted student criticized his draft-dodging friends bitterly, noting,

> I had been surrounded by friends whose mouths were full of Greater Serbia. Today, I, who identify myself as a Yugoslav, am defending this country, while they are on Cyprus or in America, or hiding out in the squares in Trešnja . . . They no longer mention Greater Serbia, and behind all these words there is just cowardice.[58]

The operational center of gravity

On the other hand, if one looks at the Serbian war effort's operational center of gravity, it seems to have been the large-sized heavy units and air-power of the JNA. A key variable in how well the break-away republics have done militarily has been the amount of heavy weaponry that they have been able to acquire. Slovenia was able to retain a significant proportion of its Territorial Defense arsenal, and handled the ineptly deployed JNA forces deftly. Croatia got nothing from its Territorial Defense arsenal, but did get some arms from those garrisons it succeeded in besieging, which enabled it to halt JNA advances in the latter phases of the war.[59] Bosnia-Herzegovina, also got very little, not only because it was unprepared for the outbreak of fighting due to a lack of foresight and a desire to avoid any provocations, but also because the JNA had had a longer period to deploy its forces beforehand to prevent any transfer or capture of arms.

In Croatia, it was the armor, artillery, and aircraft, in particular, which played the decisive role in the fighting. With some justification, one military source, for example, blamed the cessation of close air support by helicopters, due to an alleged desire to mollify foreign observers, as the deciding factor for the JNA's inability to deal with Croatian counterattacks in Western Slavonija, while Croatia's Chief of Staff singled out the JNA's artillery as responsible for repulsing a Croatian thrust across the Kupa river, both in December 1991.[60] Moreover, Yugoslav air attacks using napalm, cluster bombs, and rocket fire against large, weakly defended, stationary area targets such as cities and villages had a psychological effect disproportionate to the damage, causing civilian casualties and often forcing the inhabitants to flee. Likewise, the JNA used its artillery against towns to force the population to surrender as part of "ethnic cleansing." While the sieges of Vukovar and Dubrovnik received the most publicity, this was also the standard procedure against other Croatian towns. In the case of the town of Ilok, for example, according to a dissident draftee, "The Army gave an ultimatum for Ilok to surrender, and for all those who wanted to leave to do so . . . About 7,000 people left."[61]

Militia units and locally based reserve Territorial Defense forces, on the other hand, were of limited combat utility. One JNA officer assessed the latter as being "mostly tied to the defense of their own population centers. I think they are not well organized, and individuals and groups among them are leading a sort of private war."[62] Irregular militias, who often came to fight on a part-time basis, also proved to be of marginal military value in general. Often, they fought in conventional joint operations with the JNA, as found in the war diary of one militia volunteer, whose unit in October 1991, for example, was used for a diversionary attack by the Army and later supported Army tanks on the Slavonijan front.[63] However, the JNA leadership routinely viewed such auxiliary Chetnik units with unconcealed disdain. A weekly after-action report submitted to higher headquarters by a JNA Lieutenant Colonel operating in Croatia (dated 23 October 1991), for example, notes that:

In zone b/d 1.pgmd, there are several groups of paramilitary formations from Serbia, including the Chetniks, the "Dušan the Terrible"
units [named after the medieval Serbian emperor], and other self-
styled volunteers whose main goal is not to fight against the enemy
but to plunder people's property and to do their worst against the
innocent ethnically-Croatian population.[64]

General Colonel Života Avramović, at the time Yugoslavia's Deputy
Minister of Defense, likewise disparaged the impact of militia forces,
ridiculing those in Serbia who "attributed military successes to various
volunteer and other units." Continuing in this vein, he concluded:

> I must say that the contribution made by [such] small-sized units
> cannot be compared to the operational-strategic achievements of the
> JNA's units . . . In reality, without the JNA, not a single "guard" [i.e.,
> militia unit] would be able to defend the Serbs successfully from the
> Ustaše knife and even less so to hold on to the front dividing [our]
> people from the enemy.[65]

Perhaps not atypical was the case of one militia unit, the "Serbian Volunteer
Guard," raised in Kosovo, whose departure for the front in Croatia was
accompanied by significant local media fanfare. During subsequent training
provided by the JNA, however, its commander shot himself accidentally,
and the unit returned home without having participated in any combat.[66]

Even accounting for the JNA's concern to protect its professional image,
such assessments reflect fairly accurately the role played by such elements.
What the JNA did was to make the environment safe for the Chetnik militias
to operate by seizing territory, providing the back-up firepower, and
preventing more lightly equipped Croatian government forces from dealing
with such irregular groups as they would otherwise have done.

The JNA's critical vulnerabilities

The JNA's combat performance during the course of this war revealed
critical vulnerabilities which called into question its earlier reputation as a
formidable fighting force and undercut at the operational level its attempts
to implement the national strategy.

Morale

Morale was a central problem which dogged the Serbian war effort at the
operational as well as at the strategic level. Even those reservists who did
answer the JNA's call-up were loath to continue past the stipulated
commitment of 45 days. During the campaign in Croatia, JNA officers were
faced with demands from mobilized reservists to be allowed to return

home, as they claimed that they "did not know why they were fighting" and that they did not want to cross the Drina, the river that has marked Serbia's traditional boundary.[67] The Yugoslav military press rued the fact that "While volunteers go to the front, some others look for any means to go in the opposite direction." For example, two units totalling 2,600 reservists from the Serbian town of Valjevo deserted *en masse*, complaining that they had not been informed of the enemy's strength and disposition, that they had not been supplied properly, that JNA artillery had fired on them by mistake, and that they had not been told clearly what their mission was.[68] In their defense, other deserters claimed that they were told originally that they would be going on an exercise, not into combat.[69] In another case, an entire unit dissolved when one of the reservists, the son of a prominent politician, received an exemption before the unit was sent to the front.[70]

Even those personnel who stayed with their units were often a source of problems, with one veteran commenting that in his brigade, "No one wanted to carry [ammunition to the front], except for us fools. Everyone would run away and take cover and the commander, Topić, was forced to reorganize the first company completely . . . Everyone feared for himself, and was careful not to be in the front lines."[71]

By autumn 1991, on one part of the front in Croatia, "the reservists have practically all fled . . . According to military sources, the reservists simply do not want to fight." As a result, the JNA was obliged to form units made up solely of officers and career personnel to operate in the most critical areas.[72] Even the JNA's career personnel appear to have suffered from significant morale problems, especially after the defection or alienation of non-Serb personnel, including high-ranking officers. In at least one case, that of the Slovene commander of the 13th Army Corps in Rijeka, Croatia, General Marjan Čad, his disagreement with Serbian policy made it less likely that the JNA would operate against Istra, the peninsula that forms the extreme west of Croatia. The Air Force even had "several tens" of Serbian personnel go over to the Croatian side, allegedly because they had Croatian wives.[73] This phenomenon not only left gaps in expertise, but also compromised plans and security, and reinforced suspicions about the reliability of those who remained. In the resulting atmosphere, doubts about loyalty could reach extremes, as when a unit refused to be led by a Lieutenant-Colonel because they did not believe he was a Serb, since his name did not sound Serbian, or when a security officer was suspected of having ties to foreign intelligence services because he was Jewish.[74]

A lack of commitment also affected Serbs within Croatia, many of whom did not want to fight for either side. As one Serbian refugee who fled from Croatia to Vojvodina indicated, "I did not run away because of any threat or danger. As a Serb [however], I was threatened by the draft from two directions, both from the [Croatian] National Guard and from various [Serbian] military organizations of the so-called Krajina." In part, the split loyalties of such residents, even more so than just indifference or fear, were a deciding factor in their opting for neutrality, as in the case of the same Serbian refugee, who noted that whoever drafted him first "I would be placed in a position of shooting at people on the other side with whom I had grown up and lived with peacefully. The war will not last forever, and then we will again have to live together. What else could I do but run away?"[75]

Military sources in 1991 put the number of draft-age Serbs who had moved to Serbia from Croatian territory affected by the war, rather than staying and taking part in the fighting, at between 30,000 and 60,000. In fact, General Marko Negovanović, then Serbia's Defense Minister, was to complain that "I cannot protect the Serbs of Croatia from genocide if they do not want to defend themselves . . . their place is not here [in Serbia], but there [in Croatia]."[76] As of early 1993, at least 53,000 registered, and many more unregistered, draft-age Serbs from Croatia and Bosnia-Herzegovina remained in Serbia, despite continuing pressure for them to return home to take up arms.[77] A Serbian official in the city of Novi Sad accused many of them of not registering with the authorities with the expressed intention of avoiding the draft and of "not behaving like people who are threatened."[78]

In contrast, Croatian civilians and military personnel overall showed consistent commitment to their country's cause, and displayed remarkable resolve against heavy odds, including during the drawn-out sieges of numerous towns. As a rule, the Croatian Army does not seem to have been beset by the morale problems faced by the JNA, and fought willingly. As one Serbian veteran acknowledged about the Croatian soldiers against whom he had fought at Vukovar, "They fight like lions . . . Their bravery cannot be denied."[79] Nevertheless, the Croatian Army was also not immune to recruitment woes at times, with at least some Croatians reluctant to take part, especially at first when the fight seemed so uneven. One Croatian youth, who had gone to stay with relatives in neighboring Vojvodina to avoid the draft, for example, remarked: "I view my head as valuable as anyone else's and want to keep it." Promising that he would return to Croatia if the war continued or escalated, he concluded, however, "Until then, I think that the fight against the terrorists is a job for professional policemen and national guardsmen."[80]

Combined arms

The Yugoslav Army, although well-equipped, proved to be neither a very mobile nor an effective fighting force. The lack of a functioning combined arms capability, in particular, was a problem. In the invasion of Slovenia, armored units had been left stranded without artillery, air, or infantry support, and became easy pickings for the determined and relatively well-armed Slovenes.[81] This weakness was not fully corrected in time for the campaign in Croatia. Part of the problem was the need to minimize army casualties in order to avoid discontent, which led to a reluctance to expose infantry.[82] In addition, the departure of non-Serbs led to severe shortages of trained infantry, often forcing the JNA armored units to rely on unskilled Territorial Defense personnel or to fight alone in urban terrain, where they were vulnerable, leading to "unnecessary losses."[83] The infantry, for its part, complained about the lack of air and artillery support.[84]

Air power

The Yugoslav Air Force's performance during the war was often criticized within the military establishment, much to the chagrin of its leadership. Only thanks to a situation in which it enjoyed total air supremacy, was faced by weak air defenses, and could operate over eastern Croatia's open terrain, was the Air Force able to make the difference that it did for the JNA. Even with those advantages, the Air Force achieved much less than one could have expected from a force its size. Pilots had difficulty identifying targets, leading to the bombing of the Hungarian town of Barcs by mistake, as well as in hitting even undefended point targets. This included the Air Force's inability to destroy the bridge joining Bosanski Brod and Slavonski Brod, spanning the Sava River between Croatia and Bosnia-Herzegovina, and as reported by an administrative officer at the US consulate in Zagreb, the unsuccessful attempts to put transmission towers around the capital out of commission.[85]

Close air support was a particular problem, especially for fixed-wing aircraft. The Air Force had never viewed this as a priority mission and, as the Chief of Staff of the Air Force and Air Defense acknowledged, his aircraft were "not used according to the appropriate principles. That is, we fought in a way we did not train for . . . operating along the front lines, against snipers and mortars, and dealing with street fighting."[86] Overall performance during the fighting in Croatia was problematic, and included cases of fratricide. In one such instance, the Air Force attacked a JNA convoy, causing 80 dead and about 400 wounded, which reportedly led to "a great fall in morale everywhere where news or rumor reached about that," while on other occasions personnel reported that their own units had been hit.[87]

Command and control

Command and control was cumbersome and functioned poorly in many cases. A brigade commander, for his part, protested to his corps commander that he was not told what the military objectives were, and claimed that his unit "suffered because of that, often needlessly." He also complained that a rigid command structure robbed him of the needed flexibility and initiative, as his "hands were tied by strings whose ends were pulled from far away."[88] One Serbian veteran told a reporter that in his brigade "All our communications systems were bad, whether radio or courier."[89] As a corollary, fratricide was also a common occurrence, as in one instance in which JNA artillery firing from Bosnia hit a JNA unit operating in Croatia.[90]

Logistics

Logistics also proved problematic. Supplies came along extended lines of communication and, in some instances, Croatian forces successfully attacked JNA road columns and rail traffic specifically to obtain arms.[91] Had the Croatians had the means to interdict these lines or had the government of Bosnia-Herzegovina, over whose territory much of this traffic flowed, tried to do so, this could have created havoc with the JNA's combat effectiveness. Even without such impediments, internal bottlenecks led to shortfalls for the JNA, with reservists complaining about ineffective food distribution, defective equipment and munitions, and the lack of spare parts.[92] Ironically, even systems manufactured domestically proved to be a problem for the JNA, because of the latter's reliance on components from suppliers in Croatia and other republics. Somewhat incongruously, the manufacture of the M-84 main battle tank (a licensed version of the Russian T-72M) continued during the war as a cooperative effort between Croatian and Serbian firms, with the finished product being shipped from Croatia to Montenegro for export to Kuwait. Some observers in Croatia, however, raised questions whether these tanks were not being diverted instead by the JNA for its war effort against Croatia.[93]

Training

Providing sufficient training to reservists and volunteers in a short period was also unsuccessful, especially in areas such as armor operations.[94] In the case of the Niš Corps, 12,000 personnel went through a ten-day training course.[95] In some cases, training for reservists lasted only four or five days before their departure for the front, giving rise to frequent complaints about being assigned to equipment never seen before, which led to "catastrophic results," according to JNA sources.[96] One veteran reported that in his unit, which had only 12 days of training, "A significant number wounded themselves, since they did not know how to shoot or how to throw hand grenades."[97] Leadership shortcomings among the JNA officers exacerbated this problem, and one Serbian soldier noted that when his brigade became engaged in combat ". . . organization was hopeless, no one knew what to do nor where to be . . . Major Garača had no idea [what to do], instead only yelling 'Run away, run away!'"[98]

War crimes

War crimes played a significant part in this war. Personnel on both sides committed atrocities. However, most of those on the Croatian side seem to have been unsanctioned and isolated, the work of individuals and rogue elements. The Croatian press and opposition parties, nevertheless, were justifiably critical of the Croatian government for not acting more vigorously to prevent and prosecute all such cases. However, in proportion, crimes committed by JNA personnel and the Serbian militias were greater by far. Moreover, on the Serbian side, this conduct represented an official and systematic state-sanctioned policy designed to support "ethnic cleansing."

Although the Serbian paramilitary forces were not significant in conventional military operations, they proved to be more adept at dealing with prisoners of war and the civilian population in newly-occupied areas. One Serbian veteran summed it up thus: "The Chetniks never take prisoners, but kill them instead on the spot. That is just how they are."[99] The killing or forcible expulsion of non-Serb civilians – including members of the Hungarian, Slovak, Gypsy, and Ukrainian communities, as well Croatians – became an integral part of the Serbs' strategy in pursuit of their broader goals of territorial control. At times, however, such actions by the Serbian militia units appear to have upset even hardened JNA personnel. Colonel Milorad Vučić, commander of a JNA armored brigade which operated in Croatia, for example, acknowledged in an interview that:

> Negative occurrences happened, particularly in relation to the treatment of the population, the treatment of their property and their personal security. Personnel from some of [our] brigade's sub-units protested to me with vehemence when they witnessed first-hand the criminal behavior by some individuals from various [paramilitary] groups, and sought earnestly that a stop be put to that. They simply do not want to die for such things.[100]

This is not to say that the JNA was not also involved in war crimes, although this was not the JNA's primary military mission, unlike the case of the militia groups, for whom it was. JNA personnel, for example, were directly responsible for the massacre of wounded Croatian prisoners after the capture of Vukovar's hospital when the city fell in November 1991.[101] JNA air attacks and artillery fire, also caused large-scale destruction of population centers and many civilian casualties. In most instances, this involved attacks against targets with no military significance, including the 28 December 1991 surface-to-surface missile attack which struck Zagreb's residential suburbs. What is more, JNA units reportedly participated in acts directed against civilians along with the militias even in instances unrelated to combat operations. For example, Serbian dissident writer Nenad Čanak, drafted into the JNA, reports that:

Eighty local Croatians from the village of Lovas were arrested by the reserve unit from Lovas and by the "Dušan the Terrible" [Chetnik militia] unit. They were physically mistreated and, subsequently, four of them were killed. After the [JNA reserve] "Valjevo" unit arrived in Lovas, the local inhabitants being held in detention were used to clear minefields, resulting in the death of seventeen of them. Those local inhabitants who were wounded were refused medical help by the medical personnel at the clinic in Šid.[102]

Even after the UN-brokered cease-fire, the JNA appears to have continued to support "ethnic cleansing" in areas under its control. In one such post-cease-fire case, the JNA's information service assured reporters that Croatian villagers were departing voluntarily, since they had "developed the desire to move to areas which are to be Croatian after 'partition'."[103] Ironically, the goal of "ethnic purity" often led to the uprooting by the JNA of Serbs from parts of Croatia in which the JNA could operate but not hold onto permanently, and their forced transfer to Serb-held areas. For example, in Western Slavonija, according to the Belgrade media, Serbian peasants reportedly "did not want to leave their homes, but . . . unidentified agents and agitators pressed them into sad refugee columns headed for Baranija," while in more than one case Serbian refugees told reporters that "the Ustaše did not demolish our village; the Army did it."[104] Looting by the Army also became so widespread that, in a meeting in the Serbian Minister of Defense's office, one official mused rhetorically: "Tell me of even one reservist, especially if he is an officer, who has spent more than a month at the front and has not brought back a fine car filled with everything that would fit inside the car."[105] The JNA's conduct could give rise to instances of black humor at times, as when a Serbian tank gunner reportedly selected the best-looking houses in the Croatian village of Tovarnik for destruction, thinking they belonged to Croatians, only to find out later that most of them were owned by local Serbs.[106]

Such behavior, however, probably had a negative impact on JNA morale overall, for many average Serbian personnel were repelled by what they had experienced. The taking of the city of Vukovar seems to have been particularly traumatic for many Serbian soldiers. One veteran from Belgrade, for example, told a journalist that:

I was in the Army and did my duty. Vukovar was more of a slaughter than a battle. Many women and children were killed. Many, many. I asked him: "Did you take part in the killing?" He answered: "I deserted". I asked him: "But did you kill anyone?" he replied: "I deserted after that . . ." The slaughter of Vukovar continues to haunt me. Every night I imagine that the war has reached my home and that my own children are being butchered.[107]

The JNA and Serbia's leadership must bear responsibility for the war crimes, whether committed by JNA personnel, by the reserve Territorial Defense forces, or the militias. The JNA had direct command over the area of operations and over the forces subordinate to it, and provided to the militias arms, training, and sometimes its own officers, as well as co-operating with them in planning, intelligence, logistics, and fire support.[108] Serbia, likewise, not only supported the JNA but also many of the militias, some of whose leaders sat in the Serbian Parliament.

WAR TERMINATION AND END-STATE

Reaching the culminating point

In January 1992, the belligerents agreed to a cease-fire along the existing battle lines. Serbia did not stop the war effort, however, because of any self-imposed limit, spirit of compromise, or a wish to avoid advancing into areas that were predominantly Croatian. Rather, there is compelling evidence that Serbia and the JNA agreed to a cease-fire because they had reached their culminating point, with the momentum threatening to shift to the other side. In agreeing to the cease-fire, Milošević had to overrule many in Serbia – including the Serbian Orthodox Church – who insisted that the fighting continue.

Serbian nationalist leaders had called for taking territory up to the Karlobag–Ogulin–Karlovac–Virovitica line, representing about two-thirds of Croatia's area, including such cities as Karlovac (26.6 percent Serbs), Zadar (10.5 percent Serbs), and Dubrovnik (6.7 percent Serbs). Typically, Monte-negrin troops had marched off to war on the Dubrovnik front singing "From the Lovčen [Mountain in Montenegro], the hawk shouts for joy: 'How are you doing, Serbian Dubrovnik?'"[109] Overall, in those territories over which the Serbs managed to retain control, they constituted only a thin majority of the population (51.1 percent before the war), and in several zones were a distinct minority. Even in Vukovar, taken after months of bitter fighting, Serbs had comprised only 37.4 percent of the prewar population. Sustained military operations had been mounted in support of these broader terri-torial objectives, which were abandoned only after it became clear that the JNA could not achieve them.

Vukovar – critical battle

If there was a "critical battle" in the war, it may have been the siege of Vukovar, the river city on Croatia's eastern border with Vojvodina. Despite the fact that the Croatians ultimately were forced to give up the city, this event was critical in the sense that it apparently forced Serbia and the JNA to revise their military assessments and expectations for victory at an acceptable cost. Although subsequent recriminations in Croatia suggested that the Zagreb authorities had mishandled attempts to relieve the siege and had written off the city early, some 1,500 determined defenders – two-thirds of them local militia personnel – managed to hold out for three months until 18 November 1991 against a much larger JNA and militia force. The latter included substantial armor, artillery, river gunboats, and air assets, and was commanded by General Života Panić, later to become Chief of the General Staff. Croatian sources have estimated the attacking force at 35–40,000 personnel at its peak, and attributed to them an armored brigade, a tank regiment, an elite guard mechanized brigade, a reserve mechanized infantry battalion, three reserve infantry brigades, a paratroop company, a military police company, and other smaller regular units and militia forces.[110] In the end, the defenders were only overcome after the destruction of much of the city and bitter street-to-street fighting which reportedly caused significant JNA casualties, with one general working for Serbia's Ministry of Defense calling Serbian losses at Vukovar "senseless."[111]

Following the sobering experience of Vukovar, the JNA began to view future operations with less optimism, especially in an urban environment. JNA personnel, for example, evaluated the prospects of attacking another city in Croatia, Gospić, in terms of "a second Vukovar." One field-grade officer at the scene assessed that, while the terrain and weather would favor the attackers, "Gospić will be a hard nut [to crack]. In contrast to Vukovar, the enemy has prepared for the city's defense in a more systematic manner."[112]

Also, without the delay imposed on the JNA at Vukovar, the Croatian Army might not have had the opportunity to organize its forces, and other cities in the region, such as Vinkovci and Osijek, would have been placed at immediate risk. The unexpected breathing spell was put to good use, enabling the Croatian Army eventually to shift to the offensive in Slavonija, where the best JNA units were committed. This also raised the prospect of costlier battles, particularly as the impending winter weather would degrade the JNA's air-power advantage significantly. The JNA was being put increasingly on the defensive by December 1991 and, according to the commander of the Croatian forces in Slavonija, if the order to halt had not been issued on 26 December, the latter would have continued to advance and "Within forty-eight hours we could have been, pardon the expression, literally pissing in the Sava [River]."[113] The need to prepare for the looming crisis in neighboring Bosnia may have been an additional factor influencing the desire to avoid becoming bogged down militarily in Croatia.

The corollary of heavy Serbian casualties also threatened to undermine wavering Serbian public support and to foment discontent against Milošević. Although the JNA officially acknowledged 1,279 killed in action (of which 177 officers) during the entire Serbo-Croatian War, the actual number was no doubt considerably greater, since casualties were consistently underreported during the war. For example, in the case of one brigade, while official reports spoke of two lightly wounded after an engagement, the actual numbers were 50 killed and 150 wounded, according to the unit's intelligence officer.[114] There are indications that morale was already becoming a serious concern in the JNA in direct proportion to casualties. By November 1991, the JNA leadership was already worried that "defeatism is spreading among the people. Columns of parents who want to bring the soldiers home are being organized in precisely those parts of the country which must support the JNA's military effort."[115] The repercussions on operations were significant as, according to one JNA general, by the end of 1991, "The relatively numerous desertions from some units no doubt threaten the success of certain operations. Some actions even had to be called off [because of this]."[116] Significantly, the flight of one group of reservists reportedly had forced the "postponement of the liberation of Vukovar" for twenty days, according to JNA sources.[117]

Croatian morale, on the contrary, seems to have been peaking with the transition to the offensive, and the Croatian commander on the Slavonijan front assessed that: "I did not have a problem sending men into battle, but rather in stopping them."[118] Such considerations, along with the impending decision by Europe to recognize Croatia, were probably key in Belgrade's willingness to accept the cease-fire shortly thereafter.

Moreover, Belgrade seems to have concluded that it could achieve most of its key objectives despite the agreed-upon presence of UN peacekeeping forces envisioned by the cease-fire agreement. The reluctance or inability of the international community (whether through the UN, the European Community, NATO, or other similar body) to act more forcefully at an earlier stage – perhaps at such milestones as the initial JNA attack against Slovenia and Croatia or the sieges of Vukovar or Dubrovnik – probably led Milošević to view the international presence as only a relatively minor obstacle to Serbia's goals.

Elusive end-state

Although the war significantly affected the political and military situation, the end-state is not only far from definitive, but even quite unstable and conducive to renewed conflict in the future.

The war's impact on the JNA

For the JNA, its failure in the wars against Slovenia and Croatia and, subsequently, in Bosnia-Herzegovina, was to be a catalyst to its transformation. First, there was an internal "ethnic cleansing." During the fighting in Croatia, non-Serb cadre often left, or were eliminated, while non-Serb draftees and reservists simply refused call-ups in increasing numbers or deserted. By the end of 1991, according to one estimate, the JNA had become 90 percent Serb and the Defense Minister, General Veljko Kadijević, was headed for retirement for "health reasons."[119] Second, defeat left the JNA vulnerable to a loss of its autonomy and to its being brought back under tighter government control, this time in the form of Serbia's government, the dominant partner in the union with Montenegro which comprised the rump of Yugoslavia. Third, the JNA, renamed the Yugoslav Army, became younger and even more explicitly Serbian-nationalist in outlook. The emerging orientation was clear in the advice now being given to new officers, who "must love, above all else, their unit, their army, and their homeland – Serbia and Montenegro."[120]

In the Spring of 1992, thirty-eight generals, as well as other officers were retired, with several put on trial in Belgrade on charges of incompetence and treason. This eliminated the Army's traditional senior leadership, including many Serbs with a communist pan-Yugoslav orientation. The Yugoslav Army has also moved to become a career-based force, probably motivated by a desire to improve its quality as well as to avoid relying on Serbia's large pool of mistrusted non-Serbian draftees. Despite such changes and soul-searching, however, the vulnerabilities of the Army appear to be so deep-seated and funding so limited that it is difficult to believe that its operational problems have been overcome.

Croatia and Serbia: a tally-sheet

Although both Tudjman and Milošević, for domestic political reasons, have portrayed the war as a victory for their country, Serbia apparently gained the most. On the plus side for Croatia, it had survived and had achieved its independence. However, the war had taken a heavy toll. Over one-third of Croatia's economic infrastructure had been destroyed or damaged, 100,000 houses and apartments demolished, and large amounts of private property looted. In addition, the war had caused 18,000 confirmed casualties by the end of 1991 (of which, 1,448 military killed in action and over 10,000 wounded) and some 14,000 missing, most of whom are probably also dead. Refugees numbered 703,000 by the end of 1991 (even before the additional inflow caused by the war in Bosnia-Herzegovina).

Significantly, due to European Community pressure, the terms of the cease-fire agreement allowed the JNA to withdraw most of its heavy arms, stores, and machinery from Croatia, a good deal of it accomplished by chartering foreign ships. This provision meant a significant boost to Serbia's subsequent military capabilities, not least by enabling vital production and repair functions to continue. The JNA, for example, managed to extract almost everything from the Zmaj installation in Zagreb, the only jet aircraft refitting facility in Yugoslavia. Removed were forty-two aircraft (of which eighteen being repaired for Iraq), thirty-two aircraft engines, and 3,500 tons of equipment and supplies, valued at $700 million.[121] On balance, the Croatian government erred in not pressing the siege of the surrounded garrisons in order to force them either to surrender or to withdraw their personnel without their equipment.

What is perhaps central, however, is that a substantial part of Croatia's territory remained under occupation. As Borisav Jović, President of Serbia's ruling Socialist Party, boasted to a convention of Young Socialists, "the war was conducted far from Serbia's borders," while the Serbian leadership still managed to "liberate" the Serbian population in what "many Serbs until recently did not even know were Serbian territories."[122] Local Serbs in these territories, representing 4.7 percent of Croatia's total population, were left in control of more than one-quarter of the republic's area, including some of its best farmlands and oil and gas deposits. Moreover, the configuration of the occupied territories left Croatia virtually split into two parts, with tenuous communications and a defensive situation exacerbated by little strategic depth over a long hostile border. By its acceptance of UN peacekeepers along the cease-fire lines, rather than along its border with Serbia, Zagreb also risked relinquishing the prospect of reasserting its sovereignty over the occupied zones (the "blue zones") for the duration of their presence. Even more unpalatable was the fact that, although the Serbian-held areas could not join Serbia at the time due to international opinion, the stage had been set for them to do so potentially at a more auspicious time, as Serbian leaders suggested.[123] In addition, in the adjacent "pink zones," where Serbs accounted for only 17.4 percent of the inhabitants, the Croatian government was obliged to share control with the UN but, in the event, Serbian forces continued their occupation. Despite the unfavorable provisions implicit in the cease-fire agreement, Zagreb accepted the terms as a condition for obtaining diplomatic recognition from the West. However, since recognition entailed neither an end to the arms embargo nor the restoration of Croatia's borders, one can argue that it would have made sense, instead, for Croatia to continue the war in order to obtain better terms, as the momentum on the ground was apparently shifting in its favor, while Serbia would be embroiled in Bosnia.

Implementing the cease-fire

The UN's ineffectiveness in implementing the cease-fire, moreover, has led to a failure to achieve a viable political solution and genuine stability. In many ways, the UN presence has ended up serving as a buffer behind which the Serbs have been able to consolidate their position. To be sure, the UN has succeeded in some areas, such as stopping most of the heavy shelling of Croatia's cities, facilitating prisoner exchanges, and the delivery of relief aid. However, even UN officials have viewed their mission as a failure overall. The deployment of UN forces along the battle lines rather than along the Serbia-Croatia border probably doomed the mission from the beginning. Contrary to the envisioned retrocession of the territories to Croatian control, the UN's dealings with the local Serbian officials, who have amalgamated the territories under their control into the Serbian Republic of Krajina, have lent a sort of *de facto* recognition to the latter's authority, contrary to the UN's original intent.[124] Serbian militias have remained in control of the occupied territories, and ethnic cleansing and violence by the Serbs against non-Serbs have continued unabated.[125] Likewise, the envisioned return of refugees to their homes has been blocked and lines of communication across the territories have not been opened.

Moreover, even before the fighting in early 1993, Serbian forces in the occupied territories had remained armed. According to the Russian Commander of the UN's Eastern Sector, for example,

The Serbian Republic of Krajina controls the situation, and its leaders have refused to allow us to implement the Vance Plan in its entirety. Therefore, the disarming process is proceeding slowly . . . We have information that several thousand [Serbian] militiamen are present here . . . [some militia forces] have kept their heavy weapons and have not remained in their barracks as envisioned by the Plan . . . In short, we are living in an explosive situation.[126]

Croatia may have absorbed a lesson about the importance and effectiveness of military support for political solutions, as suggested by its subsequent conduct in relation to the Prevlaka peninsula, a spit of land at the southernmost end of Croatia, which the JNA had taken during the war. Yugoslavia was induced to withdraw its forces from Prevlaka in late 1992 because of escalating Croatian military pressure, notwithstanding a strong interest by many in Belgrade (including by Yugoslavia's Prime Minister, California businessman-turned-politician Milan Panić) and by Serbia's junior partner, Montenegro, in keeping the territory. Again, in January 1993, frustrated by the inability of the UN to enforce the withdrawal of Serbian forces from a UN-protected area which severed northern and southern Croatia, Zagreb used military force to try to reopen the lines of communication.

Croatia's geopolitical and military position has deteriorated relative to that of its Serbian neighbors since the end of the war, however. Whether it negotiates a solution directly or seeks to improve its bargaining clout first by military action, the Tudjman government will be doing so from a less favorable position than it might have achieved if it had continued the war or had cooperated with the Bosnian government while Serbia was heavily engaged in Bosnia-Herzegovina.

CONCLUSION

The Serbo-Croatian War is a valid guide to Milošević's decision-making, in particular, in relation to his cost–benefit calculus. The absence of a well-armed opponent and the perception of weak international resolve not only prolonged the Serbo-Croatian War but also may have encouraged Milošević to embark on a more aggressive policy subsequently in Bosnia-Herzegovina, and may do so again in future scenarios. In particular, the limited costs incurred because of the Serbo-Croatian War may be a factor in the Milošević government's willingness to step up the tempo of "ethnic cleansing" in areas of Serbia with large non-Serbian populations: Kosovo, Vojvodina, and the Sandžak.

However, the Serbo-Croatian War also demonstrated that Serbian national will is limited. A corollary is that Milošević would find domestic support for military escalation to be problematic, especially if he were required to call up unwilling reserves and there was a prospect of significant casualties. His dilemma would be compounded if Belgrade faced effective international isolation. In particular, Milošević would have a difficult time engaging Serbia in another costly conflict in which the latter would confront a well-armed adversary able to deal with Serbia's conventional forces – the key to military success. Central to this is that the Yugoslav Army, whatever its improvements, is still a largely ineffective fighting force with deep-seated morale problems and could not guarantee a low-cost or successful military outcome for Belgrade. Despite its weaknesses, the Yugoslav Army can still succeed if its adversaries are unable to organize an effective national defense, largely because of the international embargo on security assistance.

The conduct and results of the Serbo-Croatian War also suggest that Milošević is key to solving any of the former Yugoslavia's ethnic problems. His behavior at the end of this war indicates that, rather than being an inflexible visionary, he is sensitive to pressure and that he is a pragmatic, calculating, risk-taker. He will weigh carefully the perceived costs in pursuing Serbia's national goals – particularly in so far as they might affect his own power – and will back down if the correlation of forces is not in his favor. However, he is not likely to reverse Serbia's policies unless and until their expected cost – especially in military terms – exceeds the benefits to be achieved.

NOTES

1   Even the ultimate outcome of a war is not always to be regarded as final. The defeated state often considers the outcome merely as a transitory evil, for which a remedy may still be found in political conditions at some later date. (Carl von Clausewitz, *On War*, edited and translated by Michael Howard and Peter Paret, Princeton: Princeton University Press, 1989: 80)

2 For insightful overviews of the political background of the crisis, see Ivo Banac, "The Fearful Asymmetry of War: The Causes and Consequences of Yugoslavia's Demise", *Daedalus*, Spring 1992: 141–74; and Sabrina Petra Ramet, "War in the Balkans," *Foreign Affairs*, Fall 1992: 79–98.

3 The relevant documents were published in *Zbornik dokumenata i podataka o narodnooslobodilačkom ratu naroda Jugoslavije* [Collection of Documents and Data on the National-Liberation War of the Peoples of Yugoslavia], vol. 14, part 1 (Belgrade: Institute of Military History, 1981).

4 For example, in a 1969 survey, Serbs (and Montenegrins), accounted for 42.2 percent of the population, but held 78.9 percent of higher-level bureaucratic posts (*Ekonomska politika* (Belgrade), 27 January 1969: 12). In the military, in the early 1980s, Serbs accounted for 66.2 percent of all officers, and 70 percent of all officers major and above in 1991 (Vlatko Cvrtila, "Tko je što u Armiji" [Who Is What in the Army], *Danas* (Zagreb), 5 February 1991: 16–17). *Danas* was originally an opposition weekly but, by 1993, had begun to conform closely to the government line. On the unequal bilateral relationship pattern, see N. L. Karlović, "Internal Colonialism in a Marxist Society: The Case of Croatia," *Ethnic and Racial Studies*, July 1982: 276–99.

5 Slaven Letica, "Cetvrta Jugoslavija" [A Fourth Yugoslavia], *Danas*, 24 January 1989: 19; and Jelena Lovrić, "Nacionalna karta partije" [The Party's Nationality Card], *Danas*, 10 December 1985: 8; interview by Croatia's Defense Minister General Martin Špegelj, 29 January 1991, in Slaven Letica and Mario Nobilo (respectively a key presidential adviser and Croatia's representative at the United Nations), *Rat protiv Hrvatske* [The War Against Croatia] (Zagreb: Globus, 1991: 32); minutes of the federal government meeting at Ohrid, July 1991, *Danas*, 30 July 1991: 10.

6 The text of the *Serbian Memorandum* has been published in Bože Čović, ed., *Izvori velikosrpske agresije* [*The Sources of Great Serbian Aggression*] (Zagreb: Školska Knjiga, 1991: 297 and *passim*).

7 Ivan Stambolić, *Rasprave o SR Srbiji* [*Debates on the Socialist Republic of Serbia*] (Zagreb: Globus, 1987: 218–19).

8 For an incisive assessment of this key figure, see Sabrina P. Ramet, "Serbia's Slobodan Milošević: A Profile," *Orbis*, Winter 1991: 93–105.

9 Jelena Lovrić, "Partijski rat ili mir" [Party War or Peace], *Danas*, 18 July 1989: 13.

10 Interview by Ivica Dačić, *Epoha* (Belgrade), 17 December 1991, p. 8. *Epoha* reflects the views of the ruling Serbian Socialist Party. General Panić was rewarded with the position of Chief of the General Staff after the purges of 1992.

11 This is reported by Admiral Branko Mamula, Yugoslavia's former Minister of Defense (interview by Vanja Bulić, "Zašto nisam postao jugoslovenski Jeruzelski" [Why I Did Not Become the Yugoslav Jaruzelski], *Duga* (Belgrade), 23 November–7 December 1991: 16). General Veljko Kadijević, then Minister of Defense, was adamantly in favor of scrapping the 1974 Constitution and replacing it with a centralized authoritarian state in which the central government would be ensured the dominant political and economic role ("Za stabilnu Jugoslaviju i snaznu odbranu" [For a Stable Yugoslavia and a Strong Defense], *Narodna armija* (Belgrade), 21 December 1989: 6). *Narodna armija* was the official organ of the JNA.

12 Bishop Nikolaj, "Donosimo vam srca puna ljubavi" [We Bring You Hearts Full of Love], *Politika*, 28 June 1989: 5.

13 Jevrem Brković, *Danas*, 7 February 1989: 33; Vlado Mičunović, "Mitinzi solidarnosti u Nikšiću i Cetinju, [Solidarity Meetings in Nikšić and Četinje] *Intervju* (Belgrade), 30 September 1988: 17; and Milan Vojvodić, *Vreme* (Belgrade), 13 January 1992: 24. *Vreme* is a liberal publication.

14 Tihomir Stojanović, "Opasnost četvrtog rajha" [The Danger of a Fourth Reich], *Narodna armija*, 2 November 1991: 27.

15 Text in Čovi (see note 6), p. 293.

16 Interview by Branka Trivić, "Neću da lažem za otadžbinu" [I Will Not Lie for My Homeland], *Stav* (Novi Sad, Vojvodina, Serbia), 10 January 1992: 10. Most (62.8 percent) of Croatia's 600,000 Serbs have continued to live in areas still controlled by the Croatian government during and after the war.

17 Bogdan Ivanišević, "Vukovarski sindrom" [The Vukovar Syndrome], *NIN* (Belgrade), 13 December 1991: 12. Initially, *NIN* conformed closely to Milošević's views, but later became a liberal opposition voice.

18 Milo Gligorijević, "Pokretni kosovski boj" [The Mobile Battle of Kosovo], *NIN*, 16 July 1989: 9; and Marinko Čulić, "Kokarde opet sjaje" [The Chetnik Badges Are Shining Again], *Danas*, 18 July 1989: 10.

19 Gligorijević (see note 18), p. 9.

20 See the interview with Milić Knežević, one of the early organizers of the Chetniks in Croatia, by Vasilije Milić, "Kako smo dizali ustanak na Kordunu; Bice ustanka opet!" [How We Organized the Revolt in Kordun; There Will Again be an Uprising!], *Pogledi* (Kragujevac, Serbia), 15 May 1992: 33–5. *Pogledi* is one of the official publications of the Serbian People's Renewal.

21 The division in the Serbian community over secession versus autonomy continued well into the following year, as shown by talks conducted between Serbian officials in the territories occupied by the JNA and Serbian representatives who had returned to sit in the Croatian Parliament. Hardline leader Milan Babić openly accused on Serbia's state-run television those elected Serbian representatives in Slavonija who did not want to secede from Croatia of "leading a policy of capitulation" (Zoran Daškalović, "Sto hoće Srbi" [What Do the Serbs Want?], *Danas*, 20 August 1991: 22–4). According to Stipe Mešić, the last President of the Presidency of Yugoslavia, about 70 percent of Croatia's Serbs had voted in favor of Croatia's independence in the May 1991 referendum (*Kako smo srušili Jugoslaviju* [How We Destroyed Yugoslavia] (Zagreb: Globus International, 1992: xiii).

22 Interview "Hrvatska nema suvereniteta" [Croatia Has No Sovereignty], *Danas*, 26 March 1991: 24.

23 General Anton Tus, then Commander of the Air Force, claims to have made that request (interview by Jelena Lovrić and Mladen Maloča, "Izdaja je na drugoj strani" [It Was the Other Side Who Committed Treason], *Danas*, 31 December 1991: 16).

24 Blaine Harden, "Bank Scandal Stirs Yugoslav Outcry," *Washington Post*, 11 January 1991: A8.

25 Interview with Vuk Drašković by Stevo Batić, "Srbi su fatalisti" [The Serbs Are Fatalists], *Srpska reč (Belgrade), 2 March 1992: 24. Srpska reč* is the organ of the Serbian Renewal Movement.

26 Stephen Engelberg, "2 Yugoslav Factions Blaming Each Other for Deaths in Clash," *The New York Times*, 4 May 1991: 1, 5. According to later admissions by Chetnik leader Vojislav Šešelj, a contingent of his militia, as well as elements from another Chetnik party – the Serbian People's Renewal – had participated in the Borovo Selo "battle;" see interview with Šešelj by Dragan Alempijević, "Sada verujemo Armiji" [Now We Trust the Army], *Pogledi*, 25 November 1991: 32.

27 This is reported by Milan Djukić, President of the Serbian People's Party in Croatia, in reference to Serbs in Croatia who had refused to fight against the Croatian government (Večeslav Kočijan, "Okus kolektivne krivnje" [The Taste of Collective Guilt], *Novi Danas* (Zagreb), 31 July 1992: 29)

28 Zoran Bogavac, "Prvi srpski oklopni voz" [The First Serbian Armored Train], *Duga*, 23 November–7 December 1991: 34–8.

29 Interview, "Hrvatska mora u ofanzivu" [Croatia Must Take the Offensive], by Mladen Maloča and Darko Pavičić, *Danas*, 15 October 1991: 21.

30 According to the memoirs of Stipe Mešić (see note 21), pp. 130, 160, 193 and *passim*, and the minutes of the 18 September 1991 session of the Federal Executive Council ("Zbrisaće nas sa kugle zemaljske" [They Will Wipe Us Off the Face of the Earth], *Vreme*, 23 September 1991: 5–12).

31 Serbia's Parliament hosted a delegation from this party in July 1991, with its President, Roberto Menia, noting that his visit to Belgrade convinced him that "the Serbs support this idea [i.e., of partitioning western and southern Croatia with Italy]"; interview by Tonko Vulić ("Italija će biti do Prevlake!" [Italy will Extend to Prevlaka!], *Globus* (Zagreb), 6 November 1992: 28). Nationalist leaders in Serbia have worked to rehabilitate Italian Fascism in order to strengthen these bilateral ties; see Dragoš Kalajić ("Jedan pogled na svet: crne etikete; Ko se boji fašista još" [A Viewpoint on the World: Negative Labels; Who is Still Afraid of the Fascists?], *Duga*, 23 December 1991–6 January 1992: 77–8).

32 Blaine Harden, "Croatia Charges Army Shadows Its Officials," *Washington Post*, 19 January 1991: A11.

33 Letica and Nobilo (see note 5), p. 17.

34 Interview with Josip Manolić by Jelena Lovrić and Mladen Maloča, "Za sve jednako" [Equally for Everyone], *Danas*, 28 August 1990: 15.

35 Letica and Nobilo (see note 5), p. 72.

36 Ante Barišić, "Nemamo snage za rat" [We Are Not Strong Enough for War], *Danas*, 16 July 1991: 18.

37 Interview with General Špegelj (see note 29), p. 21.

38 See the interview with Brigadier Djuro Dečak, Commander of Croatian Army forces in Osijek, by Drago Hedl, "Neka nitko, za dragog Boga, ne podcjenjuje HV" [God Forbid that Anyone Underestimates the Croatian Army!], *Slobodna Dalmacija* (Split, Croatia), 26 January 1993: 11.

39 This was true at least in one unit, according to the interview by Rajko Lukac with veteran Milan Cvijić ("Čestitke uz pratnju artilerije" [Congratulations Accompanied by Artillery], *Spona* (Frankfurt, Germany), 15–22 April 1993: 8).

40 Interview with General Špegelj (see note 29), p. 23; Michael Binyon, "Yugoslavia Fears Grow As Army Goes on Alert," *The Times* (London), 8 May 1991: 1; Mešić (see note 21), pp. 158, 159.

41 Darko Pavičić, "Krvavo primirje" [Bloody Ceasefire], *Danas*, 3 March 1992: 24.

42 Interview (see note 29), p. 22.

43 Janez Janša, Slovenia's Minister of Defense reports this, based on his discussions with General Špegelj during the war ("Janša bi napao" [Janša Would Attack], *Danas*, 3 September 1991: 36).

44 Article by Željko Bukša, "The War Was Won by Blockading the Garrisons," based on a lecture by General Anton Tus, "Novi Vjesnik" (Zagreb), 7 February 1993, in *Foreign Broadcast Information Service – Eastern Europe-93-038*, 1 March 1993: 68.

45 Dušan Stojanović, "Serbian Leader Adopts Tone of Conciliation," *Washington Post*, 28 February 1992: A26.

46 Slavoljub Kočarević, "Srpski parlamentarac u Americi" [A Serbian Parliamentarian in America], *Intervju*, 6 March 1992: 6.

47 The minutes are those made by Dobrila Gajić-Glišić, Chief of Staff to General Tomislav Simović, Serbia's Minister of Defense (*NIN*, especially 24 April 1992: 26–7, 53; and 1 May 1992: 53).

48 Srdjan Stanišić, "Srbija medju ruševinama – drvo za Djilasa" [Serbia in Ruins – Building Material for Djilas], *Pogledi*, 27 March 1992: 24.

49 The Commander of this militia, "at the moment fighting in Bosnia and Croatia," publicly thanked the Director of Jugopetrol, a state-run firm and frequent conduit of funds for covert government activities, for "services connected with the establishment and strengthening of this armed force" (Vladan Vasilijević, "Nemoćni pridikuju moćnima" [The Powerless Are Preaching to the Powerful], *Srpska reč*, 11 May 1992: 29).

50 Interview with Milan Babić by Blagica Stopanović, *Srpska reč*, 16 March 1992: 49.

51 B. V., "The Quiet Military Coup D'Etat of the Yugoslav People's Army," *Borba* (Belgrade), 26 August 1992; *FBIS-EEU-92-181*, 17 September 1992: 39, quoting the Krajina's Deputy Prime Minister, Boško Božanić.

52 Interview (see note 50), p. 49.

53 Dragan Damjanović, "Cerska bitka drugi put" [The Battle of Cerska a Second Time], *Vecernje novosti* (Belgrade), 16 July 1992: 13.

54 Letter to the editor, *Srpska reč*, 11 May 1992: 64.

55 Bogdan Ivanišević, "Vukovarski sindrom" [The Vukovar Syndrome], *NIN*, 13 December 1991: 12.

56 Interview with Colonel Milan Milivojević by Slavoljub Kočarević, "Vreme za promene u vojnom vrhu" [Time for Changes in the Top Military Leadership], *Intervju*, 17 April 1992: 50. As a result, many units seem to have been seriously under strength. For example, one brigade had only 300 personnel instead of the intended 1,500 (*Spona*, 15–22 April 1993 (see note 39)).

57 Zlatko Čobović, "Vojni sudovi i neposlužni rezervisti" [Military Courts and Recalcitrant Reservists], *Srpska reč*, 2 March 1992: 72; Ljiljana Jorgovanović-Bulatović, "Ko finansira srpsku opoziciju? Forsiranje članstva" [Who Finances the Serbian Opposition? Pumping Up the Membership], *Srpska reč*, 13 April 1992: 11; interview with Jevrem Brković, "Prvi slovenski politicki azilant" [The First Slavic Political Refugee], *Danas*, 22 October 1991: 3. Among those who had gone abroad were relatives of the Serbian leadership, such as the nephew of General Andrija Rašeta (commander of JNA forces in Croatia), who went to London (Tanja Bulatović, "Podstanar gospodina Aleksića" [Mr. Aleksić's Tenant], *Duga*, 19 January–1 February 1992: 28–9), and the son of Serbia's Vice-President (M. D., "Ciji sinovi idu u vojsku?" [Whose Sons Go into the Army?], *Srpska reč*, 23 December 1991: 19.

58 S. Djokić, "Stvarnost druge dimenzije" [Reality of a Second Dimension], *Narodna armija*, 23 November 1991: 24.

59 The fall of the Varaždin base, for example, netted the Croatian forces 74 T-55 tanks, 61 APCs, 256 trucks, and 25,000 hand grenades, as well as substantial quantities of light arms (Nenad Stefanović, "Proces generalu Trifunoviću; Izdajnik ili pokojnik" [General Trifunović's Trial; Traitor or Deceased?], *Vreme*, 13 April 1992: 25. General Tus claims that Croatian forces captured a total of 230 tanks and more than 400 artillery pieces from the garrisons which surrendered (see note 44), p. 68.

60 Branislav Matić, "Kako su vezana čelična krila naše armije?" [How Are Our Army's Steel Wings Tied?], *Duga*, 12–25 April 1992: 39. Matić was the S-2 of the 5th Kozarska Motorized Brigade, probably the key unit on that part of the Slavonija front; and interview with General Tus (see note 23), p. 16.

61 Nenad Čanak, "Doživljaji vojnika Čanka" [The Impressions of Soldier Čanak], Part 1, *Vreme*, 23 December 1991: 23.

62 Interview with Colonel Milorad Vučić, Commander of a Mechanized Infantry Brigade, conducted by General-Lieutenant-Colonel (Ret.) Dušan Dozet, Lieutenant Colonel Nikola Ostojić, and Pero Damjanov ("Ti divni ljudi, mladi

ratnici (2)" [Those Wonderful People, Young Soldiers], *Narodna armija*, 25 December 1991: 13).

63 "Predata dobijena bitka" [Surrendering a Won Battle], *Šumadija* (Kragujevac, Serbia), 20 May 1992: 15. *Šumadija* is an official publication of the Serbian People's Renewal.

64 *Vreme* published a photocopy of part of this report, 24 February 1992: 13.

65 Interview, "Uspostavlja se moderan sistem komuniciranja armije s javnosću" [A Modern System of Communications between the Army and the Public Is Being Set Up], *Narodna armija*, 12 March 1992: 7.

66 Milovan Milutinović, "Opasnost vreba od neodgovornih" [The Irresponsible Ones Present a Threat], *Narodna armija*, 30 December 1991: 16.

67 Interview (see note 62), p. 12.

68 R. Kostov and P. Bošković, "Svi začini valjevske 'kaše'" [All the Seasonings for the Valjevo Porridge], *Narodna armija*, 2 November 1992: 11.

69 Zlatko Čobović, "Porucnik na vojnom sudu" [The Lieutenant in Military Court], *Srpska reč*, 23 December 1991: 50.

70 See the minutes from Serbia's Minister of Defense (see note 43), 24 April 1992, p. 54.

71 *Spona*, 15–22 April 1993 (see note 39).

72 "Linija Osijek-Vinkovci sada drže samo aktivne jedinice" [Only Active-duty Units are Now Holding the Osijek-Vinkovci Line], *Narodna armija*, 9 November 1991: 30.

73 Rajko Djurdjević, "Mladosrbi i jarci" [The Young Serbs and the Old Goats], *NIN*, 22 May 1992: 11.

74 Interview with Serbia's Defense Minister, General Colonel Tomislav Šimović, by M. Pantelić, "Strategija domina" [The Domino Strategy], *Narodna armija*, 2 October 1991: 10; R.I., "Gde su Slavko i Radenko" [Where Are Slavko and Radenko?], *Intervju*, 15 May 1992: 16.

75 Interview by Sanjin Pošaveč, "Izdajice i profiteri" [Traitors and Profiteers], *Danas*, 20 August 1991: 17.

76 Ljubodrag Stojadinović, "Ratnik i njegova parola" [A Soldier and His Slogan], *Narodna armija*, 6 November 1991: 9, interview by [Colonel] I[van] M[atošič], "Topola se brani u Gospiću" [Topola Is Defended in Gospič], *Narodna armija*, 16 November 1991: 4. Another source calculates that of 127,000 military-age Serbs in Croatia, only 23,000 had responded to Serbia's military call-up (B[ranko] Vučković, "Monarhija: srpski narod nije kriv" [The Monarchy: The Serbian People Are Not Guilty], *Šumadija*, 29 April 1992: 10).

77 "Apel gluvom srcu" [An Appeal to a Deaf Heart], *Evropske novosti* (Frankfurt, Germany), 16 January 1993: 6. This is the German-based edition of *Večernje novosti*, a Belgrade newspaper.

78 B.M., "Puška jača od privilegija" [The Rifle Is Stronger than Privileges], *Evropske novosti*, 20 February 1993: 13.

79 *Duga*, 7 December 1991, quoted by Ivo Banac (see note 2), p. 168.

80 Interview (see note 75), p. 17.

81 General-Major Dragoljub Arandjelović admitted this in "Pogrešna upotreba moćne sile" [The Misuse of a Powerful Force], *Narodna armija*, 10 July 1991: 19.

82 General Lieutenant-Colonel Andrija Rašeta, then Chief of Operations of the Fifth Military District, for example, gave the desire to avoid exposing infantry as the reason why armor was being deployed to Croatia (interview by Srdjan Spanović, *Danas*, 9 April 1991: 16–17).

83 Interview (see note 62), p. 13.

84 M. Marjanović and D. Glišić, "Visoka cena slobode" [The High Price of Freedom], *Narodna armija*, 21 September 1991: 10.

85 Rajko Djurdjević, "Krtice riju nebo" [The Moles are Burrowing in the Sky], *NIN*, 22 May 1992: 11; Douglas Dobson, "An Eyewitness Account of the Fighting in Croatia," *State* (Washington, D.C.), March 1992: 17.

86 Interview with General-Major Ljubomir Bajić by S. Nedeljković, "Vazduho-plovstvo po meri nove države" [An Air Force Appropriate to the New State], *Narodna armija*, 21 May 1992: 18.

87 Matić (see note 60), pp. 81–2; and Vesna Mališić, "Sa rukavom ili nogavicom više" [With an Extra Sleeve or Pant-leg], *Duga*, 23 December 1991–6 January 1992: 22; "Ratni dnevnik jednog dobrovoljca" [The War Diary of a Volunteer], *Sumadija*, 6 May 1992: 15; and Kostov and Bošković (see note 68), p. 11.

88 Matić (see note 60), p. 40.

89 *Spona*, 15–22 April 1993 (see note 39).

90 *Spona*, 15–22 April 1993 (see note 39).

91 See note 37, p. 11; interview with Major-General Ivan Basarec by Vedran Kukavica, "Tu se obranila Hrvatska" [Croatia Was Defended Successfully Here], *Hrvatski vojnik* (Zagreb), 18 December 1992: 15.

92 Kostov and Bošković (see note 68), p. 11; R. Popović, "Ne može se grlom u jagode" [One Cannot Do Things Haphazardly], *Narodna armija*, 25 December 1991: 20; M. Pantelić, "Strategija domina" [The Domino Strategy], *Narodna armija*, 2 October 1991: 10.

93 Željko Bukša, "Umjesto u Kuvajt, na hrvatska ratišta?" [Instead of Going to Kuwait, to the Croatian Battlefield?], *Vjesnik* (Zagreb), 18 February 1992: 2. The JNA confirmed this cooperation ("Stižu delovi tenka" [The Tanks Parts are Coming], *Narodna armija*, 5 March 1992: 15). One Croatian military commander complained bitterly that the new tanks awaiting shipment should have been used instead to raise the siege of Vukovar (Zlatko Toth-Feniks, "Žrtvovani grad" [Sacrificed City], *Novi Danas*, 31 August 1992: 34.

94 Interview with General Major Dragoljub Arandjelović, by Mladen Marjanović, *Narodna armija*, 2 November 1991: 4.

95 Ranko Babić, "Neminovni pad morala" [The Inevitable Fall of Morale], *Narodna armija*, 20 February 1992: 26.

96 M. Sekulić, "Propusti kao opomena" [Oversights as a Warning], *Narodna armija*, 2 October 1991: 46; Popović (see note 92), p. 20.

97 *Spona*, 15–22 April 1993 (see note 39).

98 *Spona*, 15–22 April 1993 (see note 39).

99 Mališić (see note 87), p. 32.

100 Interview (see note 62), p. 13.

101 Blaine Harden, "Serbs Accused of '91 Croatia Massacre; US Doctors Believe 200 Wounded Men Were Taken from Hospital and Shot," *Washington Post*, 26 January 1993: A-13. JNA sources gave the number of those who surrendered at Vukovar as 300 Croatian military personnel, 2,000 "unarmed Croatian military," and 5000 civilians (Colonel Nebojša Pavković, *Narodna armija*, 30 December 1991: 19). Other JNA sources have also mentioned 300 individuals from Croatia's Albanian community (whom the JNA labeled "Albanian mercenaries") taken in Vukovar's hospital who were not seen again (Nikola Ostojić, "Vukovar – slobodan grad" [Vukovar – A Free City], *Narodna armija*, 23 November 1991: 15).

102 "Doživljaji vojnika Čanka" [The Experiences of Soldier Čanak], Part 2, *Vreme*, 30 December 1991: 28.

103 "Primirje odoleva" [The Cease-fire Remains Firm], *Narodna armija*, 16 January 1992: 7.

104 Zoran Nedeljković, "Kolonizacija Baranije; seoba naroda za džakove dolara"

[The Colonization of Baranija; The Migration of People for Bagfuls of Dollars], *Srpska reč*, 6 January 1992: 21.

105 See the minutes by Dobrila Gajić-Glišić, *NIN*, 15 May 1992: 32.

106 *Vreme*, 24 February 1992: 13.

107 Interview by Huda Al-Husayni, "Milošević qada ala injazat Tito" [Milosevic Has Undone Tito's Achievements], *Al-Sharq al-Awsat* (London), 18 December 1992: 8.

108 For example, JNA officers formed and officered the First Krajina Brigade and the Second Lika Brigade, which included locals and "volunteers from Belgrade and other cities in Serbia and Vojvodina" (interview with Colonel Petar Trbović by Risto Kostov, "Tri brigade pukovnika Trbovića" [Colonel Trbović's Three Brigades], *Narodna armija*, 30 December 1991: 21). Vojislav Šešelj, leader of the Chetnik Serbian Radical Party, asked about his militia, noted that "They are cooperating with the JNA units . . . trained officers must lead them" (interview (see note 26), p. 32).

109 Dada Vujašinović, "Dje si, srpski Dubrovniče" [How Are You Doing, Serbian Dubrovnik?], *Duga*, 12–26 October 1991: 19.

110 Siniša Haluzan, "Kako je branjen Vukovar" [How Vukovar Was Defended], *Hrvatski vojnik*, 4 December 1992: 15; Karlo Jeger and Maroje Mihovilović, "Gardista razapetog na vagon gadjali su tenkovskim topom!" [They Shot with a Tank Gun at a Guard Member Spread-Eagled on a Wagon], *Globus*, 6 November 1992: 13–14.

111 The minutes from Serbia's Minister of Defense, *NIN*, 1 May 1992: 53. Croatian military sources subsequently claimed to have inflicted between 7 and 15,000 casualties, including one JNA general killed, and to have shot down 29 aircraft during the siege (Haluzan 16).

112 Quoted by B. Djurdjević, "Narod veruje samo vojsci" [The People Only Trust the Army], *Narodna armija*, 30 December 1991: 29.

113 Interview (see note 38), p. 11.

114 "U secesionističkom ratu; na strani Armije 1.279 žrtava" [In the War of Secession; 1279 Victims on the Army Side], *Narodna armija*, 12 March 1992: 12; Matić (see note 60), p. 39.

115 S. Rištić, quoting Admiral Stane Brovet, "Ratni sistem Hrvatske protiv Armije bez podrške" [Croatia's Military System against an Army Lacking Support], *Narodna armija*, 9 November 1991: 10.

116 Interview (see note 10), p. 11.

117 S.C., "Povratak ratnika" [The Soldiers' Return], *Narodna armija*, 19 March 1992: 19.

118 Interview (see note 38), p. 11.

119 Miloslav Samardžić, "Ratni zločini protiv Srbije: Istina" [War Crimes against Serbia: The Truth], *Pogledi*, 29 November 1991: 15. While two-thirds of the officer corps had been consistently Serb, the draft-enlisted personnel reflected Yugoslavia's ethnic make-up, with some weighting in favor of ethnic groups, such as the Albanians and Muslims, with higher birth rates and, therefore, larger draft-age groups, making for an overall balance of 55 percent non-Serb according to one report (Šimo Dubajić, "Sudbina JNA u srpskohrvatskom ratu; Partijska paravojna formacija" [The Fate of the JNA in the Serbo-Croatian War; A Party Paramilitary Formation], *Srpska reč*, 23 December 1991: 32).

120 Major Drago Matijašević, "Moderna vojska demokratskog društva" [A Modern Army of a Democratic Society], *Narodna armija*, 18 April 1992: 12.

121 "Evakuisana tehnološka pesnica" [The Technological Fist Is Evacuated], *Narodna armija*, 6 February 1992: 22. Croatian sources put the value at only $82 million (Karlo Jeger, "Srpski oklopni bataljuni prešli Drinu!" [Serbian

Armored Battalions Have Crossed the Drina!], *Globus*, 5 February 1993: 5). See also Milan Vego, "Break-Up of the Yugoslav Navy," *Navy International*, May 1992: 152–7. The JNA destroyed or made unusable what it could not move before handing over the installations to the Croatians, according to British peacekeepers who arrived on the scene (Laurie Manton, "They've Got the UN's Health at Heart," *Soldier* (Aldershot, England), 5 October 1992: 26).

122 Speech reported by D. Stevanović, "Jović: JNA je korišćena za zaštitu Srba" [Jovic: The JNA Was Used to Defend the Serbs], *Politika*, 4 March 1992: 1.

123 Branko Koštić, Vice-President of the Presidency of Yugoslavia, for example, clarified that Croatia would be recognized only "within those boundaries of that territory which it controls as a state, and over which it has power. Croatia at this time neither has power nor is able to control territory in the Serbian Krajina" (speech in *Narodna armija*, 22 December 1991: 6. Likewise, Serbia's Vice-President, Radoman Božović, added: "If Serbia has bound its existence and sovereignty to Yugoslavia, then it is logical that [Serbia] recognizes the same right also to other parts of the Serbian people outside of Serbia" (interview in *Epoba*, 28 January 1992: 8).

124 A Jamaican human affairs official at the UN Eastern Sector headquarters, for example, concluded that "We do not recognize the Krajina, but those of us working in the field are forced to deal with the latter" (interview (see note 107), p. 8).

125 The same source (see preceding note) also notes that whenever UN forces happen to apprehend someone suspected of murdering or kidnapping non-Serbs, the standard operating procedure is to turn him over to the Krajina authorities, who just place him on his own recognizance (interview (see note 107), p. 8).

126 Interview (see note 107), p. 8.

4

THE GENESIS OF THE
CURRENT BALKAN WAR

Slaven Letica

The idea that substantially orients the global political and social life of almost all post-communist countries is that of ethnicity. Ethnic identity, relations, distance, ethnocentrism, ethnic conflict, and finally, "ethnic cleansing," are just some of the semantic expressions of the new "renaissance" of ethnicity which – in the wake of the fall of the Berlin Wall, the end of communism, the dissolution of multinational states, as well as the chaos of ethnic war – have flooded post-communist countries.

As a result of these changes, there exists on the part of the social theorist a substantial obligation to elucidate the phenomenology of ethnic conflict in the post-communist era. The idea of ethnicity, particularly in the Western tradition of the social sciences, typically carries negative connotations. Such conceptions are most often used to explain social prejudice, ethnocentrism, nationalism, and at a higher level of generalization, authoritarianism, totalitarianism, and fascism.

The horrors of war in the Balkans, particularly those in Croatia and Bosnia-Herzegovina, will further reinforce the notion that ethnic consciousness, animated by nationalistic and/or national-socialistic ideologies, logically lead people to conflict, war, crimes, and even genocide. Post-communist ethnic conflicts of differing intensity, mild in the case of Slovaks and Czechs; confrontational in the case of relations between Russians and Baltic ethnic communities; warlike and genocidal in the case of relations between Serbs, Albanians, Slovenes, Croats, and Muslims have not attracted sufficient theoretical attention in Western scientific communities. Rather, they have typically been "theoretically" interpreted simply by way of stereotypes regarding Balkanization, that is, the allegedly inherent primitivism, tribalism, and nationalism of Balkan ethnic communities.

Given that the circumstances of war do not present ideal conditions for impartial interpretations of earlier inquiries on ethnic relations – distance, prejudice, conflict, position of ethnic communities, and the like – our scientific communities have shied away form these quagmires that go by the name of ethno-theories of post-communism. At the same time, *Realpolitik* – Croatian,

Serbian, Muslim, but also European and North American – makes constant reference to themes of ethnicity in everyday politics. Interpretations of the causes, sources and character of Balkan post-communist war(s) most often employ ethno-argumentation. Even a superficial analysis of the media, and the diplomatic and political discourses, on these conflicts yields some ideal explanatory (political and theoretical) models on the causes, sources, and character of wars (Slovenian, Croatian, and Bosnian-Herzegovinian) in the Balkans during 1991–5.

To simplify the empirical material and interpretive framework, we will limit ourselves in this chapter to the ethnic conflicts and war in Croatia. With regard to the cases, sources, and character of these conflicts, it is possible to separate two *Realpolitik* explanatory models, which will here be referred to as Croatian and Serbian. In the case of Croatia, this explanatory model is found in several sub-variations, but for the main part these coalesce into the following ideal type with regard to interpretation and argumentation: the war in Croatia by its very nature is a war of aggression and conquest behind which stand centuries of greater Serbian imperial ideology whose development has been continuous from the time of the fall of the Turkish Empire until the period of the fall of communism and Yugoslavia. Its paradigmatic documents/scriptures range from *Nacertanije* (literally, Boundaries) by Ilija Garašanin in 1844, to the 1986 "Memorandum by the Serbian Academy of Arts and Sciences," as well as an entire national-socialist movement and ideology (that was racist, proto-fascistic, and genocidal), i.e., the *Realpolitik* of Slobodan Milošević. The so-called minority problem of the Serbs in Croatia was in fact an excuse used to justify aggression and war. Under the mask of the war slogan "in defense of the Serbian people," there were hidden the following military objectives: the territorial conquest of non-Serbian territories, particularly the fertile and oil-rich fields in Baranja and eastern Slavonia, as well as the tourist and seaside resources of the Adriatic coast. A specific war objective involved the desire of the Serbian leadership and state to once again, and permanently, prevent the establishment of a stable, sovereign, and modern Croatian state. The technology behind the "production" of aggression followed the logic of so-called low-intensity conflict, and its military strategy was based on a combination of Soviet and Nazi doctrines (with the former involving the encirclement and destruction of towns and civil populations and the latter including so-called ethnic cleansing, concentration camps, and outright genocide).

The Serbian explanatory model also appears in several variations. It is possible, at least during the initial phases of Serbian aggression, to differentiate between the explanations and positions put forth by the political organs and leadership of the JNA (Yugoslav People's Army) on the one hand, and the regime of Slobodan Milošević on the other, but they both revolve around the following interpretation: that the cause and the source of the armed conflict were the secessionist and nationalistic regimes in Croatia and Slovenia, and that the former was a continuation of the fascist ideology and state-building doctrines of the NDH (Independent State of Croatia), which was in the same manner subjecting Croatia's Serbs to discrimination and persecution, so that these Serbs – having already been exposed to a half-century long process of discrimination and assimilation – were, as a result of these life-threatening hazards, led into armed uprising. In other words, the Croats as a people, and Croatia as an independent state, permanently pose a genocidal threat to the Serbian people, who therefore had to be liberated.

Western interpretations of the cause, motivation and nature of military and ethnic conflicts are presented most often in terms of rather sketchy combinations of utilitarian (*Realpolitik*) or conformist modes with clear biases and predispositions – based on history and national interest – being evident on the parts of France, England, Russia, the United States of America and Germany.

Because the post-communist Balkan Wars were from their beginning the subject of international attention – manifested in the form of *ad hoc* missions, reporters and cameramen, satellite surveillance, European Community observers, United Nations peacekeepers, intelligence services, etc. – these statistics and data on the war can today serve as an empirical foundation for substantive theoretical and political "arbitration" on the causes, source, and goals, and therefore, the nature (i.e., character: conquest vs. liberation; just vs. unjust) of the war and the responsibility for it.

Instead of such analyses – which could be undertaken by every qualified expert team of war sociologists, political scientists, and geostrategic students – foreign media and diplomatic circles continue to speak in terms of a civil war, a tribal conflict, and a religious war, in an attempt to relativize and "equitably" divide the responsibility for the conflict or find a scapegoat to carry the brunt of the blame for the subsequent horrors. During the Serbian attacks on Slovenia and Croatia in 1991, the European Community and the United States of America attempted to lay the blame and responsibility for the war on the governments of Slovenia and Croatia. The war crimes and destruction wreaked by the JNA and Serbian paramilitary formations in Croatia during the course of 1991 and 1992 forced the West to place the primary blame for war on the actual aggressor (JNA, Serbia and Montenegro). Finally, the chaos of war in Bosnia-Herzegovina in 1992, particularly the conflict between Croatians and Muslims, gradually led to Croatian authorities and Croatians themselves being labeled accomplices of the war and thereby implicated in war crimes.

A similar round of such "finger-pointing" began to be played out in the middle of 1993 between Western countries and, specifically, the bureaucratic and diplomatic circles in those countries. In mid-1993 the American administration, supported by a part of the British and American media, attempted to place responsibility for the war upon Germany (a convenient scapegoat, given the animosities engendered by its Nazi past, but also its current economic power) for its "premature recognition of Slovenia and Croatia." This game of blame-shifting continued, so that Western opinion was also confronted with two antitheses to such accusations. The first thesis: that responsibility does not lie in the premature, but rather the belated recognition of former Yugoslav states. The second (anti)thesis: that the former Secretary of State James Baker and the American administration played an active role in – and should be given significant responsibility for – the beginning of greater Serbian aggression; specifically, that the public declarations made by Baker during his visit to Belgrade in June 1991, to the effect that America would not recognize the independence of Slovenia and Croatia, and that they would support the unity of SFRJ (Socialist Federal Republic of Yugoslavia), served to precipitate the aggression of the JNA and the regime of Slobodan Milošević. Although ethnic conflicts – both latent and manifest – were present in Croatian politics from the moment of the creation of a monarchical Yugoslavia (and even earlier) until today, it is the period beginning with Tito's death, and including Slobodan Milošević's rise to power, and the end of communism, and the dissolution of SFRJ that provide us with the empirical "keys" for understanding and interpreting the ethnic and armed conflicts that led to the current Balkan war. Therefore, the primary focus will be the years 1981–91, during which the JNA and Serbia undertook all the preparations for their aggression and war.

SOCIAL POSITION OF ETHNIC GROUPS IN CROATIA

Greater Serbian political and military propaganda constantly manipulated the position of Krajina (literally, across the border) Serbs (from Kosovo, Croatia, and Bosnia) as a precursor to instigating aggression and creating a new state-political reality in the Balkans. At the heart of this propaganda lay the thesis that "the Serbian people" had been relegated to a constitutionally discriminatory position in the Yugoslav federation, and in the constitutions of Serbia, Croatia, and Bosnia-Herzegovina. In addition to this constitutional discrimination, further discrimination of Serbs was present, allegedly, within the currents of social mobility and the very social fabric. It is necessary to mention that Serbian propaganda systematically rejected empirically based analytical discourse on the social status of ethnic communities in the area of former Yugoslavia, and instead relied exclusively on anecdotal and historical arguments and "argumentation" on discrimination, endangerment, and expulsion of Serbs.

This meant, in practical terms, that the alleged social discrimination and expulsion of Serbs – for example, in Kosovo and Croatia – was "proved" by media and politicians primarily on the bases of so-called cases, or affairs, not empirical data. In Kosovo, this took the form of the "Martinović affair," while in Croatia there was the "Mlinar affair." It is obvious today that the mass psychological effects resulting from the political and media exploitation of these two cases were severe, because they directly served to create a mass psychosis – involving paranoia and persecution mania – among the rural Serb population in Kosovo and Croatia. Although the aforementioned examples deserve focussed and serious theoretical analysis, we shall be content here simply to sketch out a thesis analyzing the socio-psychological structures of these affairs.

The Martinović affair concerns a well-known, and by now legendary event which occurred on 1 May 1985, resulting in an injury or self-inflicted wound on a Serbian peasant from Kosovo, Mr. Martinović, who was found anally "penetrated" by a beer bottle. The same event, bizarre and tragic as it was, became the basis of an entire media campaign of anti-Albanian hysteria in Kosovo in the 1980s. In other words, despite the fact that preliminary findings of doctors (surgeons and psychologists) pointed to a self-inflicted injury (an explanation which the first statement by the victim himself could be seen as supporting), ultra-nationalist propaganda in the public saw this case as but one example of a pattern of systematic heinous crimes committed by a group of Albanian nationalists. The flood of latent ultra-nationalist propaganda provoked by this affair originated in the fact that Martinović's predicament evoked subconscious historical analogies with the Ottoman Turkish practice of impaling Serbs and Christians on stakes, which was viewed as the most horrific example of ritualized Ottoman military terror. Entire portions of the mythical, cultural, and national traditions and of popular aesthetics (national ballads) involve the motif of "impalement on a stake." Consequently "impalement by a beer bottle" became a metaphor for five centuries of real, but also mythical, Turkish acts of impalement, all of which was a key demonic element in the national traditions and mythology regarding the horrors of Turkish oppression. Therefore, the "Martinović affair" presented an ideal opportunity for transforming the Albanians into "Turks" in the group consciousness of the Serbian masses. To this end, leading Serbian intellectuals (doctors, psychiatrists, surgeons, photographers, journalists, and others) were positioned beforehand for the purpose of revitalizing these collective prejudices, to create feelings of endangerment, a propaganda mania, and, finally, an irrational desire for historical revenge (the second key element of Serbian national and mythical consciousness).

The "Mlinar affair" has a somewhat different psychological logic, emerging as it does from the exploitation of another Serbian revenge myth: one based on the genocidal nature of the Croatian people.

The "Mlinar affair" was intended to demonstrate to the average Serb, in Croatia and in Serbia, that a resurgence of the independent state of Croatia and its regime was imminent. On a metaphoric and symbolic level, the symptoms of and synonyms for this kind of state and regime evoked the following associations: knife, darkness, crimes, sabre, (slit) throat, massacre. All these notions coincided in the "Mlinar affair." The case concerned a young citizen of Knin, Mr. Miroslav Mlinar, who was allegedly found "seriously" injured (doctors reported a superficial clinical scar on the throat) on 18 May 1990 in Knin. Once again, in the same fashion, Greater Serbian (pre)war propaganda used the "wounding" of Mlinar to create a key *cause célèbre* with which to spread mass paranoia among the Serb residents in Knin and throughout Croatia. The "production" team involved in this case included doctors (surgeons, who gathered at Mlinar's door, as well as the Serbian psychiatrist Jovan Rašković, who projected this "affair" so as to instigate a kind of mass movement), journalists, experts on guerilla warfare, and others.

Although it was obvious from the beginning to every rational individual that what was happening was in fact a matter of war propaganda, the Croatian intellectual and political public did not adequately respond to these propaganda tricks. My own efforts to oppose this anecdotal approach with an analytical one were isolated and met with insufficient success, because analytical and empirical argumentation is dependent on reason, whereas Serbian propaganda was oriented towards emotion (frustration, fear, insecurity). A series of texts of a polemical nature which I wrote in periodicals, as well as a series of talks on Croatian TV, were practically the only protests against what was a well-thought-out and organized program of war propaganda. Not only did these efforts fail to win the support of the Croatian public, they were actually greeted as a kind of an act of sabotage, nationalistically speaking, and were suffocated by a conspiracy of silence.

The key issue is therefore the following: had the Serbian minority or ethnic community in post-communist Croatia really been relegated to a socially inferior position; subject to discrimination, forced assimilation, and even outright violence? In giving an answer to such a rhetorical question today, *ex post facto*, based on the results of the 1981 census, and the IDIS studies from 1985 and 1989, it is first worth noting the fact – though it seems at first sight a superficial one – that the head of the IDIS program, Dr. Mladen Lažić, was himself a Serb, which in and of itself serves to refute the allegation that the research was biased against Serbs and/or Yugoslavs.

The results of research carried in the second half of 1989 (the surveys themselves were carried in November) – that is, on the eve of parliamentary elections in Croatia – were presented in comprehensive detail in the book *The Status of Ethnic minorities and Interethnic Relations in Croatia* (IDIS, Zagreb, 1991). The result of IDIS research from 1985 and 1989 confirm the thesis in support of the nondiscriminatory nature of the currents of social mobility of Croatian communist society, with regard to minorities.

The so-called "cadre body politic," a variant of the Soviet nomenklature, until the very last moments of communism in Croatia (the beginning of 1991), adhered to the dogma of the so-called "cadre key," particularly with regards to ethnic-national criteria.

Given that this "cadre body politic" included all the elites – military, police, law, managerial, etc. – the social status of the Serbian minority within Croatia as far as the elite class was concerned was frequently more favorable than that of the majority population.

The authors of the IDIS research, notably Dr. Mladen Lažić, attributed this easy upward social mobility of Serbs and Yugoslavs to: (1) the relatively lower initial social status of the Serbs, which allowed for more rapid mobility upwards; and (2) historical circumstances – a relatively larger representation of Serbs and "Yugoslavs" in the Partisan movement, which led to a larger representation in the membership of the Communist Party, which in turn led to increased representation among the military, (Communist) Party, police, and political elites. Indeed, an analysis of the data from this study enables us to propose the hypotheses of the preferential and privileged status of the Serb nationality in Croatia in the 1980s, that is, the thesis of the Serbs being a sort of a ruler-nation within Croatia during the time of communism. As in other communist countries, the concentration of socio-economic power in the former Yugoslavia existed in the ideological and the political sphere. As for economics, it was totally dominated by politics, while the independent centers of power consisted of the organs of repression – the military and secret police – as well as the organs of political control (veterans' groups, youth groups, and union functionaries). Finally, unlike the countries which strictly adhered to the Soviet model of political and socio-economic organizations, there also existed the parafederal institutions, known as "self-managed interests," which served an exceptionally important role as intermediaries of power (between the party superstructures and social institutions). With regard to Western democracies, these institutions served a purpose analogous to that of insurance funds and social welfare ministries.

When one keeps in mind these preliminaries regarding the specifics of the stratificational growth of the Croatia (and Yugoslavia) of the former communist days, then it is possible to argue the status of Serbs was that of a kind of "ruling nation" in Croatia. Specifically, the results of the 1985 and 1989 censuses show the following:

1 That the Serbs, relatively speaking, were twice as likely as Croats to be members of the Communist Party, with the Yugoslavs being even more likely. Given that membership in the ruling party in a one-party regime was only partly an expression of political belief or preference, but was rather, to a great extent, a necessary precondition to upward mobility (entry into the military, political, and even the managerial elite was impossible without Communist Party membership), this data should be seen as demonstrating the latent and manifest privileged and preferential status of the Serbian "minorities."

2 A similar arrangement existed among the elites, in which was concentrated the largest share of political and financial power: military,

police, and political. Among the political elites, the Serbian representation was approximately 60–80 percent greater than their representation in the population in general. Among the military and police elites, the situation was even more favorable for Serbs. In the so-called self-managed interests, which controlled 90 percent of the financial resources allotted to intellectual production (science, culture, the media, etc.) the ethno-social structure was similar or identical.

3 The relatively larger share of Croats among the business and intellectual elites was unable to compensate for their inferiority in the political and administrative sphere, because of the subordination of the business sector to the political sector.

4 The preferential or privileged status of Serbs and "Yugoslavs" with regard to social mobility and stratification is seen to be even more extreme when one considers the fact that the "Serbian" elite originate among the lower classes in terms of social status and education level, so that the ascending social mobility is even more marked among Serbs.

5 A noteworthy, if indirect, indicator of social status of ethno-national communities in Croatia prior to the 1990s is their housing status. In a system that constitutionally does not recognize private ownership (the exception being in agricultural, handicraft, and the blue-collar service sectors), housing is the most important asset in one's personal estate. Being granted the right to inhabit housing owned by the state (either directly or by way of a state-owned business) was the most valuable social privilege that one could obtain. It was only those individuals or families who were unable to obtain housing from the state without cost who were forced to build, or buy on the open market, an apartment or house. The data show that Serbs, and even more so the "Yugoslavs," obtained state-owned housing with significantly greater ease than Croats.

To conclude, the social status and upward mobility of Serbs in Croatia during the communist era, far from being discriminatory, gave them a privileged and preferential status with regard to the majority group. The thesis of Serbs being discriminated in Croatia, put forth by Serbian propaganda during the period 1986–90, prior to the outbreak of war had the purpose of creating a sense of fear and danger among the Serbian minority and provoking them into revolt. The Croatian government at the time failed to adequately and efficaciously react to this level of fear being created by Slobodan Milošević, who after the pacification of Kosovo, decided to "export" the politics of "taking it to the streets" (i.e., revolt) to the rural Serbs of Croatia.

ETHNOCENTRISM AND THE ETHNIC DISTANCE BETWEEN CROATIA'S CROATS AND SERBS IN CROATIA PRIOR TO THE WAR

The notion of "ethnocentrism" was coined by W. G. Sumner as early as

1906 during the course of his efforts to observe and record the prejudicial attitudes of one ethnic group (racial, national, tribal, religious, linguistic, socio-cultural) towards nonmembers of that group. Ethnocentric attitudes and behavior originate in the prejudice that the attitudes, customs, and character attributes, cultural values, mores, and habits of a given group are superior with respect to a directly competing group, or often, with respect to all other groups.

We would add the notion of "ethnic distance," which signifies a specific type of social distance. Typically, the measure of ethnic distance is determined according to various ranking systems by which one quantitatively expresses degrees of toleration, attraction, or repulsion between various social (ethnic, professional, class, ideological, etc.) groups. Research on social structure in Croatia that was carried out in 1985 and 1989 captures the dynamic aspects of ethnocentric tendencies, with the longitudinal nature of these studies therefore being of crucial importance.

Results of these studies show that the social distance between Croats, Serbs, and "Yugoslavs" in Croatia was significantly less than that between ethnic groups in multi-ethnic European and American countries. Moreover, between 1985 and 1989 there is an observable trend of increasing ethnic distance. Given that the studies were taken during a period marking the growth of Slobodan Milošević's Greater Serbia movement and the complete passivity of the Croatian political community, this increasing ethnic distance can be interpreted primarily as a defense reflex of Croatia's ethnic communities in response to the growing national socialism in Serbia. This conclusion is further supported by the results of those studies which provide a broad overview of the social-cultural situation of Croatia's ethnic communities. These results suggest that lifestyles, preferences, and cultural norms of the majority and minority ethnic groups in Croatia show identical or similar tendencies.

The data suggests further that, on a local level, as far as the personal experience of the subjects is concerned, ethnic relations are ranked good or tolerable, while on the level of Yugoslavia as a whole, these relations are judged to be poor. Research on perceptions of being endangered in Croatia towards the end of 1989 is likewise enlightening. Namely, even though the notion of feeling "endangered" allows for a good deal of semantic mis-understanding and even though it was chosen for study precisely because this notion was the fundamental motivating factor in Slobodan Milošević's movement during 1986–9 (Serbian propaganda constantly spoke of the Serbs in this place or that being endangered, with Kosovo and Croatia cited as typical examples), the results of the research can still serve as at least an indicator of the feelings of the minority and majority nationalities regarding the likelihood of ethnic conflicts. At the end of 1989 in Croatia, at the most local level of the subjects' experience, there was no indication of an overpowering feeling of ethnic disorder or notion that any of the ethnic communities were "endangered."

However, given that Slobodan Milošević's movement was engineered by way of the mass media, the population came to perceive ethnic conflicts on a higher level, i.e., the republic and, at that time, federal level. This ambivalence with regard to differing levels of experience provided Milošević's exponents with a way of instilling among the Serbian minority a sense of conflict, i.e., by "exporting" it from a higher level to the local level. The technology of "exporting conflict" as practiced by the regime of Slobodan Milošević, was a very simple one: all that was necessary was to cut off the flow of information between Zagreb and the Serbian enclaves within Croatia such as Knin (it should not be forgotten that the first targets of JNA attacks were TV relays and other communications links) and install negative perceptions of ethnic relations in its stead, from the broad Yugoslav to the local (Serb) level.

ANALYSIS OF THE THESIS THAT THE "USTASHOID" BEHAVIOR OF THE CROATIAN GOVERNMENT WAS THE SOURCE OF THE WAR

Given that previous data and analyses show that the social status and ethnic distance between Croats and Serbs in Croatia could not be a reason for the war, there remains the thesis – which is prominent not only in Greater Serbian war propaganda, but also among a sector of the Western media – that it was the behavior of the newly established Croatia in the period 1989–90 (election campaigns, change of governments, constitutional change, and post-election rhetoric) which was the source and cause of ethnic and military conflicts.

The key political terminology used in Serbian propaganda was the attribute "Ustashoid government." Signs of Ustashoidism were alleged to lie in the platforms and behavior of Croatian parties and their leadership, which favored the creation of a Croatian state, and the use of the symbolism of that proposed state: the (checkerboard) coat of arms, flag, anthem, and historical Croatian political figure (especially Viceroy Josip Jelačić, and Counts Zrinski and Frankopan).

A section of Western media, particularly within America, England, and France, accepted the propagandistic theses on the "sources" of the Serbs' revolt and the "sources" of the war in Croatia. The following views expressed by *The New York Times* columnist Roger Cohen can be considered as paradigmatic in this sense:

Many of the Serbs now living in Vukovar fled persecution elsewhere in Croatia, where Mr. Tudjman's Croatian Democratic Union adopted measures in 1991 aimed largely at undermining the republic's 600,00 Serbs. Among those steps were a ban on use of the Serbs' Cyrillic script, the abrupt dismissal of many Serbs from their jobs and reintroduction of symbols formerly used by the Ustashi, or Croatian fascists, who killed thousands of Serbs when a government installed by the Nazis ruled Croatia during World War II.

(*The New York Times*, 18 April 1993)

When we today, *ex post facto*, debate whether or not the concrete or symbolic stances taken by the new Croatian government – personified in the likeness of Franjo Tudjman – were the source or the consequence of JNA and Serbian aggression on the Croatian state, on its people, and on its territory, we are able to make reference to the relatively short but the crucially important historical interval of approximately the past ten years. The chronology of these events plays a decisive role in coming to a proper understanding of the way in which post-communist wars in the Balkans are waged. To wit, the process of forming the preconditions for the overthrow of communism and the formation of democratic movements began in Croatia only in 1989, whereas Slobodan Milošević's rise to power began a full three years earlier – in 1986. This time-lag between Milošević's ascension to the presidency of Serbia and the election of Franjo Tudjman is the key to understanding the "secret" wars that played such an important role in what was to follow. These three years, 1986–9, were years of historic rebellion, accompanied by what was for the most part a political paralysis among the Croatian communist elite. At the same time, these were years in which Slobodan Milošević formed his personal nationalist socialist movement and began the precess of conquering or destroying (opting for the latter when the former was impossible) all the key federal institutions within Yugoslavia.

With this in mind, we can turn to the key war-political thesis on the sources and mechanisms of the conflicts in Croatia. At the same time as Croatia's government was undergoing a transfer of power from communism to democracy (April–May 1990), Serbia was completing a process of psychological, institutional, economic, propagandistic, and military preparation for war, or wars as the case might be. This means that the post-communist wars in the Balkans were practically unavoidable, and that they could manifest themselves in one of two different forms: 1) As a military coup carried out in order to "save Yugoslavia," which would be underpinned by the political ideology and military might of the Yugoslavian National Army; or 2) As aggression or a war of conquest for the creation of a greater Serbia which would be the "final solution of the Serbian question" whereby the mythic Serbian need to obtain historic retribution for the historic injustices the Serbs had suffered – throughout the years of the Ottoman Empire, World War II, and communist Yugoslavia – would be satisfied.

Behind these two possible scenarios for "the years of disentanglement" (which was the title of Slobodan Milošević's book) stood the two somewhat diverse political driving forces (and political motifs): the JNA and the regime/movement of Slobodan Milošević.

From a chronological perspective, the preparation of the Serbian media, the JNA, and the regime of Slobodan Milošević developed as follows:

1 The intellectual preparation of Serbia and the Serbs for aggression and warfare was completed in 1986, in the form of the renowned/notorious "Memorandum of the Serbian Academy of Science and Art" (SANU), a document which expressed a nihilistic (victim-oriented) vision of Serbia's past and present in which Serbs are seen as the perpetual losers and in which all the historic and alleged present-day injustice, victimization, discrimination and tragedy they have suffered are enumerated and itemized, and which advocates radical political action in order to change the constitutional and every other status of Serbs and Serbia in the former Yugoslavia. In order to properly understand the true nature and purpose of this document, it is necessary to keep in mind several historical analogies and incidents.

First: the document itself contains no strategy or plan of aggression, nor does it have any sort of an operative purpose; rather, it is a document intended to mobilize and motivate, and whose function was to set into motion the machinery of the Greater Serbia program: the search for leaders, the shaping of a strategy, the forging of alliances, and the selection of the proper timing.

Second: in a formal sense, the document was secret and indeed, nonexistent, thus symbolically emphasizing its kinship in purpose and nature with Ilija Garsanin's *Nacertanije*. Traditionally, in Serbian culture, such qualities of secrecy serve to enhance the importance of a document, and to endow it with mystical, conspiratorial and subversive qualities. The SANU Memorandum has, therefore, the clear purpose of reviving the "slumbering" Greater Serbian consciousness and to put it into active, political practice.

During the time in which the Memorandum was being written (1985–6), the Serbian intellectual scene was, symbolically speaking, becoming the generator of the mass consumer items of ethnocentrism and war. Homilies by clergymen in churches and out in the streets, the songs of street balladeers (*guslars*), national poetry, national painting, "literary" evenings at Francuska #7, etc. Serbian intellectuals in the mid 1980s created a critical mass of prejudice, ethnocentrism, and warmongering that made possible Slobodan Milošević's rise to power and which created the mass-psychological preconditions for aggression against Slovenes, Albanians, Croats, and Muslims. They transformed the complicated and esoteric discourse of the SANU Memorandum into a quasi-putschist populist art form. It eventually became a kind of a sacred scripture of the Serb-as-eternal-victim version of history, which served to instill terror and provide a justification for a "settling of accounts" as far as all historical injustices were concerned.

2 The ideological and political preparation for aggression was completed – as far as the regime of Slobodan Milošević was concerned – in 1986–7, while in the case of the Yugoslav Army, it was completed in 1989.

The ideological construct which Slobodan Milošević established, formally known as the "Antibureaucratic revolution" represents an eclectic combination of nationalist socialistic, Bolshevik and Titoist populism. This unusual conglomeration was not the consequence, as many believe, of any deep ideological convictions, but rather of Slobodan Milošević's opportunism and cleverness. The prevalence of authoritarianism and totalitarian communism within Serbia offered him an ideal opportunity to take his politics to the streets. The confused Serbian masses, whose confusion arose out of the crisis of communism and the end of Titoism, needed a new authoritarian leader; they did not want democratic reforms, but rather the ideological *status quo*. The Yugoslav Army, as the most powerful institution in the former Yugoslavia, likewise had no longing for pluralism, capitalism, and democracy. Thus, the ideology of nationalist–communist cooperation enabled Slobodan Milošević to obtain wide-ranging support – from the intellectuals frenzied with nationalism, from the frustrated masses and the militarily all-powerful Yugoslav Federal Army. This is why Milošević chose to take his politics to the streets with the slogan "it happens with the people."

3 The leadership's preparations for war can formally be said to have begun on 23 September 1987 at the now famous Eighth Meeting of the Central Committee of the Communist Alliance of Serbia. On this occasion, Slobodan Milošević cleansed the Communist Party of moderate communists such as Dragica Pavlović, who was at the time a member of the collective presidency of the Central Committee of the Communist Alliance of Serbia. It should be noted that this Stalinistic ritual was shown on live television. Slobodan Milošević was thus able successfully to defend two ostensibly contradictory interests: Tito's communist legacy of "brotherhood and unity," and Serbian national interests in Kosovo. A very important element of this national communist ritual/exorcism was Milošević's political reckoning with his friend, mentor and long-standing promoter, Ivan Stambolić, who was at the time the President of Serbia (the collective presidency of which accepted his resignation and replaced Stambolić three months later in December 1987.) There exists within communist tradition on one side, and in Serbian political and military history on the other, a cult and ritual of sacrifice. Indeed, the sacrifice of friends, children, brothers, or loved ones for the ideals of the "revolution" is seen as the ultimate ideal among communists, and in the case of Serbian history, it is considered the supreme demonstration of patriotism. Although Slobodan Milošević would not be elected President of Serbia until May 1989, his initiation rite and the

creation of his cult of leadership happened precisely then. His status was further confirmed by the famous slogan which he uttered at Kosovo: "No one is allowed to beat you!"

4 The mass-psychological preparation for aggression developed between 1985 and 1990. They are symbolically characterized by the already noted "Martinović affair" (Kosovo), and "Mlinar affair" (Croatia). The key factors in preparing the Serbian population to support and participate in aggression consisted of: mass meetings, which were professionally organized (the organizers and the main provocateurs were well paid), and which continued without interruption form 1986 until the famous Vidovdanski meeting on Kosovo Field on 28 June 1989; the mass media (whose refurbishment for the purpose of generating war propaganda involved replacing editors and directors within the state media in 1987 and 1988); experts in manipulation the masses – clergy, local leaders, and psychiatrists. Indeed, a key role in priming the masses for in-surrection and aggression was played by two psychiatrists; in the case of Croatia by Dr. Jovan Rašković, a specialist for group therapy, while in the case of Bosnia-Herzegovina by Dr. Radovan Karadžić, a specialist for treating paranoid states. The coordination of these well orchestrated mass-psychological war preparations allowed the regime of Slobodan Milošević as early as at the beginning of 1990 (therefore, prior to the elections in Slovenia and Croatia) to have at its disposal a wide-ranging state of mass-psychological preparedness on the part of the population, rendering it willing to approve, support, and participate in aggression.

From the very beginning, the Orthodox Church actively included itself into the psychological preparation for aggression, by way of sermons and publicity work. An important component in the Church's strategy was the ceremonial transfer of Grasanica, in Kosovo. Moreover, this several-month-long ritual included the "exodus" of the seat, along with clergy and believers along the desired borders of Greater Serbia with both Croatia and Bosnia.

5 The judicial-institutional preparation for aggression was carried out between 1988 and 1990. It began with unilateral changes to the con-stitution of Serbia in 1988 diminishing the constitutional status of the autonomous provinces of Kosovo and Vojvodina within Yugoslavia, and continued with institutional usurpation or paralysis of Yugoslav federal institutions (Central Committee of the Alliance of Communists of Yugo-slavia, Collective Presidency of SFRY, diplomatic representatives, TANJUG, the Central Bank, etc.). In the constitutive sense, the unilateral changes to the status of Kosovo and Vojvodina mark the beginning of the process of Yugoslavia's violent destruction.

6 The military preparation for aggression deserves special analysis, both as a case study of the political tactics of Slobodan Milošević, and also as an example of the Yugoslav Army's behavior in multi-ethnic conflicts.

In other words, the preparation – political, strategic and operational – of the JNA for war began at its very inception. As was the case in other communist countries, the professional mandate of the JNA was not initially limited to just the defense of the country and its borders, but also to the defense of the communist system. The constitutional and budgetary position of the Army was always exclusivist, possessing a great degree of not only precessional but also political autonomy.

The preparation of the JNA for various scenarios of military coups in order to defend "brotherhood and unity," i.e., to "save" Yugoslavia, began at the instant of Tito's death in 1980, and were especially intensified in the period between 1986–90. The organization of military jurisdictions, which was carried out in 1986, followed the typical logic of many other Greater Serbian political projects. Significantly, the entire area of Bosnia-Herzegovina, the regions of Eastern Slavonia, the Knin corpus and a good part of the Adriatic is placed under the control of the so-called "First (i.e., Belgrade's) Army". During the entire time he was consolidating his authority, Slobodan Milošević chose to leave the JNA alone, because he knew very well that political logic as well as the logic of armed conflict would inevitably bring the JNA in on the side of Serbia. The reasons for this are simple. First, the command structure of the JNA, particularly within its higher echelons, was completely dominated by Serbs and Montenegrins, which in an ethnic conflict leads to a predictable identification. Second, although the ultra-nationalistic rhetoric of the Serbian leadership in the mid-1980s was somewhat bothersome to the JNA, it was far more acceptable than the "separatist" and pluralist-capitalist rhetoric of the Slovene and Croatian leadership. The proximity of ideological positions drew the military leadership to the side of Slobodan Milošević, and the previously existing Serbian and Montenegrin predominance made the rapid Serbianization of the Yugoslav Army all the more easier.

With regard to the values and political positions of the political leadership and officer corps of the JNA, and the role the JNA played in this aggression, we have access to a very telling document, which was read out to all commanding officers of the JNA on Friday 25 January 1991, shortly before its first attempt to militarily subdue Croatia (in February). We quote only the highlights of this extraordinary document, titled "Information about the Situation in the World and in Yugoslavia and about the Imminent Tasks of the Yugoslav Army" which was signed by the Central Political commissariat of the JNA. The presentation was immediately followed by a highly inflammatory "documentary" on Serbian television which, by way of crude Bolshevik-style fabrications, purported to show how the new government of Croatia was "endangering" the Yugoslav Army. The document was published in *Vjesnik* on 31 January 1991 and subsequently by most Yugoslav newspapers. Note that the head of the new "Communist Party – A Movement for Yugoslavia" was Mrs. Mirjana Milošević, the wife of Slobodan Milošević. The document confirmed the long-held suspicion that Serbian communists considered the Yugoslav Army to be a Serbian army and, therefore, an instrument for the restoration of Communism in Yugoslavia and/or the creation of Greater Serbia on the ruins of Yugoslavia.

- The progressive forces in the Soviet Union have regrouped after realizing that "reforms" are leading to catastrophe . . . the Soviet army is becoming engaged and active – to the distress of the capitalist West.
- In Yugoslavia socialism also has not been defeated or thrown on its knees. Socialist Yugoslavia has withstood the first wave of anti-communist attacks and hysteria.
- The events in the Gulf region are not developing according to the initial scenario of the USA and the West. The USA has built its whole civilization on cheap sources of energy – the essential cause of the Gulf War. Now the War is beginning to engulf the whole region with unpredictable consequences and total uncertainty of its outcome.
- In socialist countries of Eastern Europe the situation is becoming complicated: it is improving, and is not any more under the control of the West that orchestrated and directed the upheavals.
- The Western manipulators achieved significant results in their primary objective – the destruction of communism and the socialist society. However, they did not achieve their ultimate goal at all – in most communist countries communism is neither destroyed nor defeated. Now the West is regrouping for new attacks. We can only expect even stronger attacks in the future.
- In Yugoslavia, the Western European governments and the USA will try to overthrow the communist governments in those Yugoslav republics where communists remain in power. They will organize and create social unrest as in Bulgaria and Romania, and will drive for constant democratic re-elections as long as necessary until their anti-communist fifth column does obtain power.
- Explicit proof of this strategy is the US State Department's threat that "the U.S. will energetically resist any use of force and intimidation against democratically elected governments in Yugoslavia's republics and against democratic precesses in Yugoslavia." The essence of this statement and threat is obvious – a threat to the Yugoslav Army not to resist the destruction of communism and socialism in Yugoslavia.
- The concern of the USA and Western Europe for democracy is transparent demagoguery – by democracy they really mean anti-communism.
- The Army needs to organize the progressive forces in Yugoslavia. The Yugoslav Army and its commanding officers, as an institution and as

citizens, are leading political factors of our country. Our new party, under the new name "Communist Party – A Movement for Yugoslavia," should become within the next five to six months the strongest political force and a gathering center for all left and progressive forces.

- We need to liquidate the forces that broke the lines of defense of our socialist society. We need, by our actions, to encourage the progressive forces that want to preserve socialist Yugoslavia.
- We have documents that illustrate detailed plans for attacking military installations, arms stores, and for other terrorist actions, including murder of our commanding officers and their families. Therefore, we have to act resolutely.
- We also have to resolve the issue of continued financing of the Yugoslav Army. The hostile forces have discontinued or have threatened to discontinue its further financing.
- Comrades, ask yourselves why the enemy within and outside of Yugoslavia is so against our Communist Party – A Movement for Yugoslavia. If Communism is indeed dead and finished as they say, why are they so afraid of our party?
- In some of the Yugoslav republics anti-communist "democracies" won the elections in part because of the traitors within their local communist leadership. It is especially important to liquidate such people from our party, the party that is led by our commanding officers. We should not repeat the errors made in the recent past; we should liquidate the fifth column among us.

7 The economic preparation of the JNA and Serbia for war was conducted, as absurd as it may seem, during the period of the "reformist" mandate of Ante Marković, which involved, specifically, making the Yugoslav dinar convertible and centralizing all values and foreign currency payments. This led to a flood of foreign currency into the National Bank. It led also to the systematic purchase of foreign currency on the streets of large Croatian cities. Serbian banks placed a large portion of the resultant foreign currency reserves in foreign countries, particularly in Cyprus, and throughout banks in Europe and America. The final act of Serbia's economic preparation for warfare occurred in December 1990, when Milošević's regime, without the knowledge of the Central Bank, extorted $1.8 billion of the Yugoslav dinar's hard-currency backing. Subsequently, all the resources of the Central Bank of the former Yugoslavia (foreign money, gold, and other valuables) were used for financing the War.

When speaking of the economic foundation of the Greater Serbian aggression, one should note two additional elements. First, all Serbian and Montenegrin paramilitary formations were paid during the war in

Croatia, but additionally, they were also given free license to plunder. Given that the regions of Baranja, Eastern Slavonia, and the vicinity of Dubrovnik were some of the wealthiest regions of Croatia, the plunder (in the form of automobiles, family valuables, foreign currency, livestock, farm equipment, etc.) served as a significant additional source of funding for the war. Second, for practically half a century, the Yugoslav Army, with little or no parliamentary or budget control, manufactured and bought weaponry and munitions on the basis of the preferential status which the former Yugoslavia enjoyed in the West and East throughout the cold war. The value of the military arsenal of the Yugoslav army at the start of the War amounted to between $40 billion and $60 billion. This alone gave the aggressor an enormous economic and military advantage throughout their aggression. In fact, the embargo against the import of arms into "Yugoslavia" was actually an expression of open Western support for Serbia, given that Croatia and Bosnia- Herzegovina, being totally disarmed, could obtain necessary weaponry only on the black market, with all the risks such purchases entailed, while Serbia could without worry carry on its aggression by drawing on the abundant military arsenal of the Yugoslavian army.

8 The international-political and diplomatic preparation of the aggression was insured by the very logic of the way in which the international community operated. Inertia, and an apologetic stance in favor of the *status quo* regarding international relations – in which Yugoslavia played an important role during the war – guaranteed for Serbia an initial and abiding passivity on the part of the West's approach to the aggression. Moreover, the domination of Serbs and Montenegrins in the Yugoslavian diplomatic corps enabled the instantaneous Serbianization of this body, transforming it into a crucially important diplomatic campaign team in support of aggression. Serbia's foreign relations strategy was very simple: leaning on all kinds of real and mythical historical alliances, whether ethnic (Russian) or those of "traditional friends" (France), those established through historical manipulation (demonization of Muslims as religious fanatics and Croats as Nazis), and the exploitation of the Holocaust (Israel and the Jewish community), as well as those founded on political interests opposed to disintegration (Great Britain).

If we keep in mind the background and circumstances regarding Serbian and JNA preparation for their aggression, as well as the fact that the aggression began for all practical purposes between 1987 and 1989 with an organized military coup and terrorism in Kosovo, then it is difficult to defend the thesis that the appearance of a new political elite and government in Croatia was the cause of the eruption of war in June 1991.

At the moment when people in Croatia and Slovenia were just beginning to seriously ponder multiparty elections and the overthrow of communism in the Fall of 1989, the various projects for the military overthrow and aggression on Croatia and Slovenia were already completed. As a direct witness, and for a time, a participant in these events, I can state that the Croatian government was aware of these preparations for aggression on the part of the Yugoslav Army and Serbia.

Given that the mechanism of this aggressive and imperialistic Greater Serbian attitude could not be changed, the Croatian government tried to prevent aggression by limiting the potential of ethnic conflicts, then by proposing a "confederation" designed to peacefully transform the former Yugoslavia into a commonwealth of sovereign south Slavic states.

The scholarly underpinnings of the confederation agreement were completed by August of 1990, and were drafted along the lines of the European Community prior to the 1992 model, so that they retained provisions for a customs and monetary union, a confederate judiciary for human rights, and also an organization to defend the confederation modeled after NATO.

This proposal was offered for discussion and debate to all the republics of the former Yugoslavia, but for various reasons it did not obtain their support. The proposal to peacefully transform the Yugoslav federation into a commonwealth was also submitted to representatives of the Bush administration (in the middle of September of 1991), but did not receive their diplomatic support either, and on the contrary, was opposed by a stance in favor of the unity of the Communist Yugoslavia and the reformist government of Ante Marković.

Lastly, there remains the need to answer a series of rhetorical questions on whether the new Croatian government, through any concrete political decisions, rhetoric, symbolism, or gesture, incited the Serbian minority in Croatia to armed rebellion (which formally began in Knin on 18 August 1990).

The fundamental criticisms and questions for Croatia can be reduced to several "causes" of the rebellion:

- constitutional changes, which allegedly discriminated against the Serbian minority and forbade the Cyrillic script that Serbs favored;
- expelling Serbs from positions of employment and in general discriminating against them;
- utilizing symbolism of the independent state of Croatia;
- inadequate communication and practical political links with the Serbian minority in Croatia at the beginning of 1990.

In order to determine the legitimacy of these complaints, we will strive to make use of original texts and facts as opposed to interpretations thereof.

We begin with the Croatian Constitution and its definition of sovereignty and statehood. In the new Croatia's new Constitution, which was no longer to be considered as a part of a collective state of a "higher order" – i.e., communist Yugoslavia, so that it no longer could be said to have a divided sovereignty – adopted the conception of civil sovereignty according to the logic of the American Constitution. Sovereignty is decreed in the first article of the Constitution as thus:

> The Republic of Croatia is a united and indivisible democratic and social state. Power in the Republic of Croatia derives from the people and belongs to the people as a community of free and equal citizens. The people shall exercise this power through the election of representatives and through direct decision-making.

The adoption in that article of the concept of a modern, civil sovereignty leads to the constitutional "expulsion" of all ethno-national conceptions, be they Croat or Serb, or Croatian or Serbian nations. Sovereignty at the very highest governmental level belongs to the "people" – in the sense of the civil community of all citizens. In the preamble to the Constitution, the first definition of the concept of nation-state uses the following definition:

> The Republic of Croatia is hereby established as the national state of the Croatian nation and a state of members of other nations and minorities who are its citizens: Serbs, Muslims, Slovenes, Czechs, Slovaks, Italians, Hungarians, Jews and others, who are guaranteed equality with citizens of Croatian nationality and the realization of ethnic rights in accordance with the democratic norms of the United Nations Organization and the free world countries.

Therefore, the Croatian Constitution can neither in its conception nor in its concrete formulation be said to "expel Serbs from the Constitution," but rather, explicitly names Serbs and other nations and minorities living in Croatia in the very definition of Croatian statehood.

With regard to the constitutional status of the Cyrillic script, it is established on two levels: 1) as an explicit constitutional right in Article 12, and 2) as a fundamental human and civil right in Article 15.

Article 12 states:

> The Croatian language and the Latin script shall be in official use in the Republic of Croatia. In individual local units another language and the Cyrillic or some other script may, along with the Croatian language and the Latin script, be introduced into official use under conditions specified by law.

Article 15, second paragraph, states:

> Members of all nations and minorities shall be guaranteed freedom to express their nationality, freedom to use their language and script, and cultural autonomy.

Considering Articles 12 and 15 together suggests not only that the Cyrillic script has in no way been "expelled from the Constitution" but rather that its use as an official script it sanctioned at the regional level. By the very logic of the document, it would apply to all administrative units which are ethnically mixed and in which there exists a relative or absolute majority of ethnic communities which utilize the Cyrillic script, i.e., Serbs.

Therefore, when we, *ex post facto*, analyze the phenomenology of the development of the ethnic conflicts in Croatia, what is surprising is not the fact that Greater Serbian propaganda falsified the content of the Constitution, but the fact that the Croatian government did not provide an efficient counter-propaganda response to this propaganda.

Manipulation of the historic traumas of Serbs within Croatia – specifically, their tragic fate during the course of World War II (the NDH adopted the racial legislation of Nazi Germany, and practiced a policy of genocide: deportation, concentration camps, mass executions, etc.) – was furthered by way of the thesis alleging "the return of symbols of the NDH in the Croatian Constitution."

The Constitution establishes the state "iconography" – the coat of arms, flag, anthem – in Article 11, which as can be plainly seen contains not a single symbol of the NDH. That is, the key symbol of the NDH, which was the letter "U" (the Croatian counterpart to the so-called hooked cross, or swastika, used by the Nazis), is completely absent from the Constitution. On the contrary, the flag, coat of arms and anthem "Lijepa nasa" (literally, Beautiful, our homeland) are traditional expressions of Croatian statehood, which Croats and Serbs in Croatia displayed and sang with pride for centuries.

The final complaint – that the Croatian government did not adequately communicate with the leaders of the Serbian minority and the Serbs themselves – deserves the greatest attention. Facts point to an entire series of contacts, attempts to reach a compromise, repeated offers of choice political concessions (i.e., the President of the Republic – by way of public announcements as well as private contacts – offered to place Serbs in various functions throughout the government, including: Vice-President of the Parliament, collective presidency, the government, etc.), the final responses to which were always negative. In the middle of 1990, representatives of the Serbian minority conclusively rejected further participation in the Croatian parliament, and afterwards urged their nation to collective civil disobedience, and ultimately, to armed insurrection.

The most simple and plausible explanation of this phenomenon of mistakes in communication regarding the government, the minority leadership, and the minority itself, follows form the above noted thesis that the manipulation of information and the severing of such communication links was one of the key elements of Slobodan Milošević's war strategy.

Furthermore, tracking the chronology of the ethnic conflicts and the implementation on the part of the JNA of low intensity conflict in Croatia serves to demonstrate how the destruction of communication links and communication technology, with the intent of isolating the Serbian minority, was one of the key strategic objectives prior and during the war.

Air attacks on TV relays, the construction of special transmitters which served as instruments of Greater Serbian and military propaganda, as well as other attempts to sever communication lines within the Zagreb–Knin–Beli Manastir nexus were all a part of this strategy. The moment, in May 1991, when an army of Serbian reservists under the label of the JNA came from Serbia into Croatia for the alleged purpose of "separating the warring parties" marked the end of all communication between the Croatian government, the leadership of the Serbian minority and the Serb minority itself. The tanks and other weaponry of the Yugoslav National Army became thereby not only an occupying force but also a communications barrier. A similar role was in some ways taken over by UNPROFOR units which continued the *status quo* of Serbian occupation of the Croatian territory into 1995.

Ultimately, with regard to the sources and mechanisms by which ethnic conflicts began within Croatia, one can conclude the following: the disappearance of the Yugoslavian and the appearance of the Croatian state created among Croatia's Serbs a kind of an emotional vacuum and deep frustration. The formation of a new nation-state, in this case the Republic of Croatia, inevitably involves the formation of new feeling regarding affiliation toward that new political community and loyalty to that state. The government of Slobodan Milošević, which had three years practical experience in manipulating the masses, succeeded to a greater extent than the government of Franjo Tudjman, as far as the Serbian minority in Croatia was concerned, in projecting ideas regarding affiliation to a political community (Greater Serbia) and loyalty to a state (whether toward "Yugoslavia" or the so-called Krajina, as opposed to the Republic of Croatia). Whether and how such a situation can be changed is a crucial question. A similar scenario unfolded in Bosnia-Herzegovina, and is likely to emerge in Macedonia in the near future.

5

THE RESPONSE OF THE AMERICAN MEDIA TO BALKAN NEO-NATIONALISMS

James J. Sadkovich

Let me begin by saying that this will be an incomplete and partisan survey of the media's reaction to the crisis provoked by the emergence of the aggressive neo-nationalisms following the disintegration of Yugoslavia. Let me also say that I believe that the American media has done a poor job of covering the crisis in the former Yugoslavia, and while I realize that it is easy to criticize the media, that is no reason not to do so. Indeed, as Bentham's good citizens we have a duty to censure the media that shape our behavior through their depiction of reality as freely as we do the politicians who control our lives through their occupation of government offices.[1]

Let me also note that I am not an expert on the media and my initial observations regarding the American media are limited to those characteristics that have hampered their efforts to cover the crisis in the former Yugoslavia. Since I am interested in the media's response to Balkan neo-nationalisms rather than in the phenomena themselves, I will not attempt to analyze them and only note that for our purposes they can be defined as anything that looks like, lies like, and kills like a nationalism that has been moribund for at least fifty years.[2]

Since my sources and time are limited, I shall focus on media coverage of the former Yugoslavia in 1991 and 1992, the years in which the crisis there matured as Balkan neo-nationalists captured state bureaucracies and military organizations – and the years in which we should have been striving to understand and confront these phenomena and place the bloodshed unleashed by the efforts of Yugoslavia's constituent nationalities to obtain separate states in a social, economic, and political framework so that we could formulate a viable response both as a nation and as a state to the new realities shaping the Balkans. To understand our failure to do so, we need to look at the nature of the media as well as at the quantity, quality, and distribution of media coverage of the crisis.

Although there is no consensus regarding the nature of the American media, they seem to act as a collective gatekeeper and they certainly form

113

part of national and local power structures. Reporters and editors are thus members of elites with vested interests in both the domestic and the international *status quo*, and in matters of foreign policy they are dependent on government officials, and members of universities and think-tanks that have close ties to the government. This puts them in an ambivalent position. As Carl Migdail of *U.S. News & World Report* noted, even though reporters are aware "that government facts are not facts but lies," they still prefer to support their government.[3] Consequently, they reflect the official positions of any given administration and its civilian consultants unless there are strong reasons not to do so. But in the case of the former Yugoslavia no such reasons exist.[4]

As hierarchical organizations that tend to focus on the bottom line and are owned, if not directly controlled, by a handful of corporations, the media display the structures and mentalities of large business bureaucracies.[5] The professionalism of reporters and editors is the result of a process of socialization in college and on the job that reinforces an acceptance of whatever ideology informs their particular organization – in other words, they are good employees.[6] Moreover, the conditions under which news is produced and the way in which the system of rewards and punishments is structured seem to constrain the imagination and promote conformity more than they encourage excellence or foster creativity. There is thus no incentive to depart from standard, stereotypic interpretations. As Bagdikian has noted, "the effect of a corporate line is not so different from that of a party line," even if the exercise of political intervention and control is usually subtle.[7]

The media cannot gain perspective nor analyze events, precisely because they cover events on a daily basis.[8] This lack of analytic perspective is especially applicable to television newscasts, which, as an executive at CNN observed, occur in "real time."[9] In other words, everything on the tube is ephemeral and so abstracted from the real world as to form an altogether different reality in the same way that the media form a distinct culture not accessible and often unfathomable to outsiders.[10] Getting one's "side" presented is thus difficult, and sustained analysis is impossible.

Journalists and editors tend to select sources that reinforce their own perceptions; they live for and in the momentary event; they enjoy hobnobbing with and criticizing the powerful; and they focus on personalities and concrete phenomena rather than on ideas and abstract concepts. Consequently, despite disclaimers of objectivity, fairness, and balance, news coverage often reflects corporate concerns, the hidden agenda of government officials, and the unconscious biases of journalists who filter and distort the realities being reported.[11] Put more simply, it is a lot easier for someone like Eagleburger or Kissinger to get on *Nightline* than for most of us to do so.[12]

Media coverage is shaped by the need to appeal to certain audiences, whether the average American who watches the three major networks, the college-educated viewers of CNN, the neo-conservative readers of the *National Review*, or the committed lefties of the *Nation*.[13] But because no mass audience in America – left, right or centre – has any special interest in nor any understanding of the history, culture, or fate of the various peoples who live in the former Yugoslavia, the media have balanced their coverage by giving alleged war criminals like Radovan Karadžić as much time to argue their point of view as they have the victims of Serbian aggression to make their accusations. In short, while the media claim to have no point of view in the Balkans, in reality they reflect a rather parochial American, and occasionally conservative British, perspective.[14]

Those who operate in the media thus live in a high-pressure, commercialized world that is focussed on a small group of people, nations, and events.[15] They share certain values; they have more of an interest in domestic than foreign news; they agree on which states count in the world; and they believe that viewers are fascinated with power, personalities, and the bizarre. Much news coverage is therefore little more than "political soap opera" and a large part of the world remains invisible to the media.[16] In turn, a large part of the media also remain invisible to the average American, who cannot hope to grasp "truths" that are filtered through the media prism to become so many bytes of information scattered across a vast field of electronic signals and computer-generated print, from CNN, PBS, and NPR to the dailies, weeklies, and special-interest journals that make up the American media.[17]

In general, print coverage of events in the former Yugoslavia has been more detailed, more sustained, and more analytic than that of the electronic media. This is so in part because the electronic media depend on what the *MacNeil–Lehrer Newshour* refers to as "newsmakers" – those very authority figures who tend to "issue a high quotient of imprecise and self-serving declarations," to quote Bagdikian – while the print media pay more attention to marginal actors and observers.[18] *MacNeil–Lehrer* thus runs the risk of becoming a mouthpiece for the current administration; *Nightline* of becoming a forum for a small clique of experts and authorities; and CNN of becoming a player in the diplomatic game.[19]

Not only have shows such as the *MacNeil–Lehrer Newshour* and *Nightline* presented the crisis in the Balkans through interviews with guests like Lawrence Eagleburger, David Owen, and Cyrus Vance, but they have treated these "newsmakers" with a deference evident in the use of such titles as "Lord" and "Mr. Secretary," even though it is obvious that the nature of their positions generally keeps them from speaking as frankly as we and they might wish.[20] Whether Eagleburger was beholden to Serbia, as Peter Glynn implied in *The New Republic*, is thus less important than whether by eliciting his opinions on the crisis in the Balkans, television interviewers allowed him to promote his agenda because they were unable to act as devil's advocates in fields outside their areas of expertise and incapable of filling in gaps in reasoning and knowledge that they did not even know existed.[21]

Even assuming a desire to cover all aspects of a story and to analyze it in depth, the formats of shows like *MacNeil–Lehrer Newshour* preclude analysis, and while CNN has the luxury of continuously adjusting its coverage and correcting errors, it cannot undo what has been broadcast, nor can viewers follow every update. Like CNN, the *MacNeil–Lehrer Newshour* and *Nightline* react to events, and it is difficult for them to sustain their coverage of a given crisis when others are constantly occurring. *Nightline* was particularly slow to react to the crisis in Yugoslavia, airing only one serious show on the subject in July 1991, and a second program on the religious shrine at Medjugorje in December.[22] CNN's only "special" report was a two-minute interruption of a Pentagon briefing on the Persian Gulf War to report the resignation of Yugoslavia's president, Borislav Jović, on 15 March 1991. Prior to the onset of hostilities in Yugoslavia, the crisis there was discussed only twice on the *MacNeil–Lehrer Newshour*, then twice in July after the JNA had attacked Slovenia, and eight more times by the end of the year as the fighting spread to Croatia and as cultural monuments, including much of the city of Dubrovnik, were laid waste by the JNA.[23] (See Table 1.)

Once the Vance–Carrington cease-fire took hold and the fighting diminished in early 1992, the *MacNeil–Lehrer Newshour* lost interest, airing

Table 1 Coverage by the *MacNeil–Lehrer Newshour* of the Yugoslav Crisis, 1991–2

Month	Number	Month	Number
1991		**1992**	
January	0	January	1
February	0	February	0
March	1	March	0
April	0	April	5
May	0	May	2
June	1	June	3
July	2	July	5
August	1	August	6
September	2	September	1
October	0	October	3
November	4	November	2
December	1	December	8
	12		36

only one discussion on Yugoslavia from January through March. But after the JNA's attack on Bosnia, the *Newshour* included Yugoslav topics on five shows in April, and five more in May and June, another five in July and six in August, as news of the death camps and ethnic cleansing finally permeated the filters of the US media. The siege of Sarajevo and the Vance–Owen peace plans led to at least 14 other discussions in 1992 and a spate of programs earlier in 1993.[24]

Washington Week in Review also ignored the crisis in Yugoslavia until the fighting started in mid-1991, then betrayed its domestic bias by mentioning the crisis only twice that year, twice more in the first six months of 1992, and, as the election campaigns took note of ethnic cleansing, eight times in the last half of the year. (See Table 2.) *American Interests* also covered the crisis in programs on 22 May and 19 June 1992, as did *Firing Line* in March 1991. In short, in two years, the crisis in Yugoslavia was mentioned or discussed on a total of 36 PBS programs, or once every two weeks on average. Like network newscasts, coverage tended to be reactive and to cluster around dramatic events.

The most superficial coverage has been that by the nightly newscasts of the three major networks, in part because while CNN devotes about 1:30 minutes to regular news items and up to six minutes to an interview, most networks spots vary from 20 seconds to 2:00 minutes. Consequently, while the crisis was mentioned in 173 network newscasts during 1991, any given report might be limited to as little as 20 seconds. (See Table 3.) Prior to

Table 2 Coverage by *Washington Week in Review* of the Yugoslav Crisis, 1991–2

Month	Number	Month	Number
1991		**1992**	
January	0	January	0
February	0	February	0
March	0	March	0
April	0	April	0
May	0	May	1
June	0	June	1
July	1	July	2
August	1	August	2
September	0	September	0
October	0	October	0
November	0	November	1
December	0	December	3
	2		10

Table 3 Coverage by the three major networks on the crisis in 1991

Month	Nightly news	Specials	Totals
January	2	0	2
February	0	0	0
March	10	1	11
April	0	0	0
May	2	0	2
June	21	0	21
July	39	1	40
August	20	0	20
September	26	0	26
October	13	0	13
November	24	0	24
December	15	1	16
	172	3	175

June, only 14 newscasts mentioned the crisis, an average 2.8 per month, or less that one per network per month. The three networks mentioned the fighting in Slovenia and the first skirmishes in Croatia on 61 shows in July and August, an average of 10 per network per month.[25]

The Serb–Croat War got relatively less coverage, an average of 14 broadcasts monthly from October through December, or five per network per month. Why this was so is not clear, but it seems that the crisis quickly became old hat because the rate of coverage fell steadily after the first two months of the crisis, from 30.5/month, to 23.0/month in August and September, to 18.5/month in October and November, to 15 in December. An average of 14.4 network broadcasts per month mentioned Yugoslavia in 1991, but because stories tended to run on the same days and in the same time slots, coverage averaged only about 5 days/month.

How concentrated network coverage was can be seen from Table 4. All network nightly news programs covered the crisis in Yugoslavia from 1 through 8 July, when the fighting in Slovenia was both intense and novel, and again on 14 July, when Serbian forces attacked Croatian police stations in the Krajina for the first time. Coverage then became sporadic, and if the networks did not share out the responsibility for mentioning the crisis in Yugoslavia, it seems that the "instinctive" decisions on what is newsworthy are so deeply ingrained that the networks effectively work as a single unit and do not so much cover the news in real time as define what exists in real time on any given day.[26] But if death and destruction, political crises, and human interest stories can catch the medium's attention, they cannot

Table 4 Nightly network news coverage of the crisis in Yugoslavia in July 1991

July	ABC	CBS	NBC
1	5:44:00	5:48:30	5:49:40
2	5:30:00	5:30:20	5:30:10
3	5:30:00	5:30:20	5:30:10
4	5:30:10	5:30:20	5:36:50
5	5:35:40	5:32:20	5:49:10
6	5:32:20	5:32:30	5:30:10
7	5:33:00	5:30:20	5:30:20
8	5:44:40	5:41:20	5:45:50
9	NC (No coverage)	5:43:00	NC
10	5:44:20	5:43:30	NC
13	NC	5:43:40	NC
14	5:40:10	5:44:50	5:52:10
15	NC	NC	5:50:30
18	NC	5:47:20	NC
20	5:50:30	NC	NC
22	NC	5:46:40	5:50:20
28	NC	NC	5:41:20
29	NC	5:45:20	NC
30	5:40:50	NC	NC

hold it. Episodic and focussed on the novel and the sensational, network coverage has been unable to describe, much less explain and analyze, the political forces that have emerged in the region since the mid-1980s.

Coverage in major newspapers has tended to parallel that of the major networks, but it has been more comprehensive and consistent. While three major papers *The New York Times*, the *LA Times*, and the *Washington Post*) ran front-page articles on the crisis in Yugoslavia a total of 21 of the 93 days in July, or 23 percent of the month, the networks made the crisis their lead story on only 14 days, or 15 percent of the days available. The newspapers then continued to run stories on the crisis, albeit on pages A10 or A16, missing only 24 of the 93 days (26 percent), but the networks failed to mention the crisis on 56 days (60 percent). A comparison of network transcripts would yield even a greater disparity, since a full newscast is less than the average page of newsprint. (See Table 5.)

In 1991, the *Washington Post* and the *Los Angeles Times* each published an average of 12 articles monthly on the crisis in Yugoslavia, the *Post* printing 73 articles in 59 issues and the *LA Times* 72 in 57 issues. *The New York Times* appears to have done somewhat better, publishing 109 items in 75 issues, but

Table 5 Lead stories and page-one articles devoted to Yugoslavia in July 1991

July	ABC	CBS	NBC	LA Times	Post	NY Times
1	x	x	x	NC	x	x
2	x	x	x	x	x	
3	x	x	x	x		x
4	x	x		x	x	x
5				x		x
6			x	x	x	x
7		x	x	x		
8				x		x
9	0		0	x		
10			0		0	
11	0	0	0		0	
12	0	0	0	0		
13	0		0			
14				x		
15	0	0				
16	0	0	0			
17	0	0	0			0
18	0		0	0	0	0
19	0	0	0		0	
20		0	0	0	0	0
21	0	0	0		0	0
22	0	0	0		0	
23	0	0	0	0		
24	0	0	0	0		
25	0	0	0	0		
26	0	0	0	0		0
27	0	0	0			
28	0	0		x	x	
29	0		0	x	0	
30		0	0	0	0	
31	0	0	0	0		x
	4	5	5	11	5	7

a number of the items were photographs, and the average monthly was still only 16 items.[27] In July coverage rose precipitously, and even with a drop-off in reporting later in the year, *The New York Times* published 236 items over 167 days, an average of 39 items over 28 days monthly. The *Post* printed 214 articles in 145 days (averages of 36 and 24, respectively), and the *LA Times* 136 pieces in 102 days (23 and 17 respectively). (See Table 6.)

Table 6 The appearance of newspaper articles on the crisis in Yugoslavia

Period	Washington Post	LA Times	NY Times
January–June 1991			
Total days	59	57	75
Total items	73	72	109
Days per month	9	9	12
Items per month	12	12	16
July–December 1991			
Total days	145	102	167
Total items	214	136	236
Days per month	24	17	28
Items per month	36	23	39
January–June 1992			
Total days	121	74	NA
Total items	187	103	NA
Days per month	12	20	NA
Items per month	17	31	NA
July–December 1992			
Total days	167	120	NA
Total items	371	185	NA
Days per month	28	20	NA
Items per month	62	31	NA

Coverage then fell off in the early part of 1992, but less dramatically than in the televised and periodical media. The *LA Times* published only 103 articles over 74 days, but the *Post* printed 187 pieces in 121 days, for averages of 17 articles over 12 days monthly and 31 over 20, respectively. The discovery of the camps and the focus on ethnic cleansing clearly stimulated coverage in the second half of the year, as the *Post*'s coverage doubled to 371 articles over 167 days, and the *LA Times* followed suit, publishing 185 articles over 120 days.[28]

Coverage of the crisis in periodicals followed a similar pattern, jumping from one article in June to 17 in July, falling off to 10.0/month through the rest of the year and 5.0/month in January and February 1992, then rising to 8.5 in April and May, jumping to 19 in June and 25 in July, and maintaining an average of about 25.0/month during the second half of 1992. (See Table 7.) Of special interest are the major US weeklies and periodicals, which carried pieces on the crisis in Yugoslavia in only 55 issues in 1991 (including 31 in three weeklies) and 109 in 1992 (65 in three weeklies). (See Table 8.)

Table 7 Periodicals carrying articles on the crisis in the former Yugoslavia

Publication	*1991*	*1992*
America	3	3
The American Scholar	0	1
The American Spectator	0	1
Art News	0	1
The Atlantic	0	1
Aviation Week & Space Technology	0	7
Brookings Review	0	1
The Bulletin of the Atomic Scientists	0	1
Business Week	1	2
Canada and the World	0	1
The Canadian Forum	0	1
Christian Century	2	4
Christianity Today	0	1
Columbia Journalism Review	0	2
Commentary	0	2
Commonweal	0	4
Condé Nast Traveler	0	1
Current History	0	1
Esquire	0	1
Forbes	2	1
Foreign Affairs	1	1
Foreign Policy	1	0
History Today	1	3
Jet	0	1
Life	0	1
Maclean's	12	11
Ms.	1	0
Nation	4	8
National Review	3	5
The New Leader	3	1
New Perspectives Quarterly	0	1
New Republic	5	11
New York Review of Books	2	4
New York Times Magazine	1	2
New Yorker	1	4
Newsweek	8	23
People Weekly	2	3
Policy Review	0	1
Progressive	0	2
Psychology Today	0	1
Publishers' Weekly	1	1

Table 7 continued

Publication	*1991*	*1992*
Reader's Digest	1	0
Scholastic Update	0	3
Sports Illustrated	2	1
Time	10	26
Travel Holiday	0	1
The UNESCO Courier	0	1
U.N. Chronicle	1	4
U.S. Department of State Dispatch	6	24
U.S. News and World Report	13	16
The Washington Monthly	0	1
WJR (World Journalism Review)	0	1
World Monitor	1	1
World Press Review	4	4
Major US Weeklies (*Time, Newsweek, U.S. News* and *World Report*)	31	65

Periodicals clustered their coverage, most articles appearing in the Summer and Fall months (72 of 92 in 1991 and 153 of 204 in 1992). They also seemed to respond to the dramatic, given that 72 of the 92 articles published in 1991 appeared *after* the JNA had attacked Slovenia and Croatia, and that 128 of 204 articles published in 1992 appeared *after* the US media's belated discovery of death camps and mass murder in Bosnia. Had periodicals been engaged in a systematic and sustained analysis of the crisis, there would have been a more even distribution of articles, including a response to ethnic cleansing by Serb forces in Croatia in 1991. But in the first five months of that year only 19 publications contained pieces on the crisis, and in early 1992, despite the arrival of UN forces in Croatia and the Serbian attack on Bosnia, only 32 issues had pieces on Yugoslavia. It thus seems that like television networks, periodicals responded more readily to political crises, diplomatic offensives, warfare, and atrocities than to policy issues, diplomacy, and the domestic politics of foreign countries. (See Table 9.)

If the amount of attention that the media has paid to the crisis in the former Yugoslavia has often seemed inadequate, the coverage itself has often seemed to be misinformed and superficial, when not biased and racist. It has tended to focus on the sensational rather than the substantive; it has concentrated on personalities rather than issues; and it has tended to recast what is essentially a Balkan affair in terms of American policy or the role of such international organizations as the EC, the UN, and NATO.

Table 8 Major US periodicals carrying articles on the crisis in Yugoslavia

Publication	1991	1992
The Atlantic	0	1
Esquire	0	1
Forbes	2	1
Foreign Affairs	1	1
Foreign Policy	1	0
Jet	0	1
Life	0	1
Ms.	1	0
Nation	4	8
National Review	3	5
New Republic	5	11
New York Review of Books	2	4
New York Times Magazine	1	2
New Yorker	1	4
Newsweek	8	23
Progressive	0	2
Psychology Today	0	1
Reader's Digest	1	0
Sports Illustrated	2	1
Time	10	26
U.S. News and World Report	13	16
	55	109

Yet a wide variety of opinions have found a venue in the US media, which has generally sought to "balance" coverage. The *National Review*, for example, ran pieces by both Ivo Banac, a Croatian who has criticized both Serbian and Croatian nationalists, and Nora Beloff, a staunch supporter of Serbia. Even so, much of the reporting has been biased by the location of reporters, who tend to repeat, not question, their sources; and a good deal has been rushed, leading to inaccuracies, a tendency to use simplistic explanations, and the use of stereotypes to frame complex issues and events. Given the episodic, superficial, and fragmentary coverage by both the print and electronic media, only by spending whole days in front of the TV with a Sony Walkman plugged in one ear and newspapers and periodicals at the ready for commercial breaks could the average American begin to gather enough information to make sense of events in the Balkans. Even then, because most media have related everything to American interests, presented a number of misconceptions, and cloaked their biases,

Table 9 The appearance of periodical articles on the crisis in Yugoslavia

Month	1991	1992
January	2	7
February	1	3
March	9	4
April	5	8
May	2	9
June	1	19
July	17	25
August	6	29
September	14	23
October	10	19
November	10	28
December	11	20
January–February	0	1
July–August	1	0
August–September	0	3
September–October	0	1
November–December	1	1
Spring	0	1
Summer	2	0
Fall	0	4
Winter	0	0
Trimesters		
I	12	14
II	8	37
III	40	85
IV	32	68
Total	92	204
Major US Weeklies	31	65
All others	61	139

the average reader would not be in a much better position to judge the sources of information offered or to choose among detailed arguments.

One of the most pervasive misconceptions current in the media is the belief that the ethnic groups of the former Yugoslavia have been at each other's throats for centuries, and that all sides display the same irrational prejudices and harbor the same extreme attitudes. Rather than modern nations, south Slavs are seen as "atavistic tribes" whose psyches thirst for blood, and all sides are depicted as directly or indirectly responsible for the crimes and atrocities that have characterized the crisis ever since the JNA attacked Slovenia and the Serbs in Croatia began to seize Croatian towns and villages in the Krajina. Such an approach conforms to the medias idea of being "fair," and Aryeh Neier of the *Nation* is one of the few who have warned that, "Evenhandedness in assessing a conflict in which the overwhelming share of criminal conduct has been committed by one side paints a false picture."[29]

It is thus ironic that after the revelation of Serbian atrocities in Bosnia, the *Nation* ran Alexander Cockburn's disingenuous parallel between current Serbian and earlier Ustasha ethnic cleansing, even though a more apt analogy would have been with the atrocities committed during World War II by Serbian Chetniks, who rationalized their murder of hundreds of thousands of Croats and Muslims as "ethnic cleansing." The *Nation* also provided a platform for Anthony Borden, who diluted the blame for Serbian actions in Bosnia by claiming that Zagreb and Belgrade hoped to create ethnically pure mini-empires, insisting that Croats and Serbs had both resorted to "mass killings and expulsions," asserting that the EC's findings that "Croatia's maltreatment of its Serb minority disqualified it" from being recognized as an independent state, and citing the claim by the Canadian general and UN commander Lewis MacKenzie, that the Bosnians had broken cease-fires and refused to negotiate because they preferred "intervention over negotiation."[30]

Similar efforts to tar all sides with the same genocidal brush and depict all groups as equally aggressive and untrustworthy can be found in *The New York Times*, the *Los Angeles Times*, the *New York Review of Books*,[31] the *Wall Street Journal*, the *New Yorker*,[32] the *National Journal*,[33] the *National Review*,[34] the *New Republic*,[35] *Time*,[36] *Newsweek*, *Foreign Policy*, and *Foreign Affairs*,[37] as well as on the commercial and non-profit networks.[38] For example, in the August 1992 issue of the *New Yorker*, John Newhouse claimed that the cold war had so obscured the past that "all sides were surprised to see the Balkans behaving like the Balkans," and insisted that diplomacy could not "cope with the nationalism, ethnic passions, and capricious behavior" in eastern Europe. He acknowledged that Serbia had been the "aggressor" in June 1991, but then insisted that the Croats "had embarked on a systematic destruction of Serbian villages and enclaves." Although he offered no more than diplomatic gossip as evidence for this, he concluded that, "Both groups had gone back to basics." The only difference between the two sides, apparently was their leadership. Newhouse, who dismissed Izetbegović as ineffectual, reported that "most diplomats who knew them," saw Tudjman and Milošević as "equally odious rogues," but that while the Serb was "clever," the Croat was "stupid" and consequently less dangerous.[39]

Although in late 1991 Radek Sikorski noted in the *National Review* that "we can take it for granted that the Croatian refugees from the disputed . . . areas will not be allowed to return, and their villages and towns will be settled by ethnically sounder [Serbian] elements," both the international implications and the genocidal nature of ethnic cleansing in Croatia escaped a great many commentators.[40] Perhaps because of this, rather than examine Serbian actions in the light of international law, the media has instead reported efforts to resolve the crisis diplomatically and debated the wisdom of military intervention by the West.

A number of commentators have used the conflict in the Balkans to argue for a reintroduction of a neo-imperialist system, among them David Andersen, who argued that none of the "mini-states" formed from Yugo-slavia would be "productive enough on a large enough scale to make a modern state function" and so suggested that the US, an international organization, or "a combination of several Western states should come up with a way to manage or at least control the conflict in what used to be Yugoslavia."[41] William Pfaff put forward a similar proposal, arguing that East European states be "assimilated" by an EC core, since Western Europe was the source for "modern civilizations.[42]

Eric Hobsbawm also argued in the *Nation* that small states were not viable, and Anthony Borden suggested that Bosnia be placed under "some form of UN trusteeship."[43] Gerald B. Helman and Steven R. Ratner used *Foreign Policy* to propose guardianships and conservatorships that would include assistance, delegation and governmental functions to the UN by such "failed" states as Bosnia and Cambodia.[44] Writing in the *National Review*, Paul Johnson advo-cated the creation of a new imperial order that would guarantee stability and peace, while Boutros Boutros-Ghali has indirectly supported such a position by arguing in favor of devoting more resources to peacekeeping, one of the few "growth industries" of the 1990s.[45]

A nostalgia for a vanished imperial order and an aversion to self-determination in favor of a neo-*Realpolitik* thus seems to be permeating the media.[46] Typical was the argument put forward by the editor of *Foreign Policy*, Charles William Maynes, who warned that attacking Serbia would shatter the "consensus" on the Security Council. Claiming that "when two or more populations have been reluctant to live" in a single state, the result has been power sharing, repression, or ethnic cleansing, he concluded that since the first had been rejected by the Serbs and the second by the Croats and Muslims, then only the third option of "ethnic cleansing" – which he noted had already worked well in Poland, Czechoslovakia, Greece, and Turkey – was viable.[47]

For a great many journalists and commentators, the situation in the Balkans is simply too emotional, too complex, and too Byzantine for civilized westerners to comprehend. Anthony Borden thus concluded that, "The war in Bosnia is a terrible and murky situation with no easy answers."[48] Contemplating the situation in Croatia in early 1992, Robert Guskind, was "left in shock, asking how something so horrendous could happen in modern Europe and – worse still – why no one has stepped in to definitively stop the fighting." He finally decided that "it is virtually impossible to comprehend the ferocity of what happened here, let alone to fathom the rigid politics, slug-it-out ideologies and centuries-old enmities that encouraged it."[49]

Some have thought to make sense of all this murkiness by adopting what might be called the Churchillian approach of blaming a single person; others by blaming a small coterie of evil men and fanatics or a breakdown in discipline.[50] The unthinkable thereby becomes comprehensible because it is personalized, and its description and explanation become as banal as Hannah Arendt perceived twentieth-century evil to be or as simple-minded as the latest reruns of the "A-Team," "Mission Impossible," or "Star Trek" actually are.

Such an approach has allowed commentators and correspondents to blame Tito for failing to prepare any "successors" and for having repressed Serbian and Croatian "liberals" in 1971–2 and leaving the country "to the old guard of former partisans and Communist Party apparatchiks."[51] But if Robert Guskind saw Milošević as "an unreconstructed communist" who had reacted to what he perceived as a German-led conspiracy to break up Yugoslavia, and Max Primorac saw Serbia as "a bastion of new-world-order Bolshevism," Alexander Cockburn perceived a Vatican plot and Nora Beloff combined anti-communism with anti-Catholicism by insisting that Tito and the Vatican had "colluded" to hide the "Ustashi holocaust" and warning that the old "Communist mentality is everywhere" – even in prosperous Slovenia which had failed to "legalize private enterprise," and in Croatia, where "the old apparatchiks still hold the top jobs."[52]

Noel Malcolm, correspondent for the *London Spectator*, saw the failure to remove communism, not the resurgence of nationalism, as causing the crisis in Yugoslavia, arguing that Milošević's nationalism was really a "lopsided survival of the communist-political tradition."[53] While continuity of personnel, method, and mentality underlies many of the problems that have plagued the former Yugoslav republics, the survival of a communist *mentalité* cannot fully explain the new nationalisms that have been developing there since the 1980.[54]

David Rieff saddled "the forces of Dr. Radovan Karadžić, the self-styled President of the Serb Republic of Bosnia and Hercegovina," with the blame for the carnage in Bosnia, reporting José Mendiluce's eyewitness account of massacres in Zvornik where Serbian White Eagles had been brought in "to inflict as much terror on the civilian population as possible, to destroy as much property as possible, and to target as much of the violence as possible against women and kids" in what he defined as "a war between fanatical nationalists."[55]

The media has repeatedly discussed, and thereby popularized, the argument by policy-makers that they cannot intervene in the former Yugoslavia because doing so would trigger a bloody guerrilla war against the Serbs, who supposedly held massive German and Italian forces at bay for four years during World War II.[56] The image of the Serbs as the only victims of genocide during World War II has also been accepted and popularized by the media.[57]

Alexander Cockburn thus absolved the Serbs of the opprobium of behaving like Nazis and instead stigmatized the Croats by claiming that "anywhere from 750,000 to 1.2 million" Serbs were "killed in the pogroms organized by the Nazi puppet state of Croatia," even though no more than 850,000 Yugoslavs were killed during the War, and the Serbs, who collaborated with both the Nazis and the Fascists, killed hundreds of thousands of Serbs, Croats, and Muslims. Yet Cockburn argued that while the Serbs were "taking a hammering in the press, some but not all of which [was] deserved," the Serbs in Bosnia really felt threatened and "the rhetoric of Western commentators" had gotten "entirely out of hand."[58]

As Serbian forces were overrunning Croatia in late 1991, the *The New York Times* reported only the atrocities committed by the Croatian state during World War II, largely ignored the ethnic cleansing then being carried out by the Serbs in Croatia, and failed to mention either Serbian atrocities in World War II or Serbian collaboration with the Axis.[59] Writing in the *National Journal* a month later, Guskind erroneously claimed that Croatia had "sided with the Nazis, Serbia with the Western Allies," noting that "the gruesome Ustashe World War II record," which included the murder of 500,000 to 750,000 Serbs, Jews, and Gypsies, as well as anti-Serbian and anti-Jewish remarks purportedly made by Tudjman, had lent credibility to Milošević's claim that he was "simply fighting for the unity of Serbia."[60]

This sort of inaccurate and often apologetic history not only rationalized Serbian actions, it implicated Croats and Muslims as equally guilty by blaming one group's past actions for the other's current atrocities.[61] It cannot, therefore, be dismissed, as some in the media have tried to do, as trivial and irrelevant antiquarianism.[62] The net result of imprecise reporting of historical detail has been a generally superficial level of analysis and a tendency to see the victims as carrying the same bad seed as their torturers.[63] Max Primorac was more accurate when he reported that the Serbs were "deliberately terrorizing non-Serbian populations" and waging a "Nazi-like campaign" with "death camps, summary executions, and the creation of millions of refugees."[64]

Yet the media depicted the Serbs as reacting, albeit belatedly, to Croatian atrocities 50 years earlier and as trying to avoid another 500 years of Muslim rule, reporting Serbian claims that they were simply practicing a form of self-defense and self-determination by striking at the Croats and Muslims before they once more became the victims of oppression and genocide.[65]

Serb atrocities thus became explicable as actual and preventive retaliation for perceived and possible Muslim and Croatian outrages.[66] There are even those who implied that the world should feel sorry for the Serbs, admire their military prowess and support them as the only carriers of the "Yugoslav idea."[67] Newhouse thus cited a German diplomat who saw Serbia as a "nation gone mad," but believed that in the end, theirs would be the "greatest tragedy."[68]

In April 1993, when it appeared the West might actually take some sort of military action against Serbia, *Newsweek* carried an article by Charles Lane on the "Genocide Museum" in Belgrade, dedicated to the victims of "the Hitlerite Croat Ustasha" and "recent fighting in Croatia." Noting that Milošević, not the Serbian people, was to blame for everything, and citing Vuk Drašković, who claimed that Serbs were merely fighting for their survival, Lane concluded that "Serbian protestations of innocence in Bosnia cannot be dismissed as empty posturing" and suggested that "Western policy-makers should pay a visit" to the museum.[69] That same day, Walter Russell Mead published an op. ed. piece in the *LA Times* that suggested that since the Serbs had won the war and given Clinton and the Democrats a "course in humiliation," it was time to run up the "white flag," let the Bosnian Serbs "rejoin" "Yugoslavia," and promote reconstruction and reconciliation.[70]

Although some commentators have condemned Serbia for using the JNA to create "an atavistic 'Greater Serbia'" in Bosnia, others have split legal hairs, noting that Serbia was not "in adequate control" of Serb forces in Bosnia, but merely "assisting" them, a difference that is crucial with regard to the UN Charter.[71] Stedman argued that with 19 Serb groups operating in Bosnia, it was "unclear whether there is unified command" and it would therefore make sense to attack Serbia *only* if one wanted "to deter aggression against Kosovo and Macedonia, to prevent escalation to interstate war, and to weaken Serbia's capability to carry out further attacks."[72] An ABC special on Bosnia in the Spring of 1993 conveyed a similar message, as George Kenney claimed that to "directly confront the Serbian aggression" would entail high costs and a minimum of 50,000 troops, while Jennings concluded that 400,000 troops would be needed to destroy "the hatred of three peoples for one another" and the Serbian general Božidar Stefanović threatened the defeat of the West should it take action against the Serbs.[73]

The admonitory myth of the Serb fighter thus reinforced the disingenuous legalistic argument that Serbia has no control over events outside its borders. As a result, to quote Michael Lind, "superannuated diplomats such as Cyrus Vance . . . continue[d] their internationalist shuttling to nowhere and to no avail."[74] The futility of such shuttling was made clear by David Rieff, who reported in late 1992 that when Vance arrived in Bosnia, he "was prepared to say only that he was not prepared 'to deny the existence of ethnic cleansing'" while David Owen "instructed the reporters to remember that they were "in a position to say certain things and he was not." Even so, Rieff considered such obfuscation "an improvement" over Karadžić who "categorically denied what he referred to as 'the allegation of ethnic cleansing.'"[75]

Yet the media portrayed Vance and Owen as the best hopes for peace, honest men doggedly working at an impossible task, and recently the media have begun to rehabilitate Karadžić and Milošević.[76] The efforts of diplomats have been followed closely by the media, which seems capable of comprehending the Yugoslav crisis only if it frames it in an American, British, NATO or UN context.[77] In effect, Croatia, Bosnia, and Serbia have become objects with no inner reality, the political and diplomatic equivalents to a *Playboy* centrefold or a stripper at a local bar. The *New Yorker* ran Newhouse's compilation of diplomatic gossip even though it revealed nothing, and it is clear that the actions of the UN, the US, and the EC, whether their embargo of weapons or their belated humanitarian efforts to help the victims of the embargo, have benefited the Serbs.[78]

The media has not even understood how to define "intervention" and has not realized that the United States intervened in a decisive manner when James Baker went to Belgrade in June 1991 to announce that the Bush administration looked askance at efforts to break up Yugoslavia.[79] Most journalists bought the line that the new states wanted recognition only in order to buy the weapons they needed to "fight the next phase of the civil war," and Radek Sikorski was in a minority when he argued for EC condemnation of Serbian annexation of Croatian territory and recognition of Croatia and Slovenia because "a fundamental principle of co-existence" was at stake. He condemned the "West's timidity," its "hypocritical stance," and its failure to "tell the truth" as misleading the Croats, precluding a "peaceful resolution" to the crisis, and encouraging "Serbian aggression." He was also one of the few to realize that proposals to put UN troops in Krajina might help the Croats secure their borders, but would also "safeguard" Serb "territorial gains."[80]

In fact, the UN forces in Croatia stabilized a situation that favored the Serbs, yet Vance and Owen attempted to do in Bosnia what Vance and Carrington had done in Croatia; the UN limited its role to delivering "humanitarian aid" to the beleaguered Bosnians; Boutros Boutros-Ghali boasted that Yugoslavia was the biggest peacekeeping effort ever; and Colin Powell predicted that in the future US armed forces would respond to regional conflicts with peacekeeping missions and humanitarian operations.[81] What most journalists evidently knew, but did not report, was the deliberate inactivity of the US government, whose spokespersons had taken a line that, as Brent Scowcroft put it, the Serbs had fought "long and hard" to realize a Greater Serbia and the West should recognize the *fait accompli*.[82]

But Primorac condemned the international community for allowing "the rape and murder of a nation, while piously proclaiming its commitment to

[a] 'humanitarian' aid" that only fattened the Muslim lamb for the Orthodox sacrifice.[83] And Stedman considered UN intervention in Yugoslavia "a disaster" because the "combatants" [sic Serbs] had used negotiations and cease-fires "to regroup and gain tactical advantage."[84] Of course, implying that *all* sides had broken cease-fires masks the fact that most have been undone by the JNA or Serb forces. It also generalizes and excuses Serb aggression, just as depicting all sides as fanatics committed to vendetta and ethnic cleansing excuses Serbian genocide.[85]

How little reflective thinking has gone into reporting on Bosnia was demonstrated by David Rieff, who cautioned those who had criticized Croatia's "hard-heartedness" for closing their borders to Bosnian refugees in September 1992 that "the situation was hardly so simple." Rieff quoted Peter Kessler, a UNHCR spokesman, who had informed "sour journalists" critical of Zagreb's action that Croatia was the fourth-largest receiver of refugees (after Pakistan, Iran, and Malawi) and had been inundated in under 18 months with 500,000 Bosnian refugees – "roughly the equivalent, in terms of population, of 25 million refugees coming into the United States." The consequent strain on Croatia's economy, already wrecked by Serbian bombing and shelling, had been "severe." Yet Western governments tended to be "quicker with advice than with cash donations" to help care for refugees, and while Germany had taken 220,000 refugees, the USA was willing to accept only 1,000 displaced Bosnians.[86]

By focussing on humanitarian aid and peacekeeping forces, the media has given the impression that there is no international security mechanism to deal with the crisis.[87] And by approaching the crisis from the standpoint of our national interest or the perspective of diplomats such as Vance, Eagleburger, and Owen, the media has made it seem that there is no solution capable of ending the crisis except a negotiated one imposed on the groups involved. How cynical such a solution might be became clear when Owen answered a question about lifting the arms embargo by replying that doing so would be a "disincentive to the Muslims" to negotiate seriously.[88]

Yet his response accurately reflected a diplomatic reality in which one of the leitmotivs has been that no international organization can act and that it must be made clear to the Croats and Muslims that "no western soldier is going to be sent to die over a Serb-Croat conflict," that Berlin will not help the Croats and Slovenes, and that UN forces will withdraw should they be attacked. Even so, every hint that the USA, the EC, or the UN might take decisive action has unleashed a flurry of media coverage which quickly subsides after a week or so. Ironically, the UN force that eventually was deployed hurt the Muslim cause, particularly after David MacKenzie's remarks regarding Muslim perfidy and Serbia's resistance during World War II were carried by the major networks.[89] MacKenzie's remarks were particularly damaging because they resonated for months in the media, perhaps because they reflected the thinking of both the Pentagon and George Kenney, whose opinions were presented as opposed to those of the government, whereas they were in reality merely another official scenario based on the same faulty assumptions as those reached by the Joint Chiefs of Staff.

The revelations regarding death camps, massacres of civilians by Serbian forces, and the Serbian policy of ethnic cleansing forced the media to find new rationalizations for the inaction of Western governments. Among these were claims that the US had no national interest in the Balkans, that there was little domestic support for intervention, and that there was no reasonable chance of success should outside military forces be sent to Bosnia. By recasting the crisis in American terms, commentators and journalists could avoid grappling with complex Balkan politics and Serbian atrocities by arguing that moral outrage was helpless against the stubborn realities of ancient hatreds, an impotent UN, and an indifferent and neo-isolationist American public.[90]

Consequently, although there *are* various international agreements dealing with genocide and human rights violations; and because Croatia, Slovenia, and Bosnia have been recognized as sovereign states since late 1991, attacks by Serbia or Serbian-supported forces on such sovereign states *are* covered by such documents as the UN Charter, the media have focussed attention on diplomatic maneuvres, the possibility of outside intervention, and the plight of children. By defining the situation in Bosnia as a choice between outside intervention and the continued imposition of the current embargo, the media have failed to grasp that the embargo itself is a form of intervention, just as Baker's declarations in favor of a unitary Yugoslav state were a form of intervention. These are things any diplomatic historian knows, but they seem to have escaped the notice of most commentators and journalists. Indeed, the nature of their trade seems to prevent some journalists from making coherent arguments and drawing logical conclusions. Thus, David Hackworth, who noted that even a small number of anti-tank weapons had radically shifted the balance between Croatian and Serbian forces in late 1992, argued that the UN needed to find the same resolve as it had when Iraq invaded Kuwait, even though the logic of his observations argued for lifting the embargo as the most effective way to halt Serbian aggression.[91]

But there has been a general failure of analysis with regard to the crisis in the former Yugoslavia, and the media have displayed a condescending attitude toward the Croats, Slovenes, and Muslims, just as they have dismissed such complex phenomenon as neo-nationalism in favor of stereotypical, traditional, and often racist, views of the Balkans.[92] Even Noel Malcolm, whose analyses of the events in the former Yugoslavia have been accurate and critical of the Serbians, initially perceived a surreal side to events and reported the proclamation of Slovene independence as "more like an invitation to Disneyland than a call to arms." He also criticized the Slovene government for having "done curiously little to make a clean break with the rest of Yugoslavia" and for indulging in "half-measures" – although he was not sure whether Slovene actions had been due to "incompetence" or "a genuine willingness to negotiate."[93] Rieff's definition of ethnic cleansing as a "process, not one single terrible event," and his description of that process in Banja Luka, beginning with the formation of a Crisis Committee that barred non-Serbs from employment and deprived them of their health insurance and other benefits is one of the few reports that eschewed the superficial in favor of the analytic.[94]

Rather than encourage debate and analysis, the media have tended to look for easy solutions and present simple versions of reality. Thus the *New Yorker* cited a "quiet," and presumably sane, voice from the Balkans who criticized the UN and EC peace plans as ignoring "those people who don't want to be tribal" by creating an "apartheid-style division" of Bosnia. Instead, the "quiet voice" wanted *all* parties disarmed and "protection of minority rights" by an "international administrative authority." That the voice was Serbian and the voice's demands would have tended to justify and consolidate Serbian territorial gains was not mentioned in the article, even though the implication was that Serbs are *not* adequately protected in either Bosnia or Croatia. There are, of course, few Croats or Muslims to protect in most Serbian-controlled areas.[95]

What might be called a "liberal" (or establishment) bias has also permeated media treatment of the crisis in Yugoslavia. Usually this has taken the form of favoring compromise positions on complex or contentious issues, blaming all sides equally, setting the highest priority on ending the bloodshed, or justifying inactions by the UN, USA, and EC by appealing to "reality" and noting that the national interest is not involved. There is also an aching sense of *déjà vu*, of the "old Europe" re-emerging, rather than a nasty new one being born. Joseph Joffe thus saw the formation of old blocs, as Germany and Austria lined up behind Slovenia and Croatia, while the USA, France, and Britain supported Serbia.[96]

Part of the liberal approach is to present the crisis in such a way as to reassure, rather than challenge, those who support "our" system. For example, the *New Yorker* quoted Milos Vasić on how "very easy" it is to foment war and mass murder. "First," he noted, "you create fear, then distrust, then panic. Then all you have to do is come every night and distribute submachine guns in every village, and you are ready." At first, this might not seem reassuring, but it is the stuff of most American melodramas and not a few academic treatises that deal with dictatorships and totalitarian movements, and it is useful when used in tandem with the explanation provided by Pajić, who "described a somewhat more complex process." According to the Bosnian professor, the "stable stagnation" of postwar Yugoslavia had been possible because social conflicts had been resolved "behind the scenes" within a single party or by one charismatic leader. But after communism collapsed, "all that liberals like me [Pajić] could offer was the free market and free institutions." Of course, this "terrified" those who "were not ready for these insecurities," and "the nationalists rose, exploiting social conflicts." The crisis therefore becomes merely a "new form of collective identity" and nationalism is not part of the new "liberal" order, but a continuation of the old "communist" order. Yugoslavia needs men like Pajić and Vasić, who, according to the *New Yorker*, "may have been marginalized by the war parties, but [who] continue to press for the creation of secular, democratic, multiethnic political systems." Both men blamed television for the war, which Vasić saw as "artificial."[97]

The theme of "they're a mess, but we're all right, Jack" is also struck in one of the more fanciful "liberal" explanations of the Balkan conflict by Alfred Meyer in *Psychology Today*. According to Meyer, "when the Serbs embark on a program of what they've termed 'ethnic cleansing,' it is a clear case of regression, of atavism – a desperate resort to behaviors and strategies pertinent in the past but now obsolete." In other words, the Serbs have not adapted well to being domesticated animals, and there is a lesson there for Americans. "We know," Meyer writes, "by the example of Bosnia where the deprivation of ritual can lead," so we should be content with our own admittedly imperfect political system, because it is only "the rituals of our politics – like them or not – that keeps us from expressing our differences in more aggressive ways."[98]

The existence of such an "establishment" point of view is not surprising. Bound by convention, not only has the media tended to view the crisis in Yugoslavia through a domestic lens, but their views have been shaped by and integrated into those of foreign policy, corporate, academic, and political elites who tend to be their sole or preponderant sources. Since such sources have been concerned with managing, rather than examining or explaining, events in the Balkans, the information available in most media has tended to be politically safe and analytically unsophisticated.[99]

Thus, in April 1992, the *The New York Times* reported in a front-page article that the new "Yugoslavia" had renounced all territorial claims on other republics, but it made no mention of an invitation to Krajina and Bosnia to join later, noting only that General Milutin Kukunjac had said that the JNA would stay in Bosnia as the army of those "who accept us." For those who got beyond the headlines, there was another piece on p. A10 noting that the Muslims believed that the Serbs outside Serbia intended to join Serbia and that the Serbs had become "reasonable" after taking half of

Bosnia as the Serbian Democratic Party demanded partition of Bosnia, possession of Sarajevo, and the right to join Serbia.[100] This was what might be called two-part balanced reporting, but it was still limited to "real-time" and did not remind the reader that in late 1991 the Serbs had also been anxious to negotiate a "peaceful" settlement after seizing a third of Croatia.[101]

In May 1992, the *The New York Times* published a piece by John Burns, then based in Belgrade, who reported the Serbs saw themselves as "victimized by history" and as fighting "to defend their homes," even though Muslims, Croats, and Westerners portrayed them as terrorists and aggressors. According to Burns, 100,000 Serbs had fled to avoid conscription and others were upset with Milošević's Serbian nationalism and disgusted by Serbian atrocities, but even such good, responsible Serbs blamed Croats and Muslims for the crisis. He even cited Dobriša Ćosić's claim that 300,000 Serbs had been "driven" from their homes and "dozens of predominantly Serbian towns and villages [had] been devastated."[102]

By letting his sources speak, Burns provided his American readers with some insight into the Serbian psyche and conveyed the basic rationalizations for Serbia's actions, but by not informing his readers that most of those "Serbian" towns and villages had been destroyed by the JNA or Serbian aircraft, that most refugees were Croats and Muslims, and that nothing like 300,000 Serbs had left their homes in Croatia, Burns left the casual reader with the impression that the Serbian point of view was a depiction of reality. But Burns was in Belgrade. David Rieff, who was in Sarajevo, showed considerably more skepticism when presenting the Serbian point of view.

Noting a stunning discrepancy between what his Serbian guide had told him and the physical reality both of them were observing, Rieff observed that when dealing with a politician like Karadžić, "one asked him a question, his response was a lie, he knew it, the journalists knew it, and that was that. There were no illusions on either side." But his Serbian escort's "whole world was an illusion, the product of a carefully orchestrated propaganda campaign from Belgrade," and it seemed to Rieff that "the message 'Only Unity Can Save the Serbs' [had] blocked out contradictory information" and "that minds as well as bodies were being 'cleansed' in northern Bosnia." But if the Serbs were living in a fantasy world, Rieff noted that even the "most lurid tales the Bosnian Muslims had told about the process of ethnic cleansing – stories dismissed as exaggerations during the spring and summer of 1992 – [had] turned out to have understated the slaughter."[103]

Yet for the media in general, this was good news because the crisis in the Balkans proved attractive only after it degenerated into a conflict and became sensational, allowing the media to focus attention on "human interest" stories and descriptions of carnage and destruction.[104] This proved, for obvious reasons, particularly appealing to television, but it was also true of the print media. John Burns who reported from Belgrade and Sarajevo for the *The New York Times*, regularly focussed on the "human" side of the story rather than presenting a comprehensive analysis of the situation. In mid-October, for example, he reported that about 200,000 people had been killed or wounded in Bosnia, while the casualties for a week in Sarajevo ran to 67 dead and 456 wounded. He focussed in particular on the lack of adequate medical care and the loss of the city's last flour mill to Serbian artillery.[105]

David Rieff, who provided more analysis in his piece in the *New Yorker*, none the less set the stage by depicting Banja Luka as "a sullen and frightening place" that became "terrifying" after dark as both "regulars and irregulars" got drunk and "reel[ed] through the streets, shouting and waving their Kalashnikovs and their Heckler and Koch machine pistols." Apparently the "Balkan[!] darkness" had peculiar properties that allowed "the easy settling of scores" and made "tempers flare for no particular reason" as "nonpolitical mayhem also [took] its toll," making terror "the norm in Banja Luka." According to Rieff, in Serb-controlled areas of Bosnia, "there really are signs that say 'All Weapons Must Be Checked Before Entering' or portray a pistol with a red diagonal slash across it."[106]

It seems that the media, even when they are trying to be serious, end up being entertaining, largely because they tend to be dramatic, not analytic, and to focus on personalities, not analysis of issues. Indeed, the latter are usually done in the form of comments on interviews with "newsmakers" or by commentators examining what British and American politicians have said. The data base is therefore not only narrow, but presented in a manner that tends to preclude analysis.

Typical was a short *New Yorker* article earlier this year that reduced the crisis to a conflict of personalities in which Miloš Vasić, "a large, droll man" and the editor of *Vreme*, continued to publish his newspaper "despite constant harassment from the Milošević regime." During a public meeting in New York, "some of the psychotic culture" that confronts such Balkan moderates as Mr. Vasić and his friend Mr. Pajić "suddenly put in an appearance" in the guise of a "middle-aged blonde woman with hot blue eyes." The embodiment of psychosis, as well as "the American correspondent for Belgrade television," she "angrily" interrupted the speakers "with hostile questions and remarks" and was "joined by a couple of extremely pugnacious men." According to the article, the blonde and her two companions "spoke with strong Slavic accents," which the more civilized Mr. Vasić and Mr. Pajić apparently had somehow overcome. In effect, the writer had reduced the war to a struggle of a heroic Serb journalist and his professorial friend against a harpy, two thugs, and a personal dictatorship.[107]

In late August 1992, ABC recast the conflict in Bosnia in oral and visual clichés usually associated with the Middle East when it aired a report that the Bosnians had used their mortars to kill their own people in order to get sympathy from media, then described the suffering of the Serbs with a clip of a Serbian family wailing over a single male supposedly killed in the fighting in Bosnia.[108] One of the most superficial reports on the conflict was aired by NPR's *All Things Considered* on 27 March 1993, when Susan Stamberg interviewed Tom Jelton about what it was like to cover the war. Among other valuable facts provided for the listener was that the war was "worse" than those in Central America, that Tom felt guilty leaving his "friends" in Sarajevo, that his role was crucial because the State Department only reported what appeared in the press, and that – after two years covering the crisis – he was reading Ivo Andrić's *Bridge on the Drina* and realized that hundreds of years of co-mingling had ended in Bosnia. Impressed with his professionalism, Susan thanked him for being so "vital and courageous."[109]

One of the most salient characteristics of media coverage of the Balkans is that alternate points of view are not reported and there is little opportunity to correct inaccurate coverage or rebut biased reporting and commentary. From my experience, it seems that access to the media is variable, with organizations such as NPR having an almost impregnable wall of flak-catchers and others like CNN and PBS more amenable to cooperating with those who are not members of an elite. In general, efforts to correct and rebut are repulsed or relegated to such anodyne places as the letters from readers, listeners, and viewers. As a result, there is actually little real "balance" and even less "debate," because even in the letters section, journalists who have been attacked often get the last word. Indeed, the *Nation* uses its letters section as a way to editorialize and develop partisan positions.

This is less true of the *National Review*, but it also allows the author in question the last word, no matter how feeble. Thus, when John Didović wrote a scathing letter criticizing Nora Beloff's column, she got to rebut the rebuttal. According to Didović, Serbs were only 12 percent of Croatia's population, not the 17 percent claimed by Beloff, and the majority were "in one small region." He also noted that Croatia had held a referendum on secession, that Dubrovnik was 90 percent Croatian and the EC had condemned JNA shelling of the city as "an illegal act aimed at the seizure of an indisputably Croatian city"; that the JNA officer corps was 70 percent Serbian; that Tudjman had been a partisan general, not a Nazi collaborator, and had been jailed by Tito; that the struggle was between Croatian democracy and Serbian communism; and that by depicting Croats as extremist, Beloff had become "an apologist for the Serbian Communists." Unable to argue with Didović's "facts," Beloff instead argued that the Croats had made Dubrovnik "a nationalist stronghold"; that 70 percent of the JNA's Serbian officers had been recruited from Croatia or Bosnia, that Tudjman "presides" over "a centralist, dictatorial, and collectivist regime, which has far more in common with Titoist Communism than democracy"; that his three books "all contain explicit and vicious expressions of anti-Semitism"; and that the refusal by "Tudjman (and his Vatican backers)" to admit "well-documented evidence of the slaughter of the Serbs . . . has allowed the regime to flaunt Ustasha emblems, revere the memory of Ustasha leaders, and treat their own Serb minority as disposable trash."[110] In other words, she reiterated the ideological arguments contained in her first article, and given the tenuous bases on which they rest, it is likely that Didović could have as easily demolished them, noting, for example, that Tudjman's anti-Semitic remarks were quoted out of context by Beloff and other Serbian apologists. The point is that by having his response to Beloff reduced to a letter, he lacked the chance to do so. Ironically, the *New York Review of Books* turned the tables on Beloff by reducing her criticism of Misha Glenny's article to a letter that Glenny was then allowed to rebut. Again, neither a debate nor a balanced and fair airing of an issue had occurred, because the format was structured to favor the original author, not the critic.[111]

It is now over four years since the Serbs initiated the conflict in the former Yugoslavia, and during those years the performance of the journalists and editors of the media has been lackluster, uninformed, and as biased as that of the diplomats and statesmen has been cynical, self-serving, and cowardly. The result has been not only the devastation of Croatia and Bosnia, but the destruction of a people and the evisceration of the spiritual core of the Balkans and the blatant moral failure of the West. As one old Muslim who had lost his sons told David Rieff in late 1992, Bosnia was "a dead country, at least for Muslims." It had become "Serbian," and all that was left for those Muslims who had survived was to try to emigrate to Western Europe or the United States, neither of which was anxious to have them.

José Mendiluce had complained that "we spend our time desperately trying to alert the international community to the depth of the crisis, but whether anyone is paying attention to us – serious attention, anyway – is another question entirely." In fact, as Rieff noted

> by the fall of 1992 the belief had taken hold that there was really nothing to be done for the Bosnians, just as nothing could have been done for the Beirutis before them; this belief superseded even the horror that so many had felt when the first images of the Serb concentration camps were televised.

Cynicism and "viewer fatigue" had reduced the war to "a long-running *fait-divers*," in which the cosmopolitan Muslim who could not hate was a "hero" and yet "in the context of northern Bosnia during one of the great crimes of twentieth-century Europe, [this] meant that he could only be one thing: a victim."[112] As Peter Jennings said at the end of his special on Bosnia in the spring of 1993, "most of us will go on debating," so rather than abandon the illusory "fairness" that the media had scrupulously observed for two years, he left his viewers with "twelve months of images."[113]

NOTES

1 Ben H. Bagdikian, *The Media Monopoly* (Boston: Beacon Press, 1983: xiv) considers the mass media "the authority . . . for what is true and false, what is reality and what is fantasy, what is important and what is trivial." He thus sees "no greater force in shaping the public mind." Also S. Robert Lichter, Stanley Rothman, and Linda S. Lichter, *The Media Elite* (Bethesda, Md.: Adler & Adler, 1986): 55.

2 The comment may be facetious, and if the forms being taken by Balkan nationalisms seem archaic, complete with medieval symbols and long-dormant prejudices, computers and electronics make these neo-nationalisms as different from their precursors as Stalin's authoritarian regime was from that of Ivan the Terrible. On nationalism, see Anthony D. Smith, *Theories of Nationalism* (New York: Harper and Row, 1971), and Louis L. Snyder, *Varieties of Nationalism: A Comparative Study* (Hinsdale, Ill.: The Dryden Press, 1976).

3 Landrum R. Bolling (ed.), *Reporters Under Fire. U.S. Media Coverage of Conflicts in Lebanon and Central America* (Boulder, Colo.: Westview Press, 1985: 151, 154), for Water Friedenberg's remark that the press does not take the government's word as "sacred writ." But, as David Newhouse, "Diplomatic Round: Dodging the Problem," *New Yorker*, 24 August 1992, 143, noted, the presentation of issues often depends on the availability of "authoritative sources." .

4 Reporters may question government officials closely if official versions of reality conflict sharply with the interpretations of important politicians, prestigious academics, or prominent civilian think-tanks. They may also do so if they perceive a "national interest" to be at stake. But they are less likely to take officials to task in a case like the Balkans, where their own knowledge is limited, academics and think-tanks have reinforced government policy, and they see no American interests in play.

5 According to Bagdikian, if not "monolithic," the news media still "suffer from built-in biases that protect corporate power and consequently weaken the public's ability to understand forces that create the American scene." The "doctrine of objectivity" consequently serves the interests of the powers-that-be, because stories are typically checked with either corporate executives, government officials, or "experts" and academics in a few universities and think-tanks, many of whom depend for their livelihood on large corporations and government agencies. Marginal sources tend to be ignored or discredited by more authoritative sources, and the illusion of a value-free media is created, even as it serves the interests of corporations and politicians, or in Bagdikian's terminology, "authorities" and "personalities." Bagdikian (see note 1), pp. ix, 132–3, 181–2; Lichter, Rothman and Lichter (see note 1), p. 53, see the media elite as "a largely homogeneous group that is cosmopolitan in background and liberal in outlook," and no longer "outsiders who keep the insiders straight," but "insiders themselves, courted by politicians, studied by scholars, and known to millions through their bylines and televised images."

6 Gore Vidal presented a more sophisticated argument along the same lines in the *Nation* in 1991, noting that to get to the top, reporters and editors had to have, or adopt, certain attitudes and biases.

7 Bagdikian (see note 1), pp. 37–8, and *passim*. Schulman (in John Downing et al., *Questioning the Media. A Critical Introduction*, London: Sage, 1990: 121–2), notes that the punishment for those who reject the dominant ideology is unemployment; and see Denis McQuail, *Media Performance, Mass Communication and the Public Interest* (Newbury Park: Sage, 1992: 184–95, for problems in attaining objective coverage.

8 David L. Paletz and Robert M. Entmann, *Media, Power, Politics* (New York: Free Press, 1981), 21, note that "journalists define events from a short-term, anti-historical perspective; see individual or group action, not structural or other impersonal forces, at the root of most occurrences; and simplify and reduce stories to conventional symbols for easy assimilation by audiences." Yet perspective does not necessarily guarantee understanding. Hans Magnus Enzensberger concludes that "molecular civil wars" like Bosnia have destruction as their sole goal and are "about nothing at all." See Paul Levine's review of *Civil War: From L.A. to Bosnia* in *The Nation* (23 Jan. 1995), 103.

9 Telephone interview with Gail Evans, 19 July 1993. "Culture" may be a better word, since television news tends to evolve its own manners, mores, and techniques, much as do diplomatic corps, churches, and academia. To the extent that this culture does not coincide with those of viewers, the media is seen to be biased or off-the-wall.

10 For the "transparency fallacy," the use of "clawback" to neutralize certain types of news, and a detailed discussion of the conventions of television, see John Fiske, *Television Culture* (New York: Methuen & Co., 1991), esp. 281–307; also see Martin A. Lee and Norman Solomon, *Unreliable Sources: A Guide to Detecting Bias in News Media* (New York: Carol Publishing Group, 1990), 228–337, esp. 337, for Ted Koppel's remark that reporters "are a discouragingly timid lot . . . only truly comfortable . . in a herd."

11 Edward Herman, "Media in the U.S. Political Economy," and Mark Schulman, "Control Mechanisms Inside the Media," in John Downing et al., *Questioning the Media. A Critical Introduction* (London: Sage, 1990: 75–83, 114–21). For the media's bottom-line mentality, Bagdikian (see note 1), *passim*; for the objectivity of journalists, Lichter, Rothman, and Lichter (see note 1), pp. 123–9, 294–7. Such observations also apply to NPR and PBS, which risk their funding if they offend the government or fail to attract local donors, and whose journalists and administrators come from the same pool of professionals as those of the commercial organizations.

12 This paper was originally given in August 1993 at the annual convention of the American Sociological Association in Miami.

13 Bagdikian (see note 1), pp. 111–31, noted the integrity of the *New Yorker's* editor, William Shawn, who ignored advertisers in order to continue to publish a magazine for a select audience. Of course, the commercial aspect remained, and Shawn was able to ignore the one only because he catered to the other. Bagdikian argues that newspapers actually appeal to more restricted audiences now in terms of their ability to consume than when advertising was less of a factor and papers had to appeal to a larger part of the community. Observations about the large, mainstream media also apply to small publications such as the *Progressive*, which make no secret of their biases, but seem to operate under the illusion that revealing their agenda makes them morally superior to the less forthright mainstream media. In general, the media appear to ignore pressure, or flak, from those who do not

share their ideological outlook, but seem more sensitive to criticism from those who do, especially if they advertise.

14 Philip Gaunt, *Choosing the News: The Profit Factor in News Selection* (Westport, CT: Greenwood Press, 1990), offers a good summary of recent work on the news and suggests that selection of news in regional papers in France, Britain, and the United States is governed by various factors that tend to maximize profits, but include such intangible variables as the public's image of journalism and the journalists' image of themselves.

15 Those who craft the news rarely have the leisure to think through the ramifications of what they are doing, and we can assume that the ideological slant of what one sees on television, hears on radio, or reads in newspapers is both unconscious and unintentional. Periodicals are somewhat unique, owing to the relative leisure with which they are published and the overt bias of most. Richard Gruneau and Robert A. Hackett, "The Production of T.V. News," in John Downing et al. (see note 11), pp. 281–94. Also Lichter, Rothman, Lichter (see note 1), pp. 20–53, for a "group portrait" of the media elite, and pp. 54–165 for a discussion of how the news is constructed.

16 Annabelle Sreberny-Mohammadi, "U.S. Media Covers the World," in John Downing et al. (see note 11), pp. 297–305. Occasionally, the genres of news and soap opera converge in such "soft" pieces as *Frontline*'s "Romeo and Juliet in Sarajevo," 10 May 1994.

17 The perception of bias is therefore not altogether inaccurate. Most viewers and readers receive only a few bytes of the overall "truth" conveyed in the media, because they lack the time to obtain enough bytes to construct a profound view of reality. Nor are they usually able to critique the media, since the values and techniques that inform media news coverage – from "media logic" to "visual grammar" – are usually arcane concepts to them.

18 Juan Señor tries to get a newsmaker if possible and to avoid "armchair academic analysts," while Evans of CNN was more tolerant of academic types. Bagdikian (see note 1), pp. 182–4, also notes that "at their longest" electronic newscasts contain "less information than half a newspaper page." Cassidy noted that CNN has bureaus overseas as well as free-lance staff in places such as Zagreb to sort out "who's who, what's what, and who's believable." He also noted that "everybody's pissed off" at CNN's coverage, something he takes as a good sign.

19 Telephone interview with Gail Evans, 19 July 1993. Evans noted that while CNN did not like having the leaders of the world speak to each other on its programs and being a party to negotiations, the reality is that this has happened. Indeed, she thought that for someone like Karadžić, CNN was the easiest way to talk to a variety of world leaders. On the other hand, she noted that being based in Atlanta dissolved any illusions that she was at the center of the world, because reality was waiting for her every time she left the studio.

20 Nor would journalists appear to have an interest in challenging guests such as Eagleburger, given that doing so might lead them to refuse a future invitation, and the bread and butter of *MacNeil–Lehrer* has become its ability to book powerful newsmakers who appeal to its upper-middle-class audience, just as *Nightline* depends on a restricted circle of officials and experts to make its shows on foreign policy credible, and CNN needs to convince authorities and experts to speak to its cameras. Telephone interview with Juan Señor, 16 July 1993. Señor manages European coverage for *MacNeil–Lehrer* and briefs interviewers before a program is broadcast. Señor noted that he was interested in booking people with expertise in the area, who were perceived as authorities, and who were intimately involved with

the issues and events being covered, but he was not interested in "armchair analysts" who looked at the world with an academic point of view. In short, he wanted "players" and "newsmakers," and even then he had to clear his guests with at least two editors and up to four other people. He noted that all guests were checked out and pre-interviewed, and he vigorously defended Eagleburger from charges of being pro-Serbian.

21 Peter Glynn, "Yugoblunder," *New Republic*, 24 February 1992. Interviewing reporters and academics is also normal, but merely conceals the real source of what is being discussed, since both reporters and academics depend on government officials or on the American and foreign media, whose coverage in turn is often dependent on government officials in matters of foreign policy. It is rare to get a truly "independent" point of view, which usually sticks out as idiosyncratic and occasionally iconoclastic.

22 The first show featured two Yugoslavs (the Slovene Foreign Minister, Dimitrij Rupel and the Yugoslav ambassador to the UN, Darko Silović), and an English academic (Mark C. Wheeler) who has written a study on British policy in Yugoslavia during World War II, *Britain and the War for Yugoslavia, 1940–1943* (Boulder, Colo.: East European Monographs, 1980). The second was just silly.

23 The tendency to ignore events in the Balkans was reinforced by the war against Iraq in early 1991 and the coup attempt in the USSR later that year. For example, the 23 November 1991 issue of *National Review* was devoted to the Soviet Coup and the USSR, even though by that time the coup had clearly failed and dramatic events were unfolding in Yugoslavia. It was thus clear that the media preferred to focus on large powers and strategically sensitive regions, not small powers and areas of marginal interest in terms of mineral wealth.

24 Typical of the "balanced" coverage provided by this show was its 8 February 1993 segment on Yugoslavia that featured the Croatian "Prime Minister" of Bosnia-Herzegovia, Mile Akmadžić, who reluctantly supported the Vance–Owen plan; Radovan Karadžić, who some already suspected of being a war criminal and used the appearance to promote his point of view; and David Owen, who blamed the Serbs *and* Muslims for failing to "compromise" and claimed that the Croats were "irritated" at the Muslims. Silajdžić, the only Muslim invited, had refused to go on the program, probably because it was clearly weighted to promote the Vance–Owen plan. It would have been less "biased" to have "experts" with different points of view who could have "analyzed" the plan. By inviting only players from Bosnia, the show also implied that neither Serbia nor Croatia played any role in the conflict, whereas it was common knowledge that Serbia was behind Karadžić and Croatia had forces operating in the region. This was followed by a program on 25 March 1993 that devoted a long segment to an interview with "Lord Owen," who repeated the standard line that the conflict was "fundamentally a civil war" with "a confessional aspect," that the Serbs were "testing the mettle of the international community," that the Croats were getting enough arms despite the embargo, and that lifting the embargo would be a "disincentive to the Muslims" to negotiate seriously. "Those people," Owen insisted, "have to live together," and while it was "agonizing" to watch the killing, a military solution was impossible since it would only "tilt the balance."

25 Unfortunately, I did not have available the program summaries for 1992. See *Television News Index and Abstracts* (Nashville, Tenn.: Vanderbilt TV News Archives, 1991), *passim*.

26 Paletz and Entman (see note 8), p.9, note that 70 per cent of weekday news stories on two of the three major networks are the same. The networks devote about 20 per cent of their broadcasts to foreign news.

27 Photographs, of course, can have more of an impact than printed columns, e.g., the publication of a Serbian family mourning a member killed in the fighting probably has as much, if not more, impact that a column noting that Serbian forces had devastated a number of Muslim villages, and if published in juxtaposition with the column, would tend to cancel its message.

28 I have not compiled the 1992 data for *The New York Times*, but I expect them to yield a similar position.

29 Aryeh Neier, "Watching Rights," *Nation*, 21 December 1992.

30 Alexander Cockburn "Beat the Devil," and Anthony Borden, "Bosnian Rescue?," *Nation*, 31 August–7 September 1992. Christopher Hitchens, "Minority Report," *Nation*, 29 March 1993, condemned the Croats for supposedly conniving with Owen against the Bosnian state; and the *Guardian* (UK), 2 August 1992, and television newscasts reported MacKenzie's remarks, as did Newhouse (see note 3) p.69, who also repeated the US accusations that Izetbegović had broken the cease-fire.

31 William Pfaff, "The Shame of Bosnia," *New York Review of Books*, 24 September 1992: 18–19. In a piece written for the *LA Times* and reprinted in the *New York Review of Books*, William Pfaff claimed that both Croats and Serbs "expand by aggressive war, conquest, and 'ethnic' – which in their case means religious – purge and murder." Also Nora Beloff, "Bosnia and the Balkans: An Exchange with Nora Beloff and Theodossis C. Demetracopoulos," "*New York Review of Books*, 8 October 1992: 51, who even blamed Izetbegović for the war in Bosnia because he rejected a power-sharing plan conceived by a political rival despite the fact that it was "common knowledge that the Bosnian Serbs would never willingly agree to be part of a unitary state, in which Muslims and Croats would permanently hold the majority."

Misha Glenny, "The Massacre of Yugoslavia," *New York Review of Books*, 30 January 1992: 30–2, who has written most of the pieces on Bosnia for the *New York Review of Books*, disagreed with Beloff, but he also has portrayed the Croats as guilty as the Serbs for the JNA's attack on Croatia and Serbian ethnic cleansing in both Croatia and Bosnia. Accusing Tudjman and the CDU (Croatian Democratic Union) of being "insensitive" and of discriminating against the Serbs by denying them "cultural autonomy," he claimed that most conflicts in the Krajina were "provoked by the Croat authorities" who were "intimidating local Serbs by a show of force" and he depicted the conflict as a "struggle for control" of the region by Tudjman and Milošević. Glenny portrayed the conflict as "partly a revival of the civil war" of 1941–45, and perceived a "pattern of reciprocal massacre in Yugoslavia," complaining that while the world had been alerted to "the crimes being committed by the JNA and the Chetniks at the expense of the Croats. Unfortunately, the suffering of the innocent Serbs in Croatia has had no such attention." He thus urged those "who rightly denounce the Belgrade regime for its aggression" to be "concerned about aggression against the Serbs in Croatia as well." Glenny inflated the Serbian population of Croatia to "between 12 and 20 percent," claiming that there were no reliable statistics. Aware that the war in Croatia was "largely the consequence of aggression sponsored by the Serbian regime in Belgrade and the JNA," Glenny put Zagreb on the same moral level by claiming that the war "also partly originated in the contemptuous treatment of the Serb minority by the Tudjman government."

Glenny "Yugoslavia: The Revenger's Tragedy," *New York Review of Books*, 13 August 1992: 37–38, claimed that Serbs *and* Croats were struggling to carve up Bosnia, that while "the extent of crimes committed by Serb volunteers [sic] is far greater than those for which the Muslims and Croats must bear responsibility," there had been "documented cases of Croat atrocities against Serbs" and that Croats in Hercegovina considered association with Bosnian Muslims "an insult." He even implied that Bosnian Croats were all "Ustashas." Glenny's own bias was clear in his depiction of the Bosnian Territorial Defense as comprised largely of "the lumpen proletariat and criminal fraternity of Sarajevo," and it is clear that one cannot expect much, save a little heroism, from such trash.

Glenny's point of view is similar to that of Aleksa Djilas, whose "The Nation That Wasn't" appeared in *New Republic*, 21 September 1993, along with articles by A. Husarska and N. A. Mousavizadeh.

32 In the spring of 1992, the *New Yorker* published a subtle variation on the theme of shared guilt by citing Pajić's condemnation of Serbian TV for painting Croats as Ustasha, of Croatian TV for depicting Serbs as Chetniks, and of both for playing up Muslims as "unreliable, dangerous fundamentalists." Yet both Pajić and Milos Vasić, the Serbian editor of *Vreme*, were upset with reporting that portrayed "the Balkans as a hopeless tangle of ancient blood feuds," because, "If you make all three sides equally guilty, you justify inaction," Mr. Vasić said. "Quiet Voices from the Balkans," 15 March 92, *New Yorker*. According to Pajić, a Bosnian Serb, "Serbian and Croatian propaganda scenarios" warned of "an Islamic fundamentalist state being established in Europe" and the Bosnian government was fighting "an essentially defensive war against Serbian and Croatian expansionism."

Even David Rieff, whose November 1992 essay in the *New Yorker* is a serious effort to analyze the crisis, is somewhat ambivalent regarding who, or what, is really to blame for the bloodletting. Although he begins his piece with an account of mass murder by Serbian and Montenegrin forces during the Balkan wars of 1912–13, Rieff then notes that history is merely replaying itself in Bosnia and Croatia, despite a "European conceit – born of wishful thinking and of the complacency that afflicted so much of Western Europe until the collapse of Communism made everyone take a second look – that people on the old Continent, even in the Balkans, would not go on slaughtering each other so regularly." He blames Karadžić and Milošević for "the Balkan holocaust," but he also thinks that the tendency for Serbs, Croats, and Muslims to massacre one another shows that "hatred was the real face of Yugoslavia's warring nations, and that ethnic cleansing was its emblem." There is even a sad echo of Steel's callous dismissal of events in Bosnia – that "terrible things are always happening to innocent people everywhere [sic] in the world," and the "human species thrives on violence and expresses it politically through tribal groups" – in Rieff's resigned observations that, "There is savagery in every *civil* war" and that in the former Yugoslavia "atrocities have been committed by all sides" as "the desire for revenge has taken the form of further atrocities." But Rieff also noted that if "such excesses" are part of civil wars, in Bosnia they "are also a Serb war aim."

David Rieff, "Letter from Bosnia, Original Virtue, Original Sin," *New Yorker*, 23 November 92: 82, 87, 91, 93–4, noted that in October 1992, Croat forces in Travnik turned on the Muslims there. According to Rieff, before 1941 Yugo-slavism had been only "a euphemism for Serbian dominance" and after 1945 had been imposed by Tito's regime. Thus, even Slavenka Drakulić, an intelligent dissident, "conceded that before there was ethnic cleansing, there had been ethnic thinking in all the constituent parts of former Yugoslavia," and Rieff recalled people speaking "rapturously of the nobility of their own national group and the commensurate baseness of all other national groups" well before 1991, and now even "the most liberal and soft-spoken non-combatants indulge in the same essentialist mythmaking," and are "being overcome by fantasies of original virtue for their own group and original sin for their enemies." He thus interpreted a Croatian woman's off-hand, and class-bound, remark that "we Croatians simply *detest* onions" as "the old Yugoslav complaint, as lethal in its way as the land mines on the road to Velika Kladuša or the racialist speeches of Dr. Radisav Vukić" who "had said that for him the children of mixed marriages . . . 'are already dead'" the Bosnians who saw Serbian history as "a case study in evil" and Croats as a people who did everything "as if they were wearing gloves.

33 Robert Guskind, "Letter from Croatia: Mostly They Sob," *National Journal*, 4 January 1992: 29–30, and "Ethnic Time Bombs," *National Journal*, 18 January 1992, wrote that "centuries-old enmities" had encouraged the fighting and destruction in Bosnia. He condemned both Tudjman and Milošević for unleashing "ethnic hatred" and blamed both sides for breaking cease-fires. He noted that "Croatian 'Ustashe' and Serbian 'Chetnik' irregulars roam[ed] free" near the Karlovac suburb of Turanj in "a deadly no-man's land", and he partially exculpated the JNA by claiming that there had been a "dangerous breakdown in the internal discipline" of the JNA and insisting that Chetniks and Ustashe acted on their own to commit such heinous acts as the downing on 7 January of an EC helicopter with five observers. Guskind quoted the Croatian commander, Anton Tus, who called on the world to "hurry up and come to our rescue to stop the killing of civilians and the destruction of our cities" and declared that the Croats would fight to the bitter end. Given that the Serbian Foreign Minister Vladislav Jovanovich warned that the Serbs were "ready to commit collective suicide rather than be forced to live in a Croatian state," Guskind perceived a "recipe for disaster," because the JNA would "methodically inflict any level of punishment to win" and the Croats, and presumably the Serbs, should their enemies ever get any weapons, would "suffer unthinkable casualties and destruction rather than surrender."

34 Nora Beloff, "Eastern Approaches," *National Review*, 13 April 1992, one of Serbia's most vociferous defenders, implied that all sides were to blame for the killing when she wrote that "all over Yugoslavia," which was "bristling with weapons," an "inflamed nationalism is submerging morality" while militias "on both sides" loot, pillage, and kill.

35 Ronald Steel, "Let Them Sink," *New Republic*, 2 November 1992: 15, dismissed the conflict in Bosnia as merely one of several "tribal wars," noting that "although detention camps [sic] and 'ethnic cleansing' are appalling, this reportedly takes place in Croatian-controlled areas as well" and was not as bad as what had occurred in Central America.

36 *Time*, 22 February 1993: 48–50, for Morrow, and 11 January 1993 for Nelan. Lance Morrow reported that "atavistic nationalisms, or tribalisms, may lie just beneath the civil veneer" in Bosnia, and to balance reports of mass rapes by Serbian forces, he noted that EC sources had reported "some rapes" by non-Serbs, just as Bruce Nelan had earlier reported Eagleburger's even-handed denunciation of four Serbs, two Croats, and a Muslim as war criminals.

37 Joseph Joffe, "The New Europe: Yesterday's Ghosts," *Foreign Affairs* (1992–3): 29–43, esp. 30, 31, 35, explained that Yugoslavia was an "explosive (cold war) concoction of warring tribes and nations," and therefore, even should the killing stop for a while, "Serbs, Croats, and Muslims would still be there

afterwards, full of hatred and lusting for revenge." He also inflated the Serbian population of Croatia from 11.5 percent to 17 percent. He claimed that because the Serbs were in charge of the military, bureaucracy, and secret police, "Slovenia and Croatia absconded" in 1991 and thereby triggered the subsequent slaughter.

38 One of the most extreme examples of tarring all groups with the same genocidal brush was provided by David Andersen, a former US Ambassador to Yugoslavia in a February 1992 op. ed., piece in the *Wall Street Journal*. Andersen depicted the Yugoslav crisis as the result of "tribal antagonisms" and he put a "curse" on both sides, claiming that the breakup need never have happened had there been "wiser leadership in *all* of the republics . . . less emotion and more common sense . . . and a readiness by the Yugoslavs generally to see the modern world as it is." David Andersen, "A Diplomat Explains Yugoslavia," *Wall Street Journal*, 21 February 1992: A14. He also noted that "better diplomacy by a disinterested Western Europe and U.S." would have helped to prevent armed conflict.

39 Newhouse (see note 3), pp. 60–3.

40 Radek Sikorski, "Déjà Vu/War in Europe Again," *National Review*, 16 December 1991: 40–2.

41 Andersen (see note 38), p. A14.

42 William Pfaff, "Reflections (The Absence of Empire)," *New Yorker*, 10 August 1992: 69.

43 The *Nation*, 31 August–7 September 1992. Alexander Cockburn rationalized Serbian aggression by claiming that Yugoslavia's provincial borders had been drawn to "punish" the Serbs, thereby repeating a favorite Serbian argument, put forward by Alex Dragnich, a Serbian nationalist and propagandist, as well as Emeritus Professor from Rutgers and associate of the Hoover Institute. See, for example, his *Serbs and Croats. The Struggle in Yugoslavia* (New York: Harcourt, Brace, Jovanovich, 1992): 121. In 1992 the *Nation*'s coverage of the crisis was extremely limited, with articles by Borden on 27 April, 31 August–7 September, and 12 October, a surrealist piece by Slavenka Drakulić on 15 June, two essays by Hitchens, both anti-Croatian, on 14 and 21 September, two by Neier, and one by Cockburn. The *Progressive*, one of the other standbys on the Left, devoted no articles to the crisis, but in July 1992, Erwin Knoll argued in "The Uses of the Holocaust" that he found comparisons with Bosnia "inappropriate and even offensive." Amazingly, he agreed with Ronald Steel, who argued that what was occurring in Bosnia was "not genocide and not the Holocaust." Elie Wiesel had taken a similar position on *Nightline* on 2 December 1992, while on 22 April 1993, Leon Wieseltier invoked the Holocaust and condemned the "realist analysis" as "spectacularly inadequate," noting that the genocide occurring in Bosnia was not the same as a civil war.

44 Gerald B. Helman and Steven R. Ratner, "Saving Failed States," *Foreign Policy* (Winter 1992/3): 3–20, esp. 12–16; and David A. Kay's critical letter in the Spring 1993 issue: 169–70.

45 Paul Johnson, "Wanted: A New Imperialism," *National Review*, 14 December 1992: 28–34, and Boutros Boutros-Ghali, "Empowering the United Nations," *Foreign Affairs* (Winter 1992–3): esp. 89–90. Gregory F. Treverton, "The New Europe," *Foreign Affairs* (Spring 1992): 105, argued that the crisis forced the West to choose between ignoring the crisis or intervening, i.e., enforcing the peace rather than keeping it, while Radek Sikorski advocated the latter course as early as 1991 because it was clear that diplomatic recognition and economic sanctions were insufficient to curb Serbian expansion. Radek Sikorski (see note 40), pp. 40–2. Raising the specter of Munich, Sikorski urged

the West to deliver an "old-fashioned ultimatum" to Serbia to get out of Croatia or see Europe arm and train the Croatian armed forces. "Otherwise," he warned, "this will be a long war" because neither side would "yield an inch," and while the Croats would lose, they would simply wait 20 years to fight a new war to reclaim their lost territories.

46 In the spring of 1992, Joseph Nye argued in *Foreign Affairs* that since less than 10 percent of 170 existing states are ethnically homogeneous, and half have one group that is at most 75 percent of the population, self-determination is a chimera. Later that year, Robert Cullen insisted that because US opposition to self-determination had failed in Yugoslavia, Washington should champion respect for individual rather than collective rights within existing states. Robert Cullen, "Human Rights Quandary," *Foreign Affairs* (Winter 1992/3): 81, 84–6, thought "the disastrous potential of the assertion of collective rights in the postcommunist era" argued for the granting of full rights to minorities within existing states, e.g., to Palestinians *within* an Israeli state.

Stephen John Stedman, "The New Interventionists," *Foreign Affairs* (1992/3): 3, 7–8, 14–16, ridiculed "the new interventionists" for seeking "to end civil wars [sic] and stop governments from abusing the rights of their peoples." Arguing that "civil wars" are "no more bloody" nor any more prevalent than in the past, he dismissed "humanitarian concerns" as insufficient to justify the use of force, especially since "Bosnia could rank below Sudan, Liberia and East Timor" in terms of "deaths and genocidal campaigns." According to Stedman, the war in Bosnia is "a war of secession with an internal war fought among a diverse population" and echoing Jomini, he warned that "peace-enforcement" is harder in "civil wars" than in "interstate wars," because in the former civilians and soldiers are indistinguishable. He therefore concluded that the "warring parties" in Bosnia should end the war themselves, either politically or militarily. Steel (see note 35), pp. 15–16, also rejects intervention, using many of the same arguments and warning that should the West miraculously defeat the Serbs, whom even the Germans never managed to defeat, "the Croats would rush in to take their share, and the Muslims to exact retribution," because that "is the history of the Balkans."

47 Charles William Maynes, "Containing Ethnic Conflict," *Foreign Policy* (Winter 1992–3): 7–11.

48 *Nation*, 31 August–7 September 1992.

49 Robert Guskind (see note 33, "Letter from Croatia") pp. 29–30.

50 Blaine Harden, "Serbia's Treacherous Gang of Three," *Washington Post*, 7 February 1993, blamed Milošević, Šešelj, and Ražnjatović. Also Newhouse (see note 3), p.63, who blames Milošević and Tudjman; and editorials of 18 April, 5 and 10 May, 20 November, and 23 December 1992 in the *Washington Post*.

51 David Andersen (see note 38) thought that Tito, in an effort to defuse power and "keep the Serbs from dominating" the other nationalities, compounded the problem by promulgating a constitution in 1974 that returned power to the "republican fiefdoms," without demanding "responsibility for use of this new power." In an interesting twist, Radek Sikorski (see note 40) considered the crisis to be the result of "a fusion of nationalism and post-Communist politics," blaming Churchill for allowing Tito to take power in 1943 and Milošević for using force to create a "unitary Serbian state with access to the Adriatic." But he concluded that the JNA, whose officer corps feared losing its privileged position should Yugoslavia break up, had acted on its own when it attacked Slovene and Croatian schools, churches, and hospitals. He also claimed that the Croats and Slovenes felt "that they were getting a raw deal out of the federal pork barrel," while the "entrenched post-Communist

bureaucracies" feared losing their jobs if Yugoslavia broke up. Robert Guskind agreed, citing Vuk Drašković to show that generals had enjoyed free housing, villas, and pensions in Yugoslavia.

52 Nora Beloff (see note 34), and the *Nation*, 31 August–7 September 1992. Robert Guskind (see note 33), pp. 29–30, noted that the Croats saw a Serbian plot to take over most of the former Yugoslavia. Beloff concluded that, "Neither Milošević nor Tudjman deserves sympathy – let alone military aid." Beloff even argued that the JNA was "not, legally or practically, under Miloševićs orders," and "the endless succession of broken agreements and violated ceasefires" were due to the generals acting on their own. Neither Beloff nor Cockburn was critical of the Serbian Orthodox Church. Max Primorac, "Serbia's War/Out of the Ruble" (Mostar), *National Review*, 14 September 1992: 46. Germany, Austria, the Ukraine, Hungary, and Italy favored recognizing Croatia and Slovenia in late 1991, while France and Britain opposed recognition and Bush had warned the EC against it. The claim that there is a conspiracy to reconstruct an apparently Catholic Fourth Reich is one of the favorite rationalizations used by such Serbian apologists as General Marko Negovanović, Yugoslavia's Assistant Minister of Defense in 1991. Robert Guskind (see note 33), "Ethnic Time Bombs" and *The New York Times*, 15 December 1991: A1.

53 Noel Malcolm, "On the Scene," *National Review*, 29 July 1991: 18, also saw the JNA as "out of control," and warned that the Croatians were susceptible to becoming "the very kind of resentful, vendetta-obsessed isolationists that Western policy-makers should most fear." He condemned efforts to distinguish "western" Croats from "eastern" Serbs as "over-simple" and "morally repugnant" because doing so "dooms all liberal, Western-looking, anti-Communist Serbs to a historically predetermined future" and ignores Croatian "ethnic anti-Serbian hostility." Malcolm favored recognition of Croatia and Slovenia, but claimed that the JNA had made them anti-communist, anti-federal, anti-Serbian, and pro-Western. *The New York Times*, 23 December 1991: A8, also blamed Milošević for the violence, then confused matters by noting that he was to the "left" of the Serbian nationalist Vojislav Šešelj.

54 In her paper at the *International Conference on Bosnia-Hercegovina*, Ankara, 17–19 April 1995, Patrica Forestier noted a systematic effort by Serbian leaders to use the techniques of "ethnopsychiatry" to prepare the Serbian people for war against their neighbor. At a conference on Bosnia at Chapel Hill in March 1993, Slaven Letica made a similar point regarding the use of psychology by Karadžić.

55 Rieff (see note 32), pp. 93, 85–6, discerned "a coherent strategy" that had the JNA or Karadžić's forces occupy areas only after the White Eagles had finished, concluding that "the odds favored Karadžić and the hard men."

56 Newhouse (see note 30), p. 60, noted that the "buzz words" at the Pentagon were "quagmire" and "Dien Bien Phu," and that London saw Bosnia as another Northern Ireland. For Colin Powell's fears, see *Newsweek*, 26 April and 3, 10, and 17 May 1993. In the 10 May issue John Barry noted that Powell's "doctrine of overwhelming force" had become "a pretext for overwhelming reluctance to get involved in the Balkans; and a week later David Hackworth warned that the US would only get "stuck in a bottomless swamp." "The bottom line," he wrote, "is: we don't have the right stuff to do the job; and if we did it, it wouldn't work against a guerrilla fighting in favorable terrain."

57 Aryeh Neier, "Watching Rights," the *Nation*, 18 January 1993: 43, noted that the Serbs attributed "collective guilt" to their victims and were busy avenging crimes that occurred 500 years ago.

58 The *Nation*, 31 August–7 September 1992; also Borden's remark that Izetbegović "could certainly have done more to address Serb concerns." For statistics on the number killed during World War II, see Bogoljub Kočović, *Žrtve Drugog svetskog rata u Jugoslaviji* (London: Naše delo, 1985), *passim*, who estimated that 487,000 Serbians, 207,000 Croats, and 75,000 Muslims died during the war; and Kazimir Katalinić, "Hrvatske i srpske žrtve 1941–1945," *Republika Hrvatska* (April 1988): 15–63, who estimated that 330,000 Serbians, 276,000 Croats and 96,000 Muslims perished. While Kočović thinks 334,000 Serbians died in the NDH (Independent State of Croatia), Katalinić sets the figure at 235,000.

59 *The New York Times*, 23 December 1991, A8, did report that while the Serbian uprising had begun in Krajina in the summer of 1990, there was no Croatian response until the fall of 1991.

60 Robert Guskind (see note 33, "Ethnic Time Bombs") also believed that the "roots" of conflict could be traced back 600 years.

61 Beloff (see note 34) has tried to undercut Croatian claims to independence by claiming that no "historic Croatia" existed before 1941, when Hitler created the NDH, which was ruled by Ustashi, "the Croatian equivalent of the Nazis," who killed "at least 350,000 Serbs." For Beloff, the "present resistance of Serbs to Croat domination cannot be fully appreciated without an understanding of this genocide," for which the Serbs are just now getting their "revenge." She claimed that fighting in Croatia began in 1990 when Croats "tried to take over contested regions [of historic Croatia] and were shot by Serbs," and she clearly blames the Croatians for this turn of events, claiming that Tudjman has "presided over a revival of the Ustashi's 'Croatia for the Croats' racialism" and Croatia discriminates against Serbs by taxing their properties, failing to protect "Serbs or mixed families from arson and assault," and allowing a street and a school to be named after Mile Budak, an Ustaša leader *and* one of Croatia's leading literary figures in the 1900s, a fact Beloff fails to mention. Following Beloff's logic, one would have to excise Ezra Pound from English literature.

62 A similar attitude informed much media coverage of the Falkland crisis in the early 1980s. Rieff (see note 32), pp. 83, 84, 87, 93, noted that the "Germans and their Croat allies" had practiced "ethnic cleansing" during World War II, and he reported a young Serb's remark that the "Mujadhein" who had attacked Serbians in Bosnia were worse than the "handžar" of World War II. But he did not mention Serbian collaboration or atrocities and complained that it was "almost easier to get a history lesson than to get a straight answer to what happened in this place where one is standing with one's interlocuter," because all Yugoslavs were "more likely to talk about the massacre of the Serbs by the Croat Fascists in the Second World War, or the dream of Greater Serbia, which dates back to the nineteenth century." But then, Rieff was concerned with the ethnic cleansing occurring in Bosnia in 1992, not historic rationalizations for such actions. The Handžar was an SS formation of Bosnian Muslims. Rieff reported that Serbs had divided the Muslims into: (1) professionals, local notables, and able-bodied young men – who were generally killed; (2) those being held in "intelligence camps" – who would be killed or released later; and (3) those due for release – who were housed in "open centers" accessible to the Red Cross, Caritas, and other relief organizations.

63 The Serbs have argued that the Croats and Bosnians are the aggressors, and they see the West's condemnation of their actions as unfair. *The New York Times*, 18 October 1992, Roger Cohen. How unfair the *The New York Times* can be was shown on 20 May 1993, when the paper ran an op. ed. piece by

an "anonymous U.S. official," "End the War in Bosnia Peacefully," that noted that fighting in Mostar had "reminded the world that Croatia as well as Serbia must be brought to heel if there is to be progress toward peace," then went on to argue for a policy of "safe-havens" based on the Vance–Owen plan and urged sanctions against Croatia unless it stopped "ethnic-cleansing." Clearly, the piece was not only intended to argue for a diplomatic solution that the Bosnians themselves opposed, but also to smear Croatia with the same genocidal brush as Serbia, even though "ethnic cleansing" was originally a Serbian concept carried out in both Croatia and Bosnia by Serbian forces.

64 Max Primorac (see note 52), p. 46.

65 *The New York Times*, 21 October 1992: A10, Paul Lewis, worried that the Croats might attack the Serbian "enclave" in Krajina, a not altogether fanciful notion given that the "enclave" was viewed by the Croats as a rebellious region of their state. Also Guskind (see note 33, both articles), who cited a Serbian general, Marko Negovanović, and a Croatian politician, Franjo Gregurić, but rather than explicitly condemning the JNA, whose guilt he had implied, he complained that "who was 'protected' from whom" was not clear to "an outsider unbeholden to 500-year-old ethnic hatred." He also reported that during the siege, the JNA fired 15,000 shells daily against the civilians remaining in the city, and that the JNA had attacked Osijek, whose population was 80 percent Croatian. He also quoted Franjo Gregurić's accusation that the JNA was out "to destroy the very roots of Croatia" and reported that the Serbs were "resettling thousands of refugees" in Croatia, which had seen a third of its economy destroyed, suffered $6.0 billion in damages, lost a third of its jobs, and suffered 10,000 dead and 50,000 wounded, while Serbia had undergone only 300 percent inflation. Guskind did not give the nationality of the war's 500,000 refugees, but it is unlikely that he took seriously Negovanić's claim that the JNA had "liberated" Vukovar, where Serbs were only a third of the population, in order "to free the people from the hell they were going through," nor the Serb's argument that the JNA "had the war forced upon it" by the Croats and that its "sole aim" was to prevent "the outbreak of bloody interethnic conflict and a repetition of the genocide committed in Croatia during World War II" and "to protect Serbians from the threat of genocide."

66 This, of course, is a variation on the Churchillian theme, since the idea is that the Serbian media, controlled by a few evil men, has brainwashed the average Serb. Rieff (see note 33), p. 84, reported that most Serbs refused to believe that ethnic cleansing was occurring, even though "Serb colonization" was "easy to see in Banja Luka and in other towns and villages all over northern Bosnia as well as in the Republic of Serbian Krajina." He also put down the excesses of "Serb fighters" to their belief that they were "retaliating" for Muslim atrocities, owing to biased media reporting in Serb-controlled areas. The media were very quick to note both Croatian and Muslim atrocities in 1993, e.g., *Day 1/one*, ABC, 9 May 1993, opened with a report of an atrocity committed by Croatians, and repeated the "civil war" theme of "neighbors" turning on each other.

67 The idea that the Serbs carry the "Yugoslav idea" and have a right to those areas inhabited by "Yugoslavs" as well as those occupied by "Serbs" is another theme of Serbian propaganda that has been picked up in the American media, partly from analysts like Nora Beloff, partly from the White House, whose efforts to "blame the victim" in June 1991 reinforced the image of the Serbs as trying to preserve a Yugoslav state, as Michael Lind noted in "Serbicide," *New Republic*, 22 June 1992: 16–18. Lind was the Executive Editor of the *National Interest*. Obsessed with keeping the USSR together and maintaining American

"military hegemony and political influence" in Europe, the Bush administration threatened Croatia and Slovenia and blamed them for the crisis that resulted from their secession. Beloff (see note 34), inflated the non-Croat population to 17 percent of Croatia's population, and argued that since the "hodge-podge of nationalities" in Yugoslavia make self-determination "a delusion," a third of the area claimed by Zagreb should be ruled by Serbs and "Yugoslavs" of mixed parentage. Beloff has published her point of view in the *Washington Post* and the *New York Review of Books*. In late 1991, the *The New York Times* reported that the Serbian president, Branko Kostić, wanted to maintain a "small" Yugoslavia that would include areas in both Croatia and Bosnia. It also noted that while Izetbegović had asked the EC to recognize Bosnia and requested troops from the UN, the Serbs in Bosnia had vowed to create a "Serb" republic. The impression was left of a weak Bosnian president desperate for outside help to create a Bosnian state, of a Serbian leadership that desired to maintain some sort of "south Slav" state, and of Bosnian Serbs who were acting on their own.

68 Newhouse (see note 30), p. 70.
69 Charles Lane, "The Ghosts of Serbia," *Newsweek*, 19 April 1993.
70 Walter Russell Mead, "Looking at Bosnia, Clinton Sees Only Ugly, Bad Choices," *Los Angeles Times*, 19 April 1993: M1, M6. On 2 May 1993, Senator Dole noted that it was too bad the Serbs had won on *This Week with David Brinkley*, and William Perry still favored "reconciliation" when he appeared on the *MacNeil–Lehrer Newshour* on 6 October 1994.
71 Primorac (see note 52), p. 46; and Maynes (see note 47), pp. 9–10.
72 Stedman (see note 46), pp. 14–15, implied that the Serb forces controlled Bosnia and warned that attacking them there would involve the UN in "a protracted guerrilla war."
73 Peter Jennings, "Bosnia: Land of the Demons," ABC, 18 March 1993.
74 Michael Lind (see note 67).
75 Rieff (see note 32), pp. 83, 92.
76 For example, Yigal Chazan, "Serbs Like Easing of Sanctions, Decry Split from Bosnian Kin," *Christian Science Monitor*, 27 Sept. 1994; and "The International Hour," *CNN*, 3 May 1993.
77 For example, of 33 editorials and op. ed. pieces appearing in the *Washington Post* in 1992, 14 dealt with the role of the US, EC, or UN, seven with Serbia, seven with ethnic cleansing, and one with the Croats. None dealt directly with the internal politics in Croatia and Bosnia.
78 Newhouse (see note 30), esp. p. 71, betrayed how superficial such pieces could be when he repeatedly blamed the Germans for the war owing to their push to recognize the "break-away" republics and opined that this was a grave error since "most borders in Eastern Europe are recent and arbitrary." In fact, they are neither the one nor the other, although Serb propagandists have repeatedly played up the notion that they are both.
79 *The New York Times*, 5 May 1992: A10. Through the fall of 1991, Washington threatened and cajoled the EC in an effort to prevent recognition of the secessionist republics, and not until 7 April 1992 did the United States recognize Croatia, Slovenia, and Bosnia, well after the EC had done so. Senator Dole lamented the Bush administration's error in giving Milošević a "green light" to attack Slovenia in 1991 on *This Week with David Brinkley*, 2 May 1993. David Gompert, "How to Defeat Serbia," *Foreign Affairs* (July–Aug. 1994), 34–35, tries to exonerate Baker of responsibility for the JNA's attack on Slovenia.
80 Andersen (see note 38); and Sikorski (see note 40), pp. 40–2. Guskind (see note 33, "Ethnic Time Bombs") also saw the introduction of 10,000 UN troops as

beneficial to both sides – "a victory of sorts" for the Croats who had "been pleading for foreign intervention and recognition" even though the JNA controlled a third of Croatia, and a coup for the Serbs, who had been pressing for UN forces since November. According to Guskind, a "possible reason" for the Serb "change of heart" might be that the JNA had "seized all the Croatian territory it wants, and a U.N. peacekeeping role [was] now viewed as a way to hold on to some land" in Croatia, where the Serbs were "resettling thousands of refugees." *The New York Times*, 1 January 1992, was sympathetic to Cyrus Vance's efforts to replace the JNA with 10,000 UN peacekeepers in the Krajina, portrayed the Croats as on the offensive, and noted, without specifying nationality, that 600,000 people had left their homes in Croatia since 25 June 1991.

81 Boutros-Ghali (see note 46), pp. 89–90; and Colin L Powell, "U.S. Forces: Challenges Ahead," *Foreign Affairs* (Winter 1992/3): 36–7, also repeated what has become a refrain for the US military, that before committing itself, it wanted to be assigned "clear and unambiguous objectives."

82 Roy Gutman complained that his efforts to bring the existence of Serbian "death camps" to the attention of the US government in mid-1992 were futile, while low-level State Department officials complained of being muzzled. Typically, the media presented both sides, giving Lawrence Eagleburger ample time to rebut his accusers. Peter Jennings, "While America Watched: The Bosnia Tragedy," *ABC*, 1994. For Scowcroft, and Senator Joseph Liebermann, who thought that the Serbs had done "pretty well here," *This Week with David Brinkley*, 9 May 1993.

83 Primorac (see note 52), p. 48. *The New York Times*, 21 October 1992: A10, Paul Lewis, reported that Vance and Owen had persuaded Tudjman, Izetbegović, and Ćosić to agree to work for (1) peace, (2) mutual recognition, and (3) a reversal of ethnic cleansing, as UN troops began to occupy areas of Bosnia to oversee the delivery of humanitarian aid. Rieff (see note 32), pp. 92, 85, also pointed out the shortcomings of such a policy in the *New Yorker*, noting that the UN either condemned Muslims to death by refusing to move them out of Serbian areas or became "accomplices in the process of ethnic cleansing, since the transport of this Muslim population out of the region has been the Serbs' primary goal from the start." He also cited José Mendiluce, who provided one of the few attempts to set events in Bosnia in any sort of context by noting that the first refugees "displaced by the fighting between Serbs and Croats" had been created in the summer of 1991, with more, presumably all Croatian, displaced by the "first massive campaigns of ethnic cleansing on the Serb side" after the JNA withdrew from the Krajina, and many more after the Serbs attacked Bosnia when it declared its independence. Mendiluce noted that the UNHCR was not "set up to handle such a crisis," and while "dedicated," the UN official conceded that his efforts to evacuate Muslims from certain death in places such as Zvornik had only helped the Serbian policy of ethnic cleansing.

84 Stedman (see note 46), pp. 12–13.

85 Rieff (see note 32), p. 92, noted that the European nations had written off "Bosnian refugees," that Croat "antipathy" to Muslims is "so deep" that not even the suffering of the refugees "could dilute it," and that, "To the Serbs, the Muslims are no longer human." He also implied that Yugoslavs are somehow incapable of normal feelings when he wrote that the former Yugoslavia "is a part of the world where almost the only pity on offer is self-pity." Andersen (see note 38), blamed their problems on the "Yugoslavs themselves" – "a perverse group of folks, near tribal in their behavior, suspicious of each other (with usually sound reasons), friendly on the outside

but very cynical within, ever ready for a war or a battle, proud of their warrior history, and completely incapable of coming to grips with the modern world." To "go wandering in Yugoslavia" was therefore "an adventure" in which one encountered "strange people who seemed caught up in some time-warp."

86 Rieff (see note 32), p. 88.

87 Guskind (see note 28, "Ethnic Time Bombs") noted the lack of mechanisms to enforce cease-fires; and Rieff (see note 32), noted that Mendiluce considered the refugee problems "an impossible situation," because there were no "mechanisms to deal with ethnic cleansing." Paul Johnson (see note 45), pp. 28–34, made the legalistic argument that war in Yugoslavia could not have been prevented because "there was no formal act of aggression breaking the UN charter, which does not deal with the dissolution of member-states."

88 *MacNeil–Lehrer Newshour*, 25 March 1993. Cheriff Bassiouni, who oversaw the UN investigation of war crimes in Bosnia, has accused both Owen and Boutros-Ghali of attempting to keep the investigation from antagonizing the Serbs. R. C. Longworth, "Peace vs. Justice," *Chicago Tribune*, 2 Sept. 1994.

89 Another flurry occurred in the Spring of 1993, when Clinton seemed about to act; and another followed, again owing to hints from the White House that the United States might act unilaterally. Citations from Andersen (see note 38), who believed that the Yugoslavs should be left to "exhaust themselves," while it is clear that only those besieged by the Serbs are being exhausted. MacKenzie has been on a number of talk shows and he was featured prominently while he was in Bosnia as the UN Commander in Sarajevo. His remarks regarding the inability of "thirty-seven" German divisions to defeat the Serbs and his accusations that the Muslims had shelled their own people to get media attention were duly carried by the major stations on 31 August 1992. *The New York Times*, 24 December 1991, reported that although Germany had recognized Croatia and Slovenia, it could send only civilian aid, not troops or weapons, causing Munich's *Süddeutsche Zeitung* to criticize recognition as an empty gesture and Alija Izetbegović to ask for a UN force to be deployed.

90 Joffe (see note 32), p. 33; and Maynes (see note 42), pp. 3–5, 7, 10–11, saw Yugoslavia as a test case, but of a very narrow and rather cynical set of principles. This tack was taken by Ted Koppel regarding outrage at the Serbian policy of systematically raping Bosnian women when he asked Robert Dole if the American public was ready to pay the "high cost" of getting "involved." *Nightline*, 14 Jan. 1993.

91 David Hackworth, *Newsweek*, 12 October 1992: 46–7, had reported the effectiveness of Croat anti-tank missiles as well as the imbalance in tank forces around Sarajevo, where the Serbs had 300 and the Muslims two tanks.

92 Guskind (see note 33), "Ethnic Time Bombs") was aware that there were "many conflicting views – all of them passionately held – on the most basic issues in Yugoslavia," but he saw only the "single bloody reality" that "Serbia and Croatia are stuck in a vicious circle of escalating violence and revenge, and the leaders of both republics are either willing or unable to compromise" as worth considering seriously.

93 Malcolm (see note 53), p. 18. In a rather transparent effort to show that good Serbs were suffering as much as Croats or Bosnians because they have bad leaders, the *New Yorker*, "Quiet Voices from the Balkans," reported Daniel Plesch's remark that Serbs sometimes buy the opposition newspaper *Vreme* "just to have it in their homes, so that they can point to it and feel that they are *sane* – because they are surrounded by a truly psychotic culture."

94 Rieff (see note 32), pp. 82, 86, noted that while the "presence of armed soldiers in the streets and the roar of MIG fighter jets . . . might have given the impression that here was a war like any other," the "goal of all these planes and armored personnel carriers and men with guns was ethnic cleansing," not the defeat of another armed force. He also quotes Mendiluce, who observed that "People like to simplify the problem with words" and therefore "speak of the Lebanonization of the Balkans today, just as a few years ago they spoke of the Balkanization of Lebanon." However, the UN official believed that "the reality is that at the moment no side is defeated . . . no good will exists, no stalemate has been achieved, and . . . no real international pressure exists." Thus, no solution was possible, and if refugees are not a byproduct of the war, but its aims, their plight is beyond resolution.

95 "Quiet voices from the Balkans," *New Yorker*. The voice was that of Daniel Plesch, who was promoting an Experts Committee on the Crisis in ex-Yugoslavia, which Mr. Pajić, "a longtime human-rights activist and a polished public speaker," chaired. Far from balanced, but covert in its partisanship, the article not only promoted the committee, but defended Pajić against the *The Times*, which had "described Mr. Pajić as an opponent of the Bosnian government, which he is not." Nora Beloff (see note 34), sounded a similar note when she urged "a common set of political and economic arrangements that will protect different communities."

96 Joffe (see note 37), pp. 31–2, noted that the US and EC recognized Bosnia only on 7 April, well after its declaration of independence on 29 February, and the EC's imposition of a trade embargo on Yugoslavia on 27 May.

97 "Quiet Voices from the Balkans," *New Yorker*.

98 Alfred Meyer, "Dog Eats Dog," *Psychology Today* (November–December 1992), p. 95. Silly as Meyer's piece is, it is not that unique in its view that Balkan nationalisms are anachronistic. Malcolm (see note 55), p. 18, noted that while Slovenes look like us, "Old-fashioned atavistic nationalism has not disappeared from Slovenia or Croatia (especially not from Croatia), though it no longer dresses up in peasant costumes." Atavistic nationalism, of course, is the liberal historian's Schumpeterian equivalent of a lack of ritual (Goffian?) coping mechanisms, but the neo-nationalisms that have taken hold in the former Yugoslavia seem to be different in a number of ways, including their use of sophisticated psychological techniques and their grounding in a post-communist mentality.

99 Lawrence C. Soley, *The News Shapers: The Sources Who Explain the News* (Westport, CT: Praeger, 1992), for the use of experts to manage the news, especially 24, where he notes that "unconventional" groups are not considered newsworthy and their spokesmen are dismissed as "partisan," a treatment regularly given to Croatian and Muslim leaders.

100 *The New York Times*, 28 April 1992: A1, A8.

101 The *The New York Times* seemed to bend over backward to give the Serbs a hearing in the spring of 1992. In late April, they published a letter by Alex Dragnich, the author of a number of pro-Serbian academic works, who noted that the JNA in Bosnia was in effect a Bosnian army, since Serbs from the region accounted for 80 percent of its personnel. Yet even were that the case, the JNA was still controlled by Belgrade, and it still possessed a monopoly on heavy and hi-tech weapons. Its ethnic composition was therefore beside the point, yet there was no correction nor explication with the letter. *The New York Times*, 30 April 1992.

102 John Burns, "Their Image Poisoned, The Serbs Voice Dismay" (Belgrade), *The New York Times*, 1 May 1992: A8.

103 Rieff (see note 32), pp. 88, 94. Like Rieff, Max Primorac also departed from the norm when he noted that the US military and various "experts" had compared Yugoslavia to Lebanon, Northern Ireland, and Vietnam in order "to blunt public pressure for intervention," even though air strikes against artillery, lines of communication, and other military targets are feasible. But Primorac believes our goal should be "to repel the aggressor," not "to keep peace" – nor, it is clear, maintain amiable relations on the Security Council – and he echoed the positions of the Croats and Bosnians when he insisted that they could defeat the Serbs by themselves and asked only that the embargo be lifted. But Primorac is unusual in that he criticized Eagleburger's policy to let the Yugoslavs "exhaust themselves" as making for "a one-sided slaughter;" wondered that Richard Cheney could claim that it was "unclear" who the enemy might be and the Brent Scowcroft could insist it was a "civil war" after US recognition of Bosnia and Washington's condemnation of Serbia for aggression; and ridiculed Bush for depicting the crisis as a "hiccup," a "skirmish" and a "quagmire." Primorac (see note 52), p. 48, noted that the Bosnians felt "betrayed" by the US and EC.

104 For example, *Nightline* has focussed almost exclusively on the sensational and the personal. On 10 June 1992, it looked at Sarajevo under siege, interviewing Milošević, Karadžić, the Bosnian UN ambassador, and the columnist Anthony Lewis; on 4 August, Cokie Roberts looked at the effects of the fighting on the children of Bosnia (a variant on earlier reports on the children of the Mideast and Central America) with Ilara Zorić, Karadžić and Mike Nicholson; on 6 August, it focussed on the camps, and on 10 and 11 November on reports of mass murder and death camps ("Bosnia, the Hidden Horrors," I and II); on 2 December, it carried an interview with Elie Wiesel, who was careful to deny that anything comparable to the "Holocaust" had occurred – an argument also made by the editor of *The Progressive* – and on 29 December a show on the plight of the refugees. The late-night series opened 1993 with programs on "Rape as a Weapon of War" (14 January) and "The Children of War," I and II (3–4 February).

105 *The New York Times*, 12 October 1992: A10, 18 October 1992: A1, and 19 October, John F. Burns. Although careful to note there were no precise casualty statistics, Burns reported the Bosnian government's estimate of 127,000 dead or missing, 16,000 confirmed dead, and 129,000 wounded.

106 Rieff (see note 32), pp. 83, 93, reported that a Serb had sprayed the Hotel Bosnia with an Ak-47, then pulled the pins on two grenades, killing three and wounding several in late September before Vance and Owen were to meet there with Karadžić. He was then shot by "other irregulars," but "Nobody knew why," although the Serbs blamed the Croats and Muslims, who blamed the Serbs. Robert Guskind also saw the war as grim and warned that the fighting in Karlovac and other Croatian cities was a "nightmarish glimpse into the potentially violent post-Cold War future awaiting many countries" that were emerging "from decades of iron-fisted Communist repression with centuries-old ethnic conflicts and nationalist passions intact and at explosive levels." He was particularly concerned that such conflicts might draw in other countries as well. But for Radek Sikorski, the whole affair was lighthearted at the beginning, as Croats played at war in Mazdas, Golf GTIs and Renault CTXs, with cellular phones and "perfectly fitting camouflage fatigues." It was, he observed, as "if the war had come to Scarsdale." Guskind (see note 32, "Ethnic Time Bombs"), and Radek Sikorski (see note 40), pp. 40–2.

107 *New Yorker*, "Quiet Voices from the Balkans," found her position made it "especially chilling somehow when she glared at Mr. Vasić, her fellow Serbian

journalist, and spat 'Traitor!'" The article also noted that Vasić's two oldest children from his first marriage were Croats, the next three from a second marriage were "integralist-universalists" (Yugoslavs), and the youngest from a third marriage was a Muslim. Zoran Pajić, Professor of Law at the University of Sarajevo, had a Serbian father and a Jewish mother, was married to a Bosnian Muslim and had a maternal grandmother who was Czech.

108 ABC, *Nightly News*, 31 August 1992.

109 *All Things Considered*, NPR, 27 March 1993. Two days later NPR ran another report with Linda Wetheimer and Justin Webb of the BBC in which the stress was on women and young children in Srebrenica with "lifeless eyes," but while Webb had seen "the most appalling scenes" and wondered about the ethics of transporting people from their homes because it helped the Serbs, he concluded that doing so was better than the alternative, which was death. In short, the journalist could imagine only two alternatives and carefully avoided laying any blame on the Serbs.

110 John Didović (Brecksville, Ohio), "Letter" (commenting on Nora Beloff's article of 13 April 1992), *National Review*, 24 May 1992: 2.

111 "Bosnia and the Balkans: An Exchange with Nora Beloff and Theodossis C. Demetacopoulos." Glenny simply rejected Beloff's objections and accusations, but in turn depicted Milošević as one of "three rabid Stalinists" and Tudjman as a "raving anti-Semite." Hardly objective, fair, or balanced reportage.

112 Rieff (see note 27), pp. 88, 90, 95.

113 "Bosnia: Land of the Demons." The "images" were appropriately reworked to become an artistic film montage, complete with negative frames, grainy stills, and other tricks of the video cameraman's art. In the final analysis, then, the whole business has been an interesting essay in the depiction of mass murder. *This Week with David Brinkley*, May 1993, opened with the announcement that Tony Birtley had two reports "with some outstanding pictures." But images do not seem to have the power to convince the cynical, e.g., Elizabeth Kastor, "Indelible Images? Do the Pictures of Tragedy Inspire Compassion or Complacency?" *Washington Post*, 6 Oct. 1994, a discussion of the two-month exhibition entitled "Farewell to Bosnia," by the Corcoran Gallery of Art.

6

PSYCHOANALYTIC DIMENSIONS OF THE WEST'S INVOLVEMENT IN THE THIRD BALKAN WAR

C. G. Schoenfeld

This psychoanalytically oriented study seeks to shed light upon the incredibly savage behavior of the Serbians towards their former country-men since June 1991, and to help determine why the leaders of the West failed to stop the mass murders, tortures, and rapes by the Serbians.

The barbarism exhibited by the Serbians since June of 1991 in trying to seize as much as possible of the balance of what had been Yugoslavia, coupled with their policy of "ethnic cleansing" – terrorizing and driving out all non-Serbians from such territory – might not have surprised Sigmund Freud. After all, it was he who described man's aggressiveness in his somber *Civilization And Its Discontents* in the following graphic terms:

> [M]en are not gentle, friendly creatures wishing for love, who simply defend themselves if they are attacked, but . . . a powerful measure of desire for aggression has to be reckoned as part of their instinctual endowment. The result is that their neighbor is to them not only a possible helper or sexual object, but also a temptation to them to gratify their aggressiveness on him, to exploit his capacity to work without recompense, to use him sexually without his consent, to seize his possessions, to humiliate him, to cause him pain, to torture and to kill him. *Homo homini lupus*: who has the courage to dispute it in the face of all the evidence in his own life and in history?[1]

Freud believed that man's aggressiveness – presumably a relic of primordial times, when it was necessary for survival – "perpetually menaced" civilized society with "disintegration." He stressed that when the forces in the mind that ordinarily inhibit this aggressiveness "cease to operate," men tend to abandon all restraint and reveal themselves "as savage beasts to whom the thought of sparing their own kind is alien."[2]

In *Group Psychology And The Analysis Of The Ego*,[3] Freud asserted that when people act together in mob-like groups – as have the Serbians in attacking the Croatians, the Muslims, and other former neighbors – they tend to regress and to behave far more primitively and emotionally than usual. In such groups, he declared, "individual inhibitions fall away and all the cruel, brutal and destructive instincts, which lie dormant in individuals as relics of a primitive epoch, are stirred up to find free gratification."[4]

Freud contended that the members of these groups often regress emotionally to the time of life before adequate inner controls over aggressive and destructive urges existed. This facilitates the replacement of their moral faculty with the group's leader, who becomes their shared ego-ideal. Perhaps because violence-prone groups reveal "a thirst for obedience," they tend to seek a leader who has "a strong and imposing will" – a will which, it should be noted, becomes, in effect, the group's shared "moral" guide.[5] When, as in the case of the Serbians, their leader is such a man as Slobodan Milošević or Radovan Karadžić, the worst can be expected, as has indeed occurred in the "ethnically cleansed" Bosnia.

THE CONTRIBUTIONS OF HEINZ KOHUT

If Heinz Kohut (one of Freud's most illustrious psychoanalytic successors) were alive today, he would probably contend – as he did when discussing the behavior of the Nazis – that "so long as we . . . declare [such behavior] . . . to be a reversal to barbarism, a regression to the primitive and animal-like . . . we deprive ourselves of the chance of increasing our understanding of human aggressivity and of our mastery over it."[6] Kohut (who spent a lifetime studying narcissism, self-esteem, and the development of the self) would undoubtedly have pointed out, as he did in essays on group behavior, that groups like the Serbian mobs who have uprooted their former Croatian and Muslim neighbors are held together not only by a shared ego-ideal, but more especially by "shared ambitions," shared narcissism – a "shared grandiose self."[7] And when this group "narcissism is interfered with . . . through the blocking of acceptable outlets for national prestige" – as occurred when the Serbians, who dominated Yugoslavia politically and militarily, were faced with the specter of ruling only a small and insignificant country – "deleterious consequences" follow, "particularly with regard to group aggression."[8]

Kohut also had much to say about the tendency of groups whose narcissism and self-esteem had been wounded to seek charismatic and Messianic leaders. In his words:

> Deeply rooted in our earliest childhood there remains in us a longing to merge with an all-powerful and all-knowing ideal figure. This yearning finds an apparently irresistible fulfillment for many in their total submission to a Messianic leader and to his dogmatic beliefs.[9]

Kohut believed that the Germans, whose narcissism and self-esteem had been deeply wounded by their defeat in World War I, unconsciously sought a charismatic Messianic leader who could provide the seeming omniscience and omnipotence that they craved. Hitler was such a leader:

> His convictions were absolute and, in certain areas, could not be questioned or modified . . . He knew with complete certainty what was evil and had to be eradicated . . . and what [was] good and worth preserving . . . [and most important, he] invited the participation of the German nation in this blissful self-image through . . . [an unconscious] merger with him.[10]

As for the Serbians, they are a people whose self-esteem is obviously precarious. To this very day, they feel deeply aggrieved and humiliated by – and fantasize about reversing – their defeat by the Turks in the Battle of Kosovo back in 1389 (which occurred *a hundred years before Columbus discovered America*!). That the potential dismemberment of Yugoslavia (which they controlled) would cause their self-esteem to plummet seems all too likely, as would their willingness to follow, and unconsciously seek to merge with, a ruthless and seemingly omniscient and omnipotent leader like Slobodan Milošević. As for Milošević himself (who appears to have had the abominable childhood – both his parents committed suicide – that Kohut believes most Messianic leaders are likely to have had), his personality seems to dovetail completely with that of the charismatic messianic leaders that Kohut describes in the following sentences:

> They seem to combine an absolute certainty concerning the power of their selves and an absolute conviction concerning the validity of their ideals with an equally absolute lack of empathic understanding for large segments of feelings, needs, and rights of other human beings and for the values cherished by them. They understand the environment in which they live only as an extension of their own narcissistic universe. They understand others only insofar – but here with the keenest empathy! – as they can serve as tools toward their own narcissistic ends or insofar as they interfere with their own purposes.[11]

Even more to the point are Kohut's views about "narcissistic rage," which he believes is likely to be generated when narcissistically vulnerable people with low self-esteem feel threatened. Such rage, he asserts, has traditionally been exhibited by the Japanese, "not when their principles or their freedom is challenged . . . but when they detect an insult or a detraction."[12] What characterizes narcissistic rage, according to Kohut, is its incredibly intense unforgiving fury, coupled with a "total lack of empathy" towards its victims.

> In its typical forms there is utter disregard for reasonable limitations and a boundless wish to redress an injury and to obtain revenge. The irrationality of the vengeful attitude becomes even more frightening in view of the fact that – in narcissistic personalities as in the paranoic

– the reasoning capacity, while totally under the domination and in the service of the overriding emotion, is often not only intact but even sharpened.[13]

Or, to quote from the best short study of Kohut's self-psychology that I am aware of:

[narcissistic] rage . . . pushes us to get even, to destroy the source of frustration, often without caring about the damage that may result to the self or others. In literature, Captain Ahab's uncontrolled urge to destroy Moby Dick provides a clear example of the lengths to which a person driven by narcissistic rage may go. Ahab lost his life and the lives of most of his crew and destroyed his vessel as well![14]

The foregoing quotations seem to capture the essence of the truly horrific behavior of the Serbians towards their relatively defenseless former countrymen. Indeed, herein may well be found a much-needed un-conscious key or "explanation" for the many atrocities committed by the Serbians – for the mass murders, tortures, and rapes that they have committed, and for their wanton and seemingly pointless destruction of such historically significant centers of Yugoslavian culture as Vukovar and Dubrovnik (which even the Nazis refrained from destroying). When the rage of the Serbians finally subsides, they are likely to begin to realize that they have, in effect, fouled their own nest, and have created enmities that will haunt them for generations to come. If there was ever a self-destructive (if not suicidal) course of action, the narcissistic rage of the Serbians seems to have led them to it.

NATIONALISM

Related to the foregoing is another "self"-oriented psychoanalytic approach that seeks to understand the abominable behavior of the Serbians as a manifestation of what has been termed "the scourge of Western Civilization for the last century and a half"[15] – nationalism. In presenting this approach, I will lean heavily upon a psychoanalytically oriented essay on nationalism in the *Journal of Psychiatry and Law* that I wrote back in 1974, and that seems to have been confirmed by psychoanalytic research since then.[16]

Nationalism, as many studies of it reveal, often reflects the imprint of two basic and somewhat contradictory elements: 1) the tendency to view one's nation (people or race) as an extension and enlargement of one's self; and 2) the tendency to distinguish as sharply as possible between the members of one's nation (people or race) and all other persons. These two elements of nationalism – seen, for example, in the willingness of many Germans under the Nazis to sacrifice their lives to create a larger and greater Germany, coupled with their simultaneous demand for the separation out and elimination from Germany of gypsies, Jews, and other so-called "inferior" peoples – may well express, as I will now briefly suggest, an unconsciously motivated attempt to bolster a less than secure sense of self.

Monographs by a number of scholars – including investigations by such psychoanalytic luminaries as Rene A. Spitz and Margaret Mahler – have documented the early development of the sense of self.[17] The consensus is that for the first three or four months of life, infants lack the ability to distinguish between themselves and the persons and things around them. During this phase of primary narcissism, "there is no clear distinction between psyche and soma, between inside and outside, between drive and object, between 'I' and 'Non-I', and not even between different regions of the body."[18]

Then, the "symbiotic" stage of infancy begins, in which the infant starts to differentiate himself from the persons and things in his environment – but in which *he seems to regard himself and mother (or her surrogate) as one omnipotent entity or unit*.

> The essential feature of symbiosis is [an] hallucinatory or delusional
> omnipotent fusion with the . . . mother and, in particular, the delusion
> of a common boundary of the two . . . physically separate individuals
> . . . [T]he infant behaves and functions as though he and his mother were
> an omnipotent system – a dual unity with one common boundary.[19]

Anna Freud, in particular, has documented all of this, pointing out that a young infant on his mother's lap often fails to distinguish between her lap and his own. "He is . . . surprised and indignant when the mother walks away from him as if he were suddenly left by his own body."[20] In fact, it is quite common for a one- (or even two-)year-old who likes to suck his thumb to "suddenly take the mother's thumb instead of his own; or, while feeding . . . to put the spoon into his mother's mouth."[21] Whether the infant's feeling of omnipotence at this time is a product of his "fusion" with his seemingly all-powerful mother, or is simply genetically determined (as the writings of Heinz Kohut suggest), is unclear.

After the symbiotic phase, the next stage of the development of the sense of self is that of "separation-individuation," which normally continues until some time early in the third year of life. The defining characteristic of this stage is the infant's struggle to complete the task of differentiating himself from other persons and things – of separating the "I" from the "non-I" – and, most especially, of differentiating himself completely from his mother or mother surrogate. As Richard A. Koenigsberg points out in his fascinating monograph *Symbiosis and Separation: Towards a Psychology of Culture*, accomplishing all this is by no means an easy task:

> [T]he gradual perception that one is separate from the symbiotic half
> of the self is one of the profound traumas of childhood . . . Separation

from the mother is . . . experienced as a mutilation of the self, as a shrinking of the ego . . . This "shrinkage" of the ego is extremely traumatic, since it implies the perception of one's smallness, frailty and aloneness . . . On the one hand . . . the ego strives to maintain the illusion of dual-unity, struggles to "recapture" the experience of narcissistic omnipotence . . . On the other hand, there is a struggle towards separations-individuation . . . [a] striving . . . to develop an autonomous ego whose integrity is not ruptured by that which is alien to the self.[22]

Though the conscious and unconscious results of the struggle for separation-individuation undoubtedly vary from child to child, they almost always reflect the presence and influence of such involuntary unconscious "defense mechanisms" as denial, introjection, projection, and repression. As a result of the automatic use of these defense mechanisms, vestiges of the struggle for separation-individuation remain in "the unconscious," and (particularly when this process has been especially traumatic) constantly seek to re-enter consciousness and thereby trigger what Heinz Kohut has described as the most intense and intolerable form of anxiety: the anxiety that erupts when the self is threatened with what is perceived as the danger of "disintegration."[23]

The two basic elements of nationalism – the tendency to view one's nation (people or race) as an extension and enlargement of one's self, and the tendency to distinguish as sharply as possible between the members of one's nation (people or race) and all other persons – offer crucial help in preventing the eruption into consciousness of the repressed and otherwise unconscious vestiges of the struggle for separation-individuation (and the related threatened generation of intolerable anxiety). Like neurotic symptoms (so-called "compromise formations"), these two basic themes of nationalism help to provide symbolic expression to the unconscious symbiotic desire to merge with the mother (one's "country or nation . . . is a fundamental symbolic object in modern life, serving, for great numbers of persons, as a 'container' for the dream of omnipotence, the dream of symbiotic fusion"),[24] while at the same time expressing the somewhat contradictory goal of separating the self from the mother and all others. In providing this symbolic expression to both the symbiotic and separation-individuation phases of infancy – in enabling Nazi German nationalists, for example, to seek the enlargement of Germany's borders, while simultaneously demanding the expulsion of the Jews; and in encouraging Irish nationalists to be willing to die for their country, "providing that they can thereby take the life of some of the English soldiers stationed in Northern Ireland"[25] – nationalism is able to calm down threatening unconscious vestiges of the struggle between symbiosis and separation-individuation and thereby minimize the likelihood of these vestiges endangering the sense of self and causing the appearance of intolerable disintegration anxiety.[26]

I believe that the Serbian attempts to expand the borders of Serbia by seizing as much as possible of what had formerly been Yugoslavia, coupled with their ruthless and barbarically executed policy of "ethnic cleansing," can be thought of in these terms. The Serbian conquest of parts of the internationally recognized countries of Croatia and Bosnia-Herzegovina for example, may well be unconsciously regarded by them as attempts to extend the boundaries of the Serbian self; and the Serbian policy of terrorizing, decimating, and driving out the Croatians and Muslims from the seized territories may also be regarded symbolically and unconsciously by the Serbs as attempts to re-work successfully the crucial task of separating the Serbian self from all else. As to what precipitated the nationalistic behavior of the Serbians in the first place, it is tempting to speculate that the break-up of what was once Serbian-controlled Yugoslavia into a number of small countries was symbolically and unconsciously interpreted by many Serbians as an assault on the stability and integrity of their sense of self. For many Serbians, permitting the break-up of Yugoslavia may well have been the symbolic unconscious equivalent of permitting the disintegration and destruction of their sense of self.

By no means is the foregoing analysis intended to suggest that the barbaric and inhumane behavior of the Serbians (for example, their declaredly intentional – and almost gleeful – bombing and shelling of helpless Bosnian children in playgrounds, schools, and hospitals) is in any way justifiable or forgivable. Contrary to the well-known French aphorism *tout comprendre, c'est tout pardonner*, it simply is not true that to understand all is to forgive all. Also, the discussions in the preceding pages are not the only possible psychoanalytic approaches to the actions of the Serbians. For instance, one might analyze the Serbian onslaught against their former countrymen in light of the views expressed by Jovan Rašković, a psychiatrist who, before his death two years ago under mysterious circumstances, was the leader of the Croatian Serbs. In his book *Luda Zemlja* (Crazy Country) published in 1990, Rašković contended that the Serbians are a hate-infused "*Oedipal* people, aggressive and authoritarian . . . who identify Serbia with Yugoslavian internationalism, large borders, [and] a big role in the world."[27] However, instead of exploring additional psychoanalytically oriented approaches to the behavior of the Serbians (whose Bosnian leader the Montenegrin-born Radovan Karadžić, is also a psychiatrist associated with the mysterious London-based Tavistock Institute of Human Relations), it might prove more helpful here to consider, from a psychoanalytic point of view, appropriate responses to the atrocities inflicted by the Serbians upon their former neighbors.

CRIME AND PUNISHMENT

Before returning to private life, where, as a member of Kissinger Associates, he had entered into business ventures with the Serbs that may have been interpreted by some as a possible conflict of interest,[28] Lawrence Eagleburger – then acting Secretary of State of the United States under President Bush – set in motion a process to have the leaders of Serbia declared war criminals.[29] The presumed purpose of this process was to prepare the ground for international criminal trials of the Serbian leaders, much as the leaders of Nazi Germany had been tried and convicted at the Nuremberg Trials that followed World War II. Whether, in seeking to have the Serbian leaders branded war criminals, Eagleburger was seeking to obscure his own role in preventing the United States from taking the actions needed to halt the Serbian attacks on their neighbors may never be known.[30] Still, implicit in the process that Eagleburger set in motion is the premise that good reason exists to believe that the Serbian leaders, like those of Nazi Germany, are criminals who need to be brought to justice.[31]

If, as seems evident, Slobodan Milošević, Radovan Karadžić, and their henchmen are indeed criminals[32] guilty of genocide (as were Hitler and the group around him that ruled Nazi Germany) – then certain psycho-analytically derived insights about crime and punishment immediately become relevant.

To begin with, psychoanalytic studies strongly support the view that the desire to retaliate for crimes is instinctual. The punishment of criminals, according to Franz Alexander and Hugo Staub, reflects "an instinctive demand which is active in every living being and is independent of social agencies . . . Every animal strikes back with hate at the one who attacks it."[33] Or, in the words of David Abrahamsen: the punishment of criminals expresses "the self-preservation instinct within the group."[34] What the law has traditionally tried to do is to *substitute vengeance by society for private vengeance*, and in so doing, secure order and keep the peace.[35] As America's greatest legal scholar and (perhaps second to John Marshall) its greatest jurist, Oliver Wendell Holmes, Jr., pointed out in his masterpiece, *The Common Law*:

> The first requirement of a sound body of law is, that it should correspond with the actual feelings and demands of the community, whether right or wrong. If people would gratify the passion of revenge outside of the law, if the law did not help them, the law has no choice but to satisfy the craving itself, and thus avoid the greater evil of private retribution.[36]

Or, as the renowned legal philosopher Morris R. Cohen once expressed it:

> The sentiment that injuries should be avenged . . . cannot be ignored within the life of any community . . . If the natural desire for

vengeance is not met and satisfied by the orderly procedure of the criminal law, we shall revert to the more bloody private vengeance of the feud and of the vendetta."[37]

The point is that if appropriate legal procedures are not found and employed to deal with the many horrendous crimes committed by the Serbians, unending retaliatory vengeance by the victims of these crimes and their families seems almost certain. For peace and order to return to what was once Yugoslavia – where (to paraphrase Thomas Hobbes) every man seems to be enemy to every man – the Serbians, who have wantonly, and in cold blood, murdered, tortured, and raped their former countrymen must be put on trial and punished. Otherwise, life in this so-called "tinderbox of Europe" is likely to continue to be violent, brutal, chaotic, and a perpetual threat to world peace (World War I began, it will be recalled, after the Bosnian terrorist Gavrilo Princip, under Serbian direction, assassinated Archduke Ferdinand of Austria in Sarajevo).

Other psychoanalytically derived insights that are relevant here pertain to the effect of the trial and punishment of criminals upon the moral faculty or super-ego of the average law-abiding person. To understand and appreciate these insights, it is helpful to be aware of the psychoanalytic discovery that "we are all of us born criminals in the sense that we are extensively endowed with impulses which, if unchecked, lead to anti-social conduct."[38]

[S]ide by side with loving attitudes and peaceful contentment, there are always to be found [in infants and young children] mental processes reminiscent of the most primitive aspects of savage life of an intensity that is only faintly mirrored later on by the distressing aspects of our international relations, including even the tortures and other atrocities. Violent and ruthless impulses of destruction (i.e., murder in adult language) follow on the inevitable minor privations of this period. The jealousies, hatreds, and murderous impulses of which signs may be detected in childhood are, in fact, the weakened derivations of a very sinister inheritance we bring to the world and which somehow has to be worked through and chastened in the painful conflicts and emotions of infancy.[39]

Unfortunately, these primitive and savage urges do not simply disappear during infancy and early childhood. Rather, they are often rendered unconscious by repression or some other involuntary defense mechanism. And while unconscious, these "criminal" tendencies exist in their original form – unaltered by the passage of time – and are kept in check and prevented from becoming conscious largely by the super-ego (which pressures the ego to act).

Perhaps because these criminalistic or antisocial desires exist to some extent in the unconscious of most law-abiding persons, there is a tendency for such persons to identify themselves unconsciously with criminals.[46] When this happens (typically, when a notorious crime is given excessive media attention or when, as in Yugoslavia, horrendous crimes are reported daily in the media), the antisocial wishes in the unconscious of the law-abiding become aroused and seek access to consciousness and expression in action. Their super-ego then springs into action, expressing its alarm by generating a variety of anxiety known as "guilt."

Demanding that criminals be tried and punished helps to dampen these guilt feelings and to calm the anti-social urges that had aroused them. "[T]he demand that the lawbreaker be punished is . . . a demonstration against one's own inner drives, a demonstration which tends to keep these drives amenable to control . . . [P]unishment [acts] as an intimidating example . . . against one's own primitive . . . repressed instinctual drives."[41] Also, punishing criminals aids the law-abiding in coping with their own guilt: "Unconsciously they identify with the criminal because of their own latent anti-social tendencies and somehow vicariously demand and accept the punishment to relieve their own guilt feelings."[42]

Further, for the super-ego of the law-abiding (in conjunction with the ego) to prevent anti-social urges from entering consciousness and finding an outlet in criminal conduct, it needs concrete evidence that its punitive responses are being acted upon – evidence that the punishment of criminals (with whom the law-abiding have unconsciously identified them-selves) is capable of providing. If the public believes that criminals, and particularly vicious criminals, are not being punished or punished suffi-ciently, then – as psychoanalytic studies indicate – the moral faculty or super-ego of the law-abiding begins to atrophy and disintegrate, and is increasingly unable to induce the ego to prevent anti-social desires from becoming conscious and expressing themselves in outright criminality.[43]

The relevance of all this to the situation in what was once Yugoslavia is plain: Slobodan Milošević, Radovan Karadžić, and the other Serbian cut-throats who have run wild in Slovenia, Croatia, and Bosnia-Herzegovina must be tried and punished for their crimes. To fail to bring these criminals to justice would be to court the danger of seriously weakening and undermining the moral faculty not only of the Bosnians, Croatians, and Muslims – and of those Serbians who still retain some shreds of moral decency – but also of peoples all over the globe who read newspapers, see television, and who have been made acutely aware of the Serbian atrocities that have gone unpunished. Unless sincere and timely efforts are made to bring to trial, and to convict and punish, the Serbian criminals, a multitude of once-hidden barbaric and primitive urges in the unconscious of many persons (both in Yugoslavia and in other parts of the world) may well become conscious and express themselves in behavior just as savage and as loathsome as that of the Serbians.

167

WESTERN INACTION(?)

...rue, then why the inaction of the West. Why have the leaders
...t failed to stop the mass murders, tortures, and rapes by the
...Why, for example, did the West stand idly by when such a
...wn Serbian terrorist and fugitive from justice as Željko
Raznjatović (known as "Arkan" and wanted by Interpol) organized and
directed *open and public* massacres, tortures, and rapes of literally tens of
thousands of utterly defenseless Croatians, Bosnians, and Muslims,
followed by the plundering of their churches, schools, mosques, and
homes, and the sale of the plunder in Belgrade.

But are we really dealing only with Western inaction? For instance, was
it Western inaction or action when President Bush's Secretary of State,
James A. Baker, visited Belgrade on 21 June 1991 and publicly declared that
the United States would refuse to recognize an independent Slovenia or
Croatia – an action followed within five days by the Serbian invasion of
Slovenia, and shortly thereafter by the Serbian attack upon Croatia?[44] Was
it Western inaction or action when, in September of 1991, the United States
and the European Community – *in response to a request by Serbia* – pushed
through United Nations Resolution no. 713 imposing an arms embargo on
all the participants in the Yugoslavian conflict, even though the Serbians
(who have one of the largest armies in Europe) were armed to the teeth,
and their Bosnian and Muslim victims were largely defenseless? And was it
Western inaction or action when the United Nations – at the instigation of
the English and the French – sent so-called "peacekeeping" troops to
Bosnia-Herzegovina under the leadership of arguably pro-Serbian
commanders such as Major-General Lewis MacKenzie (who has since
participated in a speaker's tour funded by a Serbian-American advocacy
group)?[45] To continue: Was it inaction or action when the commanders of
the forces of the United Nations in Bosnia Herzegovina enforced the arms
blockade against the Bosnians, but looked the other way when, at night,
Serbians looted arms warehouses that belonging to the UN and shipped
truckloads of heavy armor and munitions into Bosnia; when these UN
commanders ordered the cut-off of escape routes to airports and otherwise
prevented the Bosnians from leaving so-called "safe havens," while doing
nothing about constant Serbian bombardments of these supposedly
UN-protected zones; and when these UN officials deployed their "peacekeeping" troops in such a way that periodically threatened American air
strikes upon Serbian positions would inevitably cause casualties among the
UN forces and were therefore never carried out?[46]

The point is that regardless of whether the behavior of the leaders of the
West in response to the bloodbath in Yugoslavia is characterized as active
or inactive (or a combination of both) – or is described as covertly
pro-Serbian, or as simply a "hands-off" policy – the result has been to allow

the Serbians to engage in what amounts to genocide towards their former countrymen. Just as Neville Chamberlain and Eduard Deladier failed to lift a finger when Hitler started to destroy the Jews, so have Britain's John Major and France's François Mitterrand failed to do anything even remotely effective to halt the Serbian onslaught upon their former neighbors. In fact, if one were to use as a yardstick the behavior of the British and French, one might well conclude that the British and French leaders have followed a course of action designed to ensure a Serbian victory. But whether or not this is so, I believe that the refusal of the leaders of Britain, France, Russia, and the United States to take the necessary steps to stop (and earlier to prevent) the mass murders, tortures, and rapes by the Serbians is, by any standards, immoral.

"So what?" would probably be the response of many of today's practitioners of *Realpolitik* – the doctrine propounded by Henry Kissinger throughout his career (first as a scholar, and later as President Nixon's National Security Adviser, and as Secretary of State under Presidents Nixon and Ford) that a nation's foreign policy should be based upon its interests, and not upon moral principles.

> Kissinger's conservative realpolitik, as reflected in his dissertation, was based on the principle, taught by realists from Karl von Clausewitz to Hans Morgenthau, that diplomacy cannot be divorced from the realities of force and power. But diplomacy should be divorced, Kissinger argued, from a moralistic and meddlesome concern with the internal policies of other nations. Stability is the prime goal of diplomacy. It is served when nations accept the legitimacy of the existing world order and when they act based on their national interests: it is threatened when nations embark on ideological or moral crusades.[47]

Historically, *Realpolitik* is closely associated with the diplomacy of Austria's Prince Klemens von Metternich, Britain's Viscount Castlereagh, and Germany's Prince Otto von Bismarck; and its recent practitioners appear to include John Major, François Mitterrand, James A. Baker, and Lawrence Eagleburger.

As Henry Kissinger once presciently noted, future historians are likely to find it next-to-impossible to discover the truth about a modern nation's diplomatic maneuvering:

> Kissinger's tenure in power coincided with two trends that seemed designed to flummox future historians: the rise of the Xerox machine and of the posterior-protecting memo. This meant that the documentary record became both voluminous and misleading. Future scholars, Kissinger himself noted, will have "no criteria for

determining which documents were produced to provide an alibi and which genuinely guided decisions."[48]

Still, there can be little doubt that, since the turn of the century, the leaders of Britain and France have worried (with reason) about possible German expansionism; and they have viewed a strong Serbia – and more particularly, a *united* Yugoslavia – as a bulwark against this expansionism. Indeed, so long as these leaders were able to justify their conduct publicly, they (as well as the leaders of the United States) opposed the decision by Germany and the European Community to recognize the democratically-elected regimes in Slovenia, Croatia, and Bosnia-Herzegovina.[49] In short, it seems likely that discouraging the break-up of Yugoslavia, and supporting Serbia in its efforts to prevent the disintegration of Yugoslavia, would have been viewed by John Major and François Mitterrand as consistent with the national interests of their countries: and as practitioners of *Realpolitik*, they would presumably have felt obligated to pursue these interests vigorously and at the expense of moral principles and concerns.

By no means is this to suggest in any way that *Realpolitik* and its implicitly rejection of morality as a guide to action is the only rational or realistic approach to foreign policy. There is a highly regarded opposing school of thought (numbering among its many supporters such distinguished figures as Immanuel Kant, Woodrow Wilson, and Daniel P. Moynihan) that envisions a crucial role for morality in foreign affairs. And though it would be absurd to suggest that this is the time and place to decide whether morality has a legitimate place in foreign affairs (and what its role should be), I think that it would be helpful to pause here and try to determine whether psychoanalysis – which, for almost a century, has shed light upon the origin and influence of man's moral faculty – has something of value to contribute to the question of whether morality should play a role in foreign affairs, particularly in the light of Serbian atrocities in Yugoslavia during the past few years.

THE ROOTS OF MORALITY

In *Totem and Taboo*, the anthropological study in which Freud (drawing upon the research of Charles Darwin) suggested that the "primal horde" may have been mankind's original family or social group, he declares unequivocally that "the beginnings of . . . morals" are to be found "in the Oedipus complex."[50] In the eighty or so years that have passed since this pioneer anthropological work was first published in 1913, Freud's view about the origin of morality have been endlessly confirmed by psycho-analytic research.

The phrase "Oedipus complex" was coined by Freud to describe his discovery that children between 3½ and 5½ years of age tend to be drawn erotically to the parent of the opposite sex and to experience jealousy and hostility towards the parent of the same sex. The classic description of the Oedipus complex is undoubtedly that to be found in *The Interpretation of Dreams*, published in 1899, in which Freud draws upon Sophocles' great tragic drama *Oedipus Rex*.

> If the *Oedipus Rex* is capable of moving a modern reader or playgoer no less powerfully than it would the contemporary Greeks, the only possible explanation is that the effect of the Greek tragedy does not depend upon the conflict between fate and human will, but upon the peculiar nature of the material by which this conflict is revealed. There must be a voice within us which is prepared to acknowledge the compelling power of fate in the Oedipus . . . And there actually is a motive in the story of King Oedipus which explains the verdict of this inner voice. His fate moves us because it might have been our own, because the oracle laid upon us before our birth the very curse which rested upon him. It may be that we were all destined to direct our first sexual impulses towards our mothers and the first impulses of hatred and violence towards our fathers; our dreams convince us that we were. King Oedipus, who slew his father Laius and wedded his mother Jocasta, is nothing more or less than a wish-fulfillment – the fulfillment of the wish of our childhood. But we, more fortunate than he, insofar as we have not become psychoneurotics, have since our childhood succeeded in withdrawing our sexual impulses from our mothers, and in forgetting our jealousy of our fathers. We recoil from the person for who this primitive wish of childhood has been fulfilled with all the force of the repression which these wishes have undergone in our minds since childhood. As the poet brings the guilt of Oedipus to light by his investigation, he forces us to become aware of our own inner selves, in which the same impulses are still extant.[51]

I can still remember some of the intense opposition that Freud's discovery of the Oedipus complex generated, particularly among anthropologists influenced by the extreme cultural determinism of Franz Boas and by the now largely discredited study of the Samoans by his then 23-year-old student and acolyte Margaret Mead;[52] and as late as 1966, I felt compelled to write an article for the *Journal of Nervous and Mental Diseases* dissecting the utterly illogical and absurd arguments against the Oedipus complex to be found in the otherwise notable and valuable works of Erich Fromm.[53] But all of this now seems like water over the dam, except, perhaps, for occasional sneering references to the Oedipus complex still discoverable in the books of James Q. Wilson and other diehards.[54] Very few knowledge-able students of human nature today would even think of disputing the statement in Charles Brenner's *An Elementary Textbook of Psychoanalysis* that "the best evidence which is available at present speaks for the existence of incestuous and parenticidal impulses and conflicts about them in every culture we know of."[55]

Undoubtedly, the mainspring of the opposition to acknowledging the existence of the Oedipus complex has been man's moral faculty or super-ego. This became understandable once psychoanalysts discovered that when the super-ego begins to stabilize and morality becomes an inner matter at about the age of 6 – exactly when the Oedipus complex disappears from consciousness – the unconscious nucleus of the super-ego's prohibitions is "the demand that the individual repudiate the incestuous and hostile wishes"[56] that constitute his Oedipus complex.

Related, perhaps, is what I have always regarded as a potent "intellectual" argument against the existence of the Oedipus complex: the contention that there is no discernible logic or sense in the appearance of parricidal and incestuous urges at the age of 3½, when they are hardly likely to be consummated; urges which then disappear from view at the age of 6 or so when the super-ego begins to stabilize and the so-called "latency" period begins; and which, as psychoanalysts have learned, suddenly reappear just before puberty begins (along with a host of other infantile desires); and finally, are normally abandoned during adolescence. As I discovered when I investigated the roots of the Oedipus complex back in the early 1960s, the logic of all this is the "logic" of evolution – the same logic that, since the pioneer investigations of Charles Darwin, has enabled us to understand why, for example, gill clefts and a rudimentary tail appear and then disappear during the growth of the human embryo; and why, after birth, a child often loses the hair with which he was born, and his thymus gland eventually disappears along with his milk teeth. Research by such giants of evolutionary anthropology as Ernst Haeckel appears to have confirmed that human development, both embryonic and post-embryonic, proceeds in accordance with the principle that "ontogeny recapitulates phylogeny" – that an individual's fetal and post-fetal development retraces, albeit fleeting and incompletely, man's racial history.

Once it is realized that a person's pre-adult development retraces to some extent the evolutionary history of the human race, then the existence of the Oedipus complex becomes understandable, particularly if one takes into account Darwin's and Freud's belief that in primordial times, men (like many species of monkeys and apes who mature today at the age of 4 or so) lived in small groups or "primal hordes." Typically, the groups or hordes consisted of a powerful and ferocious adult male who ruled and totally dominated it (and monopolized its women), his harem of wives and daughters, and youngsters of both sexes. If and when the growing sons aroused the sexual jealousy of their brutal sire, he would have killed, castrated, or driven them from the horde. The exiled sons presumably lived together with their brothers in small bands, possibly in a polyandrous relationship with one or more stolen females.

Unlike Freud, Darwin believed that, sooner or later, one of the exiled sons returned to the primal horde and fought his father – if necessary, to the death – for control over it. If the son proved to be the victor (and either killed or drove off his father), he became the new ruler of the primal horde and, as such, took sexual possession of all its mature females, including his mother and sisters. Inexplicably, Freud seems to have overlooked completely the obvious kinship between the urges and passions that presumably governed the members of the primal horde and what he labeled the "Oedipus complex." As I stressed, in an article dealing with this and related matters in *The American Imago* back in 1962:

> [I]t can be argued that the erotic wishes little girls now direct towards their father and the hostility they feel for their mother may be remnants of the powerful emotions experienced by grown daughters in the primal horde when they competed with their mother for the sexual attention of the only mature male available – their father. Similarly, the hatred small boys experience concerning their father, as well as the erotic desire they have for their mother, may be traces of the insistent emotions that ruled the mature son who challenged his father for mastery of the primal horde and sexual possession of all its women, including the mother."[57]

As ethological studies reveal, the "Oedipus complex" is constantly being acted out in the animal kingdom – not simply by monkeys and apes, but also by a large variety of herd mammals. For instance, seals, wild horses, deer, kangaroos, and zebras appear to have essentially the same "family" unit as that in Freud's and Darwin's primal horde, and to exhibit much the same intrafamilial sexual and aggressive behavior. A particularly striking illustration of the centrality of the "Oedipus complex" in the life-cycle of such herd mammals is to be found in Walt Disney's unforgettable documentary film *Seal Island*, which depicts the sexual and related aggressive conduct of the fur seals who, for part of each year, inhabit the Pribiloff Islands in the Bering Sea.

Man, unlike these other herd mammals, has presumably abandoned the Oedipus complex as the moving force in his life-cycle; and, as noted earlier, has developed an inner moral faculty – the super-ego – to help guard against the activation of vestigial Oedipal wishes. In fact, as psychoanalysts have learned, the demand that hostile and incestuous Oedipal urges be rejected "persists throughout life . . . as the essence of the superego."[58] Further, as Freud attempted to reveal in *Totem and Taboo*, both traditional religion and its predecessor totemism have served to reinforce man's moral sense by enjoining the bedrock evolutionary "crimes" of incest and parricide, as have the "laws" of the most primitive societies that anthropologists have been able to study.[59]

By no means is this to suggest that mankind's "natural" or innate morality pertains only to forbidding patricide and incest – or, in more general terms, to forbidding murder and sexual license. Psychoanalysts have discovered that there also seem to be archaic innate "moral" prohibitions against cannibalism (against eating human flesh and drinking blood, for example), and against castration and related mutilations.[60] In fact, the moral faculty or super-ego of most persons – certainly by the age of 6 or so – contains stringent prohibitions against the "thoughtless" cruelty exhibited by very young children who "pull off the arms and legs of the dolls . . . puncture their eyeballs . . . smash whatever is breakable . . . [and] when put together in a playpen . . . bite each other, pull each others hair and . . . [steal] each others toys, without regard for the other child's unhappiness."[61]

THE DEVELOPMENT OF THE SUPER-EGO

Man's moral faculty or super-ego, as psychoanalytic investigations reveal, does not exist at birth and for some time thereafter. Precursors of the super-ego begin to appear during the first year or two of life, however, and consist largely of parental admonitions and prohibitions that the infant alternatively internalizes and externalizes.

> Typically, we try to disown the fiercely aggressive wishes that assail us from within [discussed earlier in the section on Crime and Punishment] by projecting them onto our parents. But once we do this, our parents seem to be so threatening and ferocious that we introject them (that is, we internalized the distorted image that we have formed of them). Then, however, we become so terrified of the introjected parents "within" us that we feel compelled to re-externalize them. And the process starts all over again. In fact, psychoanalysts believe that this alternating process is continually repeated until we reach the age of about six. At that time, we internalize the image we have formed of our parents on a more or less "permanent" basis. This internalized parent image becomes our superego and, in effect, takes over many of the "guiding" functions previously performed by our parents.[62]

Normally, the super-ego continues to develop to a limited extent after the age of 6 or so – during the latency period, adolescence, and even in young adulthood – but at an extremely (and increasingly) slow pace. These later super-ego changes usually reflect the influence of parent substitutes: teachers and public figures, for example, as well as high social ideals.

A properly formed super-ego performs a number of related functions that include setting moral and ethical standards, evaluating the thoughts and actions of one's self and others in light of these standards, praising and seeking to reward moral conduct, and condemning and demanding punishment for unprincipled behavior. The super-ego of Immanuel Kant, for example, demanded that: "Even if a Civil Society resolved to dissolve itself with the consent of all its members . . . the last Murderer lying in prison . . . [had to] be executed before the resolution was carried out."[63]

The super-ego acts in a sense like a policeman whose job it is to monitor a person's hostile and destructive urges – particularly those derived from the Oedipus complex and other phylogenetic sources – and to make sure that they fail to erupt in delinquent and criminal behavior. As Franz Alexander and Hugo Staub express it in their classic psychoanalytic study of criminality: "[W]ithin every law-abiding citizen there must live [such] a police officer, for it is practically impossible to keep law and order only by means of external compulsion."[64]

Implicit in all this is the conclusion, amply confirmed by psychoanalytic research, that if a person's moral faculty or super-ego is healthy and normal, he is highly unlikely to engage in murder, rape, mayhem, and other serious violent crimes, nor is he likely to stand idly by if he has the opportunity to prevent the commission of these crimes. Conversely, if his super-ego is weak, incomplete, or malformed – and hence unable to exert sufficient control over his archaic and infantile criminalistic urges – he may well become a murderer, rapist, and sadistic torturer, and fail to prevent others from acting in a similarly savage and bestial manner.[65]

Implicit as well in the foregoing sketch of psychoanalytic discoveries about the origin and contents of man's super-ego is the conclusion that a normal person is one with a moral faculty strong enough to counter the "pull" of the Oedipal and other vestiges of mankind's violent and savage past – a moral faculty that not only repudiates and seeks to prevent murder, rape, mayhem, and the like, but also acts as a necessary guide to life in civilized society. In short, the psychoanalytic evidence that has now been collected for almost a century strongly suggests that man – if only because of his phylogenetic or racial history – is essentially, and intrinsically, a moral being.

MORALITY, REALPOLITIK, AND YUGOSLAVIA

If all that has been presented so far about the origin and development of man's moral sense is sound, then it seems patent that those who preach *Realpolitik* in foreign affairs – with its implicit abandonment of morality as guide to action – bear the burden of proving why man should repudiate his normal, phylogenetically determined morality in the field of international affairs. Bearing this burden of proving that morality has no place in foreign affairs seems particularly compelling in the case of what was once Yugoslavia, where the Serbians have violated practically every norm of morality known to mankind (with the possible exception of the ban on cannibalism).

The reality is, however, that – in accordance with the traditional *Realpolitik* penchant for secrecy[66] – the leaders of the West have done their best to avoid public discussion and justification of their policy towards Serbia,

Slovenia, Croatia, and Bosnia-Herzegovina. Indeed, ever since the European community recognized these newly formed countries early in 1992, such putative Western practitioners of *Realpolitik* as John Major, François Mitterrand, James A. Baker and Lawrence Eagleburger have been most reluctant to explain publicly just what the goals of their foreign policy are in regard to what was once Yugoslavia.

This "stonewalling" of inquiries about US foreign policy towards Serbia and its neighbors has continued in the Clinton administration under Secretary of State Warren Christopher (who had been an Assistant Secretary of State under Cyrus Vance, the Secretary of State during the Carter administration in the late 1970s). Despite campaign rhetoric by presidential *candidate* Clinton questioning the morality of US policy towards Yugoslavia, *President* Clinton – under the guidance of Warren Christopher – has followed what is essentially the same *Realpolitik* Yugoslavian policy as that of the previous Bush administration.

Devising possible "*Realpolitik* reasons" for the unwillingness of the current leaders of the West to openly share their real foreign policy objectives towards Yugoslavia with the public requires little perspicacity. One can surmise, for example, that these leaders may be trying to cope with what they perceive as the possible danger of a resurgent German expansionism, while seeking to avoid giving public offense to the Germans whose economic cooperation they need. Also, they may fear the spread of Islamic fundamentalism and want to demonstrate – without publicly embarrassing the Muslim governments of the oil-rich countries of the Middle East – that an anti-Western policy carries high costs for the Muslims living in Europe (even though the Muslims who were slaughtered by the Serbians in Bosnia-Herzegovina were anything but Islamic fundamentalists). In addition (and like Neville Chamberlain of Britain and Eduard Deladier of France who, at Munich in 1938, "sacrificed" much of Czechoslovakia to Hitler), the *Realpolitik*-oriented leaders of the West may believe that secretly sacrificing the interests of Croatia, Slovenia, and Bosnia-Herzegovina is a small price to pay for helping Boris Yeltsin to survive in Russia, where even the hint of an anti-Serbian Western policy might be used by his enemies to try to bring him down.

"*Realpolitik* reasons" of this sort aside for pursuing a covert pro-Serbian policy, I believe that the basic reason why Western leaders are unwilling to expose publicly their real policy towards what was formerly Yugoslavia is that they rightly feel that their own countrymen would probably be revolted by it and demand that it be replaced by a morally oriented policy (and, indeed, that *they* be replaced as well). In short, I believe that the leaders of the West are fully aware of the immorality of what appears on the surface to be their dithering response to the massive Serbian atrocities, and are afraid of what would happen if the putative secret roots of their Yugoslavian policy were exposed to public scrutiny. Consider, for example, how the public in Britain might respond if they learned of, and gave credence to, reports that British mercenaries had deliberately stirred up trouble between the Croatians and the Bosnian Muslims so as to make the Yugoslavian conflict appear to be a civil war rather than one provoked by Serbian aggression.[67]

Whether or not such reports prove to be accurate, there can be no doubt that a number of Western officials who presumably have "inside" information about the events in Yugoslavia have recently tried to distance themselves from the conflict. Cyrus Vance, for example, who served as a so-called "impartial" mediator for the United Nations, suddenly resigned. And, one by one, a total now of five US State Department officials familiar with the creation and implementation of American foreign policy towards Serbia, Croatia, Slovenia, and Bosnia-Herzegovina have resigned for reasons of "conscience."[68] Though unprecedented and persuasive, these resignations, by themselves, admittedly fail to "prove" that current Western policy in what was once Yugoslavia is morally corrupt. After all, President Clinton's current National Security Adviser – Anthony Lake – who resigned in 1970 as an assistant to the then National Security Adviser Henry Kissinger to protest the US Invasion of Cambodia, still appears able to stomach (and may even advocate) US inaction in the face of the atrocities committed by the Serbians.

However, regardless of the weight assignable to resignations of officials familiar with Western intentions towards Serbia and its neighbors, and regardless of the demands voiced by such former leaders of the West as Margaret Thatcher[69] and Ronald Reagan (and his Secretary of State George Shultz) that the victims of Serbian terror ought to be allowed to obtain the weapons they need to defend themselves, and even though it is uncertain whether Western policy towards Serbia et al. is truly that of dithering inaction, or is really covertly pro-Serbian, there is no disputing the psycho-analytically derived conclusion that man – if only because of his phylo-genetic or racial heritage – is essentially and intrinsically a moral being; and that the failure of Western leaders to use their power to stop the mass murders, rapes, and tortures by the Serbians violates mankind's bedrock morality. Simply put, persons with a normal moral faculty or super-ego do not stand idly by and wring their hands if they have the means and ability to prevent their fellow human beings from being murdered, raped and tortured. The Serbians have behaved worse toward their former country-men than the inhabitants of Sodom and Gomorrah did towards strangers; and – to remind the current leaders of the West who seem to have forgotten the vivid moral lessons taught by the Old Testament – God did not simply stand by and deplore the wickedness of the inhabitants of Sodom and Gomorrah, rather, he rained fire and brimstone upon them and eliminated them from the face of the earth.[70]

One would suppose that the current *Realpolitik*-oriented leaders of Britain, France, Russia, and the United States regard themselves as wiser and infinitely more knowledgeable about international affairs than their fellow countrymen. I would remind them, however, that (as noted earlier) not only is there a respectable school of thought that envisions a significant role for morality in foreign affairs, but that, historically, *Realpolitik* has often proven to be disastrous. As Walter Isaacson points out in his recent and brilliant biography of Henry Kissinger, an open and moral foreign policy – rather than one based upon Kissinger's *Realpolitik* – would probably have averted disasters for the United States in Vietnam, Cambodia, and Pakistan.[71] Also – and of immense importance for mankind – *Realpolitik* and its unfortunate consequences, first in Sarajevo and then at Munich, helped to precipitate World War I and World War II. If one adds to all this the arrogant refusal of the leaders of the West to justify publicly their obviously immoral policy towards what was once Yugoslavia, the conclusion seems inescapable that these leaders have failed – certainly from a psychoanalytically oriented point of view – to act in a morally normal and acceptable manner. One hundred years of psychoanalytic research on the origin and contents of man's moral sense or super-ego leads ineluctably to the conclusion that current Western policy towards Serbia, Slovenia, Croatia, and Bosnia-Herzegovina is intrinsically unnatural and immoral; and as such, should be changed to conform to mankind's basic phylogenetically derived moral sense.

SUMMARY

Using a psychoanalytic perspective to shed light upon 1) the abominable and inhumane behavior of the Serbians towards their former countrymen since June 1991; and 2) the failure of the leaders of the West to prevent or stop the butchery and "ethnic cleaning" by the Serbians, has been this study's purpose. To accomplish this purpose, Freud's views about the "dark" and brutally aggressive side of man's nature – particularly when acting in mob-like-groups – were presented, as were the theories of Heinz Kohut about how savagely men may act, especially in groups led by charismatic and Messianic leaders, when their narcissism, self-esteem, and sense of self seem threatened. Highlighted in the discussion was Kohut's description of "narcissistic rage," which, as noted, seemed "to capture the flavor or essence of the truly horrific behavior of the Serbians towards their relatively defenseless former countrymen."

Then, psychoanalytic insights about nationalism were delineated, and an attempt was made to reveal how Serbian attempts to expand the borders of Serbia, coupled with their ruthless and barbarically executed policy of "ethnic cleansing," were unconsciously related to the crucial stages of symbiosis and separation-individuation in the development of the sense of self, and to the two basic (and somewhat contradictory) elements of nationalism.

The next section of this study dealt with psychoanalytic insights about crime and punishment. It was concluded that unless the Serbian criminals were brought to trial and punished, "a multitude of once-hidden barbaric and primitive urges in the unconscious of many persons (in both Yugoslavia and in other parts of the world)" might reach consciousness and find expression in conduct "just as savage and as loathsome as that of the Serbians."

The chapter then turned to the failure of the leaders of the West to stop the mass murders, tortures, and rapes by the Serbians. Implicit in the discussion offered was the suspicion – which, with every passing day of Western "inaction," is turning into a conviction – that the leaders of the West have not simply dithered while the Serbians have bathed what was once Yugoslavia in blood, but that these leaders have actually been implementing a covert "*Realpolitik*" pro-Serbian policy.

A large section of this chapter was devoted to presenting psychoanalytic discoveries about the roots of the Oedipus complex and its centrality in the development of man's moral faculty or super-ego. This was followed by a discussion of the appearance and functions of the super-ego. It was contended that the failure of the leaders of the West to prevent or stop the bloodletting by the Serbians violated mankind's fundamental racially based morality.

The relationship of all this to *Realpolitik* was explored, and it was concluded – particularly because Western leaders have studiously avoided public disclosure or discussion of their policy towards Serbia, Slovenia, Croatia, and Bosnia-Herzegovina – that current Western policy towards what was once Yugoslavia "should be changed to conform to mankind's basic phylogenetically-derived moral sense."

Unfortunately, the policy of the leaders of the West towards Serbia and its neighbors seems unlikely to change in the near future. What appears to be going on now is a concerted effort by these leaders to pressure the victims of Serbian aggression to accept defeat. In the short run, such a course of action may well prevent further carnage. Yet, there can be little doubt that, in the long run, the damage that has been done to man's moral faculty, both in what was once Yugoslavia and elsewhere, is likely to prove catastrophic. Not only have the less-than-moral leaders of the West lost an historic opportunity to begin to create a "New World Order" – and given Muslims all over the world a "*cause célèbre*" – but they have helped to create an unstable mess (reminiscent of Freud's description of the id as a "cauldron of seething excitement"[72]) that will surely haunt mankind for generations to come. Seneca and Shakespeare were all too accurate when they declared: "What fools these mortals be!"

NOTES

1 S. Freud, *Civilization And Its Discontents* (London: Hogarth Press, 1955: 85).
2 Freud (see note 1), p. 86.

3 S. Freud, *Group Psychology And The Analysis Of The Ego* (New York: Liveright Publishing, 1951).

4 Freud (see note 3), p. 17.

5 Freud (see note 3), p. 21.

6 H. Kohut, "*Thoughts on Narcissism and Narcissistic Rage,*" in P. H. Ornstein (ed.), *The Search For The Self: Selected Writings of Heinz Kohut: 1950–1978* (New York: International Universities Press, 1978, vol. 2: 615, 635).

7 Kohut (see note 6), p. 658.

8 Kohut (see note 6), p. 658.

9 Kohut, "Psychoanalysis in a Troubled World," in Ornstein (see note 6), pp. 511, 532.

10 Kohut, "Creativeness, Charisma, Group Psychology: Reflections on the Self-Analysis of Freud," in Ornstein (see note 6), pp. 793, 833–4.

11 Kohut (see note 10), p. 834.

12 Kohut (see note 6), p. 638.

13 Kohut (see note 6), pp. 639–40.

14 H. S. Baker and M. N. Baker, "Heinz Kohut's Self-psychology: An Overview," *American Journal of Psychiatry*, vol. 144, no. 1 (1987): 6.

15 G. Kurth, "Politics: Unconscious Factors in Social Prejudice and Mass Movements," in H. Kurth (ed.), *A Handbook of Psychoanalysis* (Cleveland, Ohio: World Publishing, 1963: 297–305).

16 C. G. Schoenfeld, "International Law, Nationalism, and The Sense of Self: A Psychoanalytic Inquiry", *Journal of Psychiatry and Law*, vol. 2 (1974): 303, 317. See, e.g., R. A. Koenigsberg, *Symbiosis and Separation: Towards a Psychology of Culture* (New York: Library of Art and Social Science, 1989).

17 See, e.g., R. A. Spitz, *The First Year of Life* (New York: International Universities Press, 1965); M. S. Mahler, *On Human Symbiosis and the Vicissitudes of Individuation* (New York: International Universities Press, 1968).

18 Spitz (see note 17), p. 35(n).

19 Mahler (see note 17), p. 9.

20 A. Freud, "Some Remarks On Infant Observation," in *The Psychoanalytic Study of the Child* (New York: International Universities Press, 1953, vol. 8: 9, 14).

21 Geleerd, "Clinical Contribution to the Problem of the Early Mother–Child Relationship," in *The Psychoanalytic Study of the Child* (New York: International Universities Press, 1956, vol. 11: 336).

22 Koenigsberg (see note 16), pp. 6–8.

23 See, e.g., Kohut, *The Restoration Of The Self* (New York: International Universities Press, 1977: 104–5).

24 Koenigsberg (see note 16), p. 52.

25 Schoenfeld (see note 16), p. 313.

26 It is of interest to note that in both *Civilization And Its Discontents* (p. 90) and in *Group Psychology And The Analysis Of The Ego* (p. 55), Freud briefly mentions the second of the basic characteristics of nationalism discussed in this article. Yet he never relates it to the development of the sense of self.

27 Private communication (letter of 6/6/93) from Professor Stjepan Meštrović, Texas A&M University.

28 See, e.g., the references to Eagleburger and Scowcroft in Walter Isaacson's *Kissinger: A Biography* (New York: Simon & Schuster, 1992) and Patrick Glynn's "Lawrence of Serbia", *New Republic*, vol. 206, 24 February 1992: 16.

29 See, C.A. Robbins, "Balkan Judgements. World Again Confronts Moral Issues Involved in War-Crimes Trials." *Wall Street Journal*, 13 July 1993: A1: "What triggered me was conversation I had with Elie Wiesel, Mr. Eagleburger says.

"He persuaded me that these people needed to be named and that this conduct could not go on. It was my last opportunity to do it, and I did it on my own."

30 Similar motives may, for example, have played a part in the sudden intervention of the United States in Somalia.

31 P. Lewis, "UN Panel Accuses the Serbs of Crimes Against Humanity," *The New York Times*, 3 June 1994: A1.

32 See C. Sudetic, "Rival Serbs are Admitting Bosnia-Croatia Atrocities," *The New York Times*, 13 November 1993: A6: R. Thurow, "Milosevic Retains His Grip on Power in Serbian Vote," *Wall Street Journal*, 21 December 1933: A4; J. Kifner, "In Serbian Election, Nationalism, is Unchallenged," *The New York Times*, 20 December 1933: A3.

33 F. Alexander and H. Staub, *The Criminal, The Judge, And The Public* (Glencoe, Ill.: Free Press; revised edn, 1956: 218).

34 D. Abrahamsen, *The Psychology of Crime* (New York: First Science, 1964: 3).

35 This insight is also expressed by the most famous founding father of sociology, (David) Emile Durkheim, in this theory of crime and punishment found in the *Division of Labor in Society* (New York: Free Press, [1895] 1963). This theme is elaborated in S. G. Meštrović, *The Balkanization of the West* (London and New York: Routledge, 1994).

36 O. W. Holmes, Jr., *The Common Law* (Boston, Mass.: Little, Brown, 1881: 41).

37 M. R. Cohen, *Reason and Law* (New York: Collier Books, 1961: 54).

38 J. C. Flugel, *Man, Morals, and Society: A Psychoanalytical Study* (New York: Compass Books, 1961: 190).

39 E. Jones, *Hamlet And Oedipus* (New York: Doubleday Anchor, 1955), 85.

40 See e.g., Abrahamsen (see note 34).

41 Alexander and Staub (see note 33), p. 215.

42 Abrahamsen (see note 34).

43 See, e.g., S. Asche, "Some Superego Considerations in Crime and Punishment," *Journal of Psychiatry & Law*, vol. 2 (1974): 169–70.

44 26 June 1991, the day of the invasion, is also the anniversary of the Battle of Kosovo, in which, on 26 June 1389, the Serbs collaborated with, and then lost, to the Turks.

45 Norman Cigar, *Genocide in Bosnia: The Policy of Ethnic Cleansing* (College Station, Tx., Texas A&M University Press, 1995: 149) writes: "Mackenzie, however, upon leaving Sarajevo had became a lobbyist and was being paid hefty fees by a Serbian-American political action committee while he was also meeting with the media and government officials. His affiliation with this group should have, at the very least, raised questions about a conflict of interest." See also Roy W. Gutman, *A Witness to Genocide* (New York: Macmillan (1993): 168), who writes: "Mackenzie acknowledged in telephone conversation from Ottawa that his tour was funded by the group SerbNet, but said he didn't know how much he was paid . . . SerbNet later confirmed that it had paid him $15,000 plus expenses to give more than a dozen speeches and interviews in Washington two days last month (May 1993). In his public appearances, including congression testimony last month, MacKenzie never disclosed SerbNet's support."

46 In general, UN actions of various sorts failed to deter Serbian genocidal aggression. See especially P. Lewis, "U.S. Says U.N. Officials in Balkans Lack the Will to Oppose Serbs," *The New York Times*, 2 May 1994: A5; R. Cohen, "Embargo Leaves Serbia Thriving," *The New York Times*, 30 May 1994: A3; C. Sudetic, "U.N. Blocks Air Raids," *The New York Times*, 24 April 1994: A1; M. R. Gordon, "With NATO Set to Strike, U.N. Officials Sought to Warn Economy Network," *Wall Street Journal*, 7 June 1994: A1.

47 W. Isaacson, *Kissinger: A Biography* (New York: Simon & Schuster, 1992: 75).

48 Isaacson (see note 47), p. 827.
49 See J. Darnton, "Thatcher Tells of 1989 Plan With Paris to Rein in Bonn," *The New York Times*, 18 October 1993: A10: "Worried that a reunified Germany would dominate Europe, the leaders of Britain and France took tentative steps in December 1989 and January 1990 to create a British-French entente to 'check the German juggernaut,' Lady Thatcher has written in her memoirs . . . A special concern was over eventual German hegemony over the countries of Eastern Europe."
50 S. Freud, *Totem and Taboo* (New York: Norton, 1952: 156).
51 S. Freud, *The Interpretation of Dreams* in *The Basic Writings of Sigmund Freud* (New York: A. A. Brill, 1938: 308).
52 See generally D. Freeman, *Margaret Mead and Samoa: The Making And Unmaking Of An Anthropological Myth* (Cambridge, Mass.: Harvard University Press: 1983).
53 C. G. Schoenfeld, "Erich Fromm's Attacks Upon The Oedipus Complex – A Brief Critique," *Journal of Nervous and Mental Diseases*, vol. 141 (1966): 580.
54 See, e.g., J. Q. Wilson, *On Character: Essays by James Q. Wilson* (Washington, DC: AEI Press, 1992: 67, 68).
55 C. Brenner, *An Elementary Textbook of Psychoanalysis* (New York: International Universities Press, revised edn, 1973: 115).
56 Brenner (see note 55), pp. 123–4.
57 C. G. Schoenfeld, "God the Father – and the Mother: Study and Extension of Freud's Conception of God and as an Exalted Father," *The American Imago*, vol. 19 (1962): 214, 219.
58 Brenner (see note 55), p. 124.
59 Freud (see note 50), p. 143(n) (quoting Robertson Smith).
60 See, e.g., Karl Abraham, "The First Pregenital Stage of Libido," in D. Bryan and A. Strachey (eds), *Selected Papers of Karl Abraham* (New York: Basic Books, 1953, vol. 1: 248, 251, 257); B. O. Rubenstein and M. Levitt, "Some Observations Regarding the Role of Fathers in Child Analysis," in M. Levitt (ed.), *Readings in Psychoanalytic Psychology* (New York: Appleton-Century-Crofts, 1959: 375–87).
61 See, e.g., C. G. Schoenfeld, "What is Law? A psychoanalytically-oriented Study," *Journal of Psychoanalysis and Law*, vol. 7 (1979): 71, 83.
62 C. G. Schoenfeld, *Psychoanalysis Applied To The Law* (Port Washington, N.Y.: Associated Faculty Press, 1984: 56).
63 I. Kant, "Philosophy of Law," in M. R. Cohen and F. S. Cohen, *Readings in Jurisprudence and Legal Philosophy* (Englewood Cliffs, N.J.: Prentice-Hall, 1953: 320, 322).
64 Alexander and Staub (see note 33), p. 13.
65 See Alexander and Staub (see note 33) generally. See also C. G. Schoenfeld, "A Psychoanalytic Theory of Juvenile Delinquency," *Crime and Delinquency*, vol. 17 (1971): 469.
66 See, e.g., Isaacson (see note 47), pp. 206–7. "*Realpolitik*" has been used in this article to refer not simply to the foreign policy theories associated most notably with Henry Kissinger, but also to what is known more generally as "realism." For in-depth explorations of the realist tradition in American foreign policy thinking, see J. H. Rosenthal, *Righteous Realists* (Baton Rouge, La.: Louisiana State University Press, 1991), and M. J. Smith, *Realist Thought from Weber to Kissinger* (Baton Rouge, La.: Louisiana State University Press, 1986).
67 See translations of news reports in Croatian newspapers about attempts by English mercenaries to provoke clashes between the Croatians and Muslims in Bosnia. *Electronic mail summaries dated 8/22/93 by Stanko Barle.*

68 See "State Department Balkan Aides Explain Why They Quit," *The New York Times*, 26 August 1993: A5: "Mr. Western: 'You can't read through the accounts of [Serbian] atrocities on a daily basis, add them up and see what's happening and not be overwhelmed. It calls into question your morality.' . . . Mr. Harris: 'This Administration has used and manipulated the media and public opinion on Bosnia' . . . Mr. Walker: 'The signal sent to the Serbs was we're doing everything we can, go ahead, have a good time.'"

69 See M. Thatcher, "Stop the Serbs. Now. For Good." *The New York Times*, 4 May 1994: A12.

70 *Old Testament*, Genesis, 19: 24–5.

71 See the references to these countries in Isaacson (see note 47).

72 S. Freud, *New Introductory Lectures On Psycho-Analysis* (New York: Norton, 1933: 104).

7

COLLECTIVE PUNISHMENT AND FORGIVENESS

Judgments of post-communist national identities by the "civilized" West*

Thomas Cushman

My purpose in this essay is to consider in a very preliminary way the cultural dimension of Europe's judgment of the countries of the former Yugoslavia. This task is vitally important, for such judgments play an integral role in Europe's response – or perhaps more accurately, its lack of response – to the current conflicts in the Balkan countries. Most theorists of international relations and practitioners of *Realpolitik* alike hold that the hesitance of the countries of Europe to repel Serbian aggression in Bosnia is purely a function of the respective interests of the parties involved: on this view, France and Britain hesitate to get more involved in Balkan conflicts because they fear expansion of the War, because they fear intensification of conflict with Germany, or they do not wish to agitate pro-Serbian Russian allies.

To be sure, within existing theoretical frameworks that are used to analyze international relations, interests are the crucial independent variable that guide the actions of European nation states in relation to the Balkan War. This is why, as Stjepan Meštrović (1995) argues, the response to the war has a "post-emotional" quality; it seems as if Europe's response is purely rational and not made with any reference to moral or cultural frameworks which should ideally guide Western policy toward the Balkan conflict. A purely interest-based, rational-choice view, however, ignores the fact that actors often base their action on substantive, cultural considerations (Weber 1978). From a sociological perspective, it is vital to consider the independent role of culture in shaping and guiding not only choices, but concrete actions (Swidler 1986, Griswold 1986), even if the latter seem to be purely rational actions or choices. This appreciation of the role of culture in foreign affairs constitutes the distinctive aspect of the present analysis. I argue that the interactional dynamic between the more advanced nations of Western Europe and the newly independent nations

*This chapter is derived from a paper originally presented at the 20th Annual Congress of the International Academy of Law and Mental Health, Montreal, Quebec, Canada, 16 June 1994.

of the former Yugoslavia is conditioned by cultural dynamics of collective punishment and forgiveness. More specifically, I hold that underlying the response of Western European nations toward the Balkans are very real and powerful *collective judgments* regarding both the nature and character of Western European nations themselves and of the new nations in the Balkan region. It is this dialectic between the Western European "self" and the Balkan "other" which is, in part, responsible for Western ambivalence toward the Balkan conflict.

Let us begin with a few basic questions. What do Western nations see when they look at the nations of the former Yugoslavia? Or, more appropriately, how do they judge and assess the identity of the Balkan nations that are currently embroiled in conflict with one another? If one examines the rhetoric of the Western press, a very clear pattern emerges. The conflict is seen as a situation in which "all sides are equally guilty" and are getting what they deserve: these nations are acting in a way which is "tribal," "irrational," and "uncivilized" (Gamson 1995). The very use of the term "Balkanization" in the Western political vocabulary to convey a sense of the dissolution of previously united entities into a hostile units makes it all the more likely that a Balkan country is, by nature, a stranger that is hostile to the Western project of modernity in which the principles of unification and federalism are held to be sacred. According to this cultural logic, the most practical course of action for a "civilized," "rational," and "enlightened" West is to let the Balkan countries remain entrapped in their own interminable conflicts. To help one side or the other would be to "Balkanize" Western Europe itself. In the West's view, there are no victims or aggressors, only combatants in a "civil" war in which each party deserves much of what it gets. In the act of constructing the Balkan other as "uncivilized," the nations of the West construct their own cultural essence as "civilized" and "rational." Thus, in addition to the concrete and seemingly interest-based affairs of international relations, lies a powerful cultural dynamic which not only reproduces the cultural identity of both self and other, but existing status hierarchies within the world-system itself.

As a way of exploring this dynamic, I would like to offer a case study of European judgment of one Balkan nation that is currently at war with Serbia, Croatia. Though it is vitally important, I will leave the question of the European judgment of Bosnia aside. To be sure, the cultural dimension of Western indifference to Bosnia is a continual subject of discussion; the fact that Bosnia is primarily Muslim is seen as crucial to understanding the indifference of a non-Muslim Europe.[1] Yet the Croatian case is interesting because, of all the Balkan nations (with the exception of Slovenia), Croatia lies firmly within the cultural tradition of Middle Europe. In a sense, the West European judgment of Croatia is, objectively, an act of judging "one of its own" yet, as we shall see, it is, subjectively, an act of making one of its own a stranger (in the sense used by Georg Simmel 1971).

As a starting point I would assert that Europe views Croatia in the present as not having been able to shed the central or essentialist identity of its fascist past. As such, it cannot be trusted at this point to join the community of civilized nations of Europe. This judgment, however, has been forged without any clear reflection on Europe's part in its own fascist history, Croatia's anti-fascist movement in World War II, or the degree of responsibility of each European nation for the course of events up to and during World War II. The facts about complicity with Nazis and other fascists by all countries in Europe during World War II are clear. While there were strong resistance movements in all European countries, in virtually every country a proportion of the population supported fascist governments and, knowingly or unknowingly, the atrocities which they committed. The question which is of central interest here is this: *why is the responsibility of some nations "absolved" or "forgiven" while the complicity of other nations is made the center of collective punishment?* The answer to this question offers a preliminary framework for understanding what is arguable one of the most important cultural processes of the current *fin de siècle*: the social construction of the identities of formerly communist nations which are now seeking autonomy, independence, and integration into the world community of nations.

In what follows I explore the phenomenon of Europe's absolution or forgiveness of itself, and its judgment and condemnation of what might be called the Balkan other. My thesis is twofold: I argue that the collective memory of fascist complicity in some of the main fascist protagonists of Europe was and is obliterated and occluded by a socially constructed discourse of a "civilized" and "rational" Europe. Conversely, this discourse is used as a standard by which to construct the identities of various nations of the post-communist world. Many of the nations of Europe – quite literally – got away with murder because they were able to reconstruct their identities by drawing on elements of their widely known and respected cultural past and using elements of that past in the construction of *discourses of absolution*. Such discourses are *rhetorical strategies* which work to reconstruct in more favorable and positive terms the identities of European states that supported fascism. Many of the newly independent countries of East and Central Europe are, like the countries after World War II, seeking to redefine their identities and join the European cultural community. To do this, they must demonstrate that they are "civilized." Yet many of these countries lack the cultural memory and traditions from which a discourse of absolution can be constructed. And because of this, for the new nations of the post-communist world, the tasks of reconstruction, of shedding the past in order to face the future, are quite formidable.

The sociological point here is that European national histories of guilt, complicity, and collaboration with fascist powers are subsumed within a longer culture history characterized by cultural preeminence within the world-system. That is to say, *collective forgiveness* of complicity and colla-boration depends to a great extent on the existence of a strong cultural tradition of contributing to world civilization, the elements of which can be used in the construction of a discourse of absolution of the various sins on the twentieth century. In other words, having done something "good" in the past is a crucial precondition for being able to make claims that a country should be absolved or forgiven for having done something "bad" in the present. As applied to the current situation, this thesis leads us to predict that only some countries, by virtue of their pre-fascist past, are "allowed" to shake off the memory of their fascist complicity – and indeed – reconstruct their identities in exactly the opposite direction.

Consider the commemoration of the 50th anniversary of D-Day which took place in 1994. During the ceremonies, French President François Mitterrand offered a glimpse of the construction of a discourse of abso-lution from the elements of a romanticized cultural past. Even though Germany was not invited to the ceremonies, Mitterrand stood on the shores of Normandy and reconstructed the identity of Germany as a land which was a repository of a great and important culture which had been corrupted by the Nazi blight. The French president urged the world to look at Germany and see not its villains, Hitler, Goebbels, Himmler, and the like, but its heroes, Bach, Beethoven, Schiller. I would like to argue that the *possibility* of absolution from national sins depends fundamentally on the possession of a visible cultural memory from which a discourse of absolu-tion can be plausibly constructed. By extension, one can easily see how countries which seem to lack such "cultural capital" would find it difficult to create a discourse of absolution which would work to reconstruct their spoiled identities. All things being equal, forgiveness of an "uncivilized" past, an essential precondition for acceptance in a "civilized" present, is greatly facilitated by the existence of a cultural past which is worthy of being deployed in the service of absolution.

For purposes of brevity, let us focus on a comparison between two interesting cases. This comparison illustrates in greater detail the selective dynamics of collective punishment and forgiveness in contemporary Europe. These cases are Italy and Croatia.

GOOD ITALY: BENEDETTO CROCE'S RHETORICAL RECONSTRUCTION OF ITALIAN IDENTITY

On the eve of its defeat in World War II, Italy faced the daunting task of reassessing and rehabilitating its identity. More importantly (and perhaps more pragmatically) it faced the task of avoiding the collective punishment of the rest of Europe. Reconstruction for Italy went far beyond rebuilding a war-torn country. It involved rebuilding the country's reputation and convincing the European victors that it was worthy of inclusion again in the community of civilized nations. A principal means of this identity-reformation was the construction of a discourse of absolution. A key figure in the production of this discourse was the statesman and philosopher Benedetto Croce.[2] As the end of the war approached, Croce, in a series of speeches, began the process of the rhetorical reconstruction of Italy's identity and reputation. His argument, most generally, was that Italy was a great European country which had contributed a great deal to European culture and civilization. For Croce, fascism was only a temporary "foreign invasion," a virus imported into Italy by the authoritarian and illiberal Germans. Fascism had corrupted Italy and its long tradition of liberal humanism. This virus, however, had been defeated and, Croce argued, Italy was now immune from the threat of further fascist invasion. Croce promoted the view that Italy's experience was the same as that of the rest of Europe and that it would be unfair to single out Italy for special punishment for its sins. He viewed fascism as a disruption of the normal path of Italian history and used elements of Italy's pre-fascist history as basis for the reconstruction of Italy's identity as a "civilized" European nation. Not only that, Italy – rather than being punished for its involvement in the war – should be forgiven and its cultural traditions should be used to reconstruct a "civilized" Europe. Italy was the cultural capital of Europe and ought to lead the way in postwar reconstruction. The upshot of Croce's argument was simple: Italy really was *in essence* a "civilized" society – perhaps the most civilized in Europe – in spite of its rather egregious and demonstrable incivility in, first, supporting Mussolini's fascism and, then, in allying with Hitler in the war.

Croce emphasized Italy's long cultural tradition as a civilized nation as a means of arguing for the *absolution* of the Italians of their guilt and responsibility for their actions in the war. Croce's rhetoric was compelling: who could resist his argument when presented with the cultural evidence from the resplendent Italian Renaissance? The Renaissance, after all, was perhaps the central defining moment in European history. Who could argue against the positive power of Italy's *Risorgimento*, the period of cultural nationalism and political activism in the nineteenth century that let to the unification of Italy and the demonstration that federalism represented civility triumphant over uncivil Balkanization and particularism. Even in light of its fascist sins, Croce aimed to reconstruct Italy as a victim whose purity had only been temporarily polluted by the virus of fascism. Above all, because of its cultural past, Italy remained worthy. Croce's rhetorical strategy ensured that questions about the relations between Italian fascism and Italian nationalism would never be raised, even though there was obviously a connection between the two.

The most important question here is, of course, the extent to which Croce's rhetorical strategy actually had any effect on the collective mind of the rest of Europe. Italy's post-war fortunes indicate that Croce's rhetoric was quite effective. Italy was absolved almost immediately and re-incorporated back into the community of civilized nations of Europe. It is fascinating to note how quickly Italy was absolved of guilt for its trans-gressions. More than that, the cunning of Croce's argument was that it actually *preserved* Italian nationalism as a positive force which could do battle with fascism and other foreign ideas. Who now equates con-temporary expressions of Italian fascism with historical expressions of fascism? Even in 1994, when neo-fascists won 40 percent of the Roman vote, such expressions were written off as anomalies, aberrant cultural expressions which were, like those of the past, a product of anything but resplendent Italian culture.

BAD CROATIA: A RHETORIC OF ABSOLUTION FALLING ON DEAF EARS

Let us now compare the experience of the collective European judgment of present-day Croatia with that of post-war Italy. In 1991, Croatia emerged from the communist federation of Yugoslavia as an independent state. Croatian aspirations to independence were motivated as much by the nation's dislike of a communist federation as it was by its resentment of Serbian national hegemony in Yugoslavia.[3] A central task of the newly independent, post-communist states of the former Yugoslavia was to pitch themselves to the dominant players in the world-system in order to seek recognition and status in the world community of nations. In this task, Croatia worked rather closely with the major European powers in its plans to declare independence and gain recognition. In spite of that, a common critique emanating from Western European intellectual circles is that world recognition of Croatia's independence was premature. Predictably, those countries who were at one time Croatia's enemies (or the enemies of Croatia's friends) were the first to criticize Croatia's independence. France, Russia, and Britain were suspicious and critical of Germany's intentions in recognizing Croatia, thus evoking in the post-communist present the animosities of the pre-communist past.

From Croatia's standpoint as a new nation, however, its central task was to gain legitimacy and acceptance by the very same Europe which squabbled over European interests in the region and which dredged up age old alliances in the face of independence movements in East and Central Europe. Croatia was posed with a formidable task, namely to seek collec-tive forgiveness by explaining its complicity with the fascists in World War II. Like Italy, Croatia had a past which needed some explanation. Unlike Italy, however, Croatia had been immediately incorporated into the Yugo-slav federation and, thus, moved immediately from fascism to communism. In this respect it was not able to absolve itself since it had moved from one "deviant" classification, fascism, to another, communism. Unlike Italy, and even Germany, Croatia never had the chance to be forgiven by the community of "normal nations," the hegemonic core nations of post-war Europe. Unlike Italy, Croatia could not, publicly and in the Western media and press, separate the perpetrators from the innocent or assess the role of Croatians as a people in the events of World War II. While the nations of Western Europe rehabilitated themselves, Croatia lay buried under the weight of its fascist past as well as the weight of a Serb-dominated communist present. As it emerged from communist hegemony, Croatia embarked on a program of identity reconstruction and maintained that it had been a victim of a whole series of misfortunes in the twentieth century: the Axis-supported fascist Ustasha during World War II, the communists afterward, and, in the present, Serbian nationalistic aggression. Many of the arguments made by Croce in defense of Italy were made by Croatians in defense of Croatia. The Ustasha was a foreign import (ironically, an Italian import only later supported by the Nazis). Communism and its totalizing ideology of federalism was foreign to the Croatian national idea of independence and autonomy. Serbian aspirations in Croatia thwarted Croatian autonomy. In the rhetoric of the new state, all of these things had corrupted a simple desire on the part of Croatia to exist as an independent and autonomous nation-state.

What is crucial to point out here is that Croatia's arguments in defense of the positive qualities of its national character and of rights to exist were treated in quite a different manner than the same arguments made by Italy in defense of its right to exist as a nation and to make a contribution to civilized Europe. Croce's rhetoric of fascism as an external virus was not easily supportable by empirical data. On the contrary, in spite of what Croce said, Italy's fascism was home-grown and supported by the majority of the Italian population. Ironically, there is a great deal of evidence that fascism in Croatia *was* clearly a foreign import, just like it was in Norway, France, or Belgium. The Ustasha was a small faction which enjoyed very little popular support and there is compelling evidence that the anti-Ustashe movement was among the strongest and most committed in Europe (see Almond 1994, Cohen 1992a, Cohen 1992b, Malcolm 1994). What was the collective response to such evidence? While specific research is necessary to assess the position of Croatia in the European collective conscience, I would like to suggest that the discourse of absolution constructed by Croatia did not convince the community of nations which were so crucial for acceptance of Croatia as an entity worthy of inclusion in the civilized community of European nations. Within the context of an unresolved past, any and all Croatian actions, in particular those which could be defined as nationalistic, were interpreted as expressions of some inherent tendency toward fascism. Croatia could not escape its past, because its past had never been adequately explained or absolved or, ultimately, forgiven. As a result, in spite of its independence, Croatia was condemned to live within a web of circulating fictions about the essentially negative identity of Croatians and Croatia.

To be sure, there are a variety of actions taken by the new Croatian state which could be described as nationalistic. President Franjo Tudjman is clearly a nationalist. What is interesting, though, is that in the Western consciousness contemporary expressions of Croatian nationalism are so easily elided with expressions of nationalism during the fascist period. Very seldom did any Western commentators on the new state make any distinction between Tudjman and the fascist characters of the past; instead, Tudjman's nationalism is rather easily equated with the fascist nationalism of the independent state of Croatia. Very seldom was Tudjman's activity as a fighter in the anti-fascist Partisan movement brought up. Nor was his status as a political prisoner in the late years of the Tito regime. Rather, some of the overtly nationalistic actions of the young Croatian state were adjudicated rather harshly and this judgment, I would argue, had something to do with the persistence of the collective representation of the "Croatian as Nazi." One of the most interesting cases of this concerns the attack on Tudjman's (1989) book *Bespuca povijesne zbiljnosti (The Wastelands of Historical Reality)*. In the book, which is primarily a kind of postmodern critique of history as a mode of inquiry, Tudjman raises the question of the number of Serbs killed in the infamous concentration camp of Jasenovac. The purpose of Tudjman's discussion, if one reads it carefully, is to counter exaggerated Serbian claims of Ustasha atrocities, claims which were convenient in justifying all manner of atrocities against Croats by Serbs in the present. While any contestation of numbers of people killed in genocidal campaigns might *ipso facto* be infelicitous, Tudjman's discussion was made even more infelicitous by being taken out of its proper context. Tudjman's body-counting, which was meant to counter Serbian use of past genocide as propaganda to ground their own genocide, was recast by many as Holocaust revisionism.[4] Notwithstanding the difficulty of shaking such a label in the present-day world, the accusation of revisionism could, within the context of the collective representation of "Croatian-as-Nazi," be seen as further evidence of a Croatian affinity for Nazism and anti-Semitism.

There are other examples of collective punishment for events which, while perhaps politically imprudent or infelicitous, were certainly not in and of themselves evidence of a present-day affinity for fascism. One example concerns the adoption of the kuna as the currency of the new Croatian state. The controversy seems to revolve around the fact that the kuna was the currency used by the Ustashe-dominated independent state of Croatia. What is not said in such critiques is that, after World War II, both Italy and Germany continued to use, respectively, the lira and the mark as their currency. If, in fact, the use of the kuna, whose origins can be traced back to the fourteenth century, was an expression of affinity for fascism then why was that not the case as well with continued use of currency used by fascists in Italy and Germany? Another controversy raged about the adoption of the Croatian coat of arms as the basis for a new national flag. This coat of arms was used by the Ustasha with the addition of a U symbol above it. Of course, the new Croatian state struck the "U" from the flag, but continued to use the coat of arms. This was seen, again, as evidence of affinity for fascism. Yet what went unsaid was that this coat of arms was used as a symbol of Croatian nationhood from medieval times and was even used to identify Croatia as a republic within the Yugoslav federation. Such historical facts were never brought into a discussion of the collective judgment of Croatia by the West.

The above are only a few representative examples of a more general and persistent tendency of the West to make any and all expressions of nationalism in Croatia resonate with the negative images of Croatia which exist in the collective conscience of "civilized" Europe. The effectiveness of Serbian propaganda is partly responsible for the West's response to Croatia. Images of Tudjman as supporter of genocide, of the kuna as fascist money, of the Croatian coat of arms as the flag that will fly over new Croatian concentrations camps built to kill Serbs – all are part of the mainstay of Serbian propaganda which has grounded Serbian aggression and expansionism in the former Yugoslavia. A crucial question here is: why is Serbian propaganda so effective in the West? The effectiveness of Serbian propaganda is conditioned in part by Europe's own judgments of itself and its collective judgments of others. Serbian stories about, say Croat atrocities – both then and now – are made more believable by the pre-existing imagery of nations such as Croatia which already exist in the European collective conscience and by Europe's own belief in its own cultural superiority and the inferiority of lesser, Balkan nation-states.

It would be difficult to imagine that contemporary displays of French nationalism on Bastille day would be linked to Marshal Petain's support of fascism in France. No one would think of the French obsession with protecting its language and art from American influence as a prelude to a fascist resurgence in France. Similarly, would the nationalism expressed by Norwegians during the 1994 Winter Olympics be seen as an omen foretelling a return to a Quisling Nazi puppet state in Norway? French nationalism, Norwegian nationalism, and the nationalisms of the rest of the civilized world are viewed as positive, innocuous, or "good" nationalisms, whereas the nationalisms of the Balkans are, *ipso facto*, seen as negative or "bad" nationalisms. An important sociological question is this: why are some nationalisms, to paraphrase Claude Lévi-Strauss, "good to think" while others are "bad to think"? The same argument that Croce used to defend the Italians after the war – that fascism was a foreign tumor which could be irradiated by the splendid Italian cultural past – could not be used as a technique of absolution by the Croatians. This is not so much because there are no "good" habits of the Croatian heart – to paraphrase Alexis de

Tocqueville (1875) – but because the Croatians lack a visible cultural history which could be used to construct a plausible discourse of absolution. The sins committed by the Ustasha during the war remain sins because there is little known in the West from Croatia's cultural history that could be used – in the manner of Italy – to make the argument that Croatia was *essentially* above sin and evil. The greater European collective judgment of Croatia is based on the idea that it is, at its core, a "bad seed," unworthy of inclusion in the community of civilized nations no matter what it does, and therefore worthy of whatever evil happens to befall it.

The real problem with the judgments of countries such as Croatia from the community of "civilized" European nations is that it leaves Croatia – as well as the other countries which are the victims of Serbian aggression in the area – open to further onslaught. For example, Tudjman's recent decision to banish UNPROFOR forces from Croatia will undoubtedly be seen as further evidence of Croatia's inability to comply with the norms of civilized nations. The irony is, of course, that Croatia's intended expulsion of UNPROFOR is grounded in a recognition of the fact that UNPROFOR, the supposed metaphor of Western civility, has actually facilitated Serbian aggression and incivility in the region and created great hardships for Croatia. Croatia will be blamed for any misfortune which befalls it as a result of its rejection of Western civility. All of this would not be so maddening if the same countries who construct Croatia's reputation as "uncivilized" did not obliterate their own uncivilized pasts in rhetorical discourses of civility. Unfortunately, this pattern of collective hypocrisy runs deep in European history: Christian crusaders slew a variety of infidels on the way to fight the Holy Wars. German Nazis paused often to reflect on the great German contributions to civilization made by Goethe, Kant, Schiller, and Wagner even as they slaughtered millions in the name of that civilization (one can't help but think of the scene in the film *Schindler's List* in which the Nazi liquidators of the Krakow ghetto stop to revel in German civility by banging out a Mozart *étude* – or was it by Bach? – on a piano in the apartment of those whom they were hunting).

In spite of all of this selective process of judgment and forgiveness, it is remarkable that Croatia should still wish to be included in a European community whose hypocrisy has been exposed in such a glaring way. Croatia has been excluded from the "club" even though it has persistently met all of the criteria which Europe has set for its inclusion. The only criteria it cannot possibly meet is that of placing itself at the center of European civilization. If what I have said of Europe is true, it might be said that Croatia should be glad to be excluded from the European community, since its inclusion would entail an acceptance of the hypocritical bases of inclusion and exclusion and of selective punishment and forgiveness which guide the interactions and of European nations at present. Yet Croatia's response has been otherwise. As Croatian writer Pavao Pavličić (1994) notes in his essay "Lament over Europe," Croatia cannot itself forgive Europe, but it can at least live up to the best ideals of Europe and, thus, strive to be more European than Europe itself.

NOTES

1 In this sense, no less a figure than Richard Nixon (Nixon 1994) becomes a sociologist of culture in arguing in his last work that if the Bosnians were Christian or Jewish, Europe would have come to their aid. From a sociological standpoint, it is not only interests, but the culture of the other which guides the response of the self.
2 I am grateful to my colleague David Ward for making drafts of his work available to me. The following discussion is based on Ward's elaboration of Croce's speeches during this time. The sociological interpretation of Croce's rhetoric as a discourse of absolution is mine.
3 As two measures of this hegemony, we can consider that Serbs constituted 75 percent of the military and were disproportionately members of the Communist Party, both inside Croatia and in the federation as a whole. See Hashi (1993).
4 For a good example of this decontextualization of Tudjman's arguments, see Kaplan (1991).

REFERENCES

Almond, M. (1994). *Europe's Backyard War: The War in the Balkans*. London: Heinemann.

Cohen, P. J. (1992a). "Holocaust History Misappropriated." *Midstream* 38(8): 18–21.

Cohen, P. J. (1992b). "Desecrating the Holocaust: Serbia's Exploitation of the Holocaust as Propaganda." *Unpublished manuscript* (7 November 1993).

de Tocqueville, A. (1875). *Democracy in America*. London: Longman.

Gamson, W. (1995). "Hiroshima, the Holocaust, and the Politics of Exclusion: 1994 Presidential Address." *American Sociological Review* 60: 1–20.

Griswold, W. (1986). *Renaissance Revivals: City Comedy and Revenge Tragedy in the London Theatre, 1576–1980*. Chicago: University of Chicago Press.

Hashi, I. (1993). "Regional Polarization in Postwar Yugoslavia and the Impact of Regional Politics" in R. Ali and L. Lifschultz (eds), *Why Bosnia: Writings on the Balkan War*. Stony Creek, Ct.: Pamphleteer Press: 300–30.

Kaplan, R. D. (1991). "'Croatianism'." *The New Republic* 205(22): 16–18.

Malcolm, N. (1994). *Bosnia: A Short History*. New York: New York University Press.

Meštrović, S. (1995). "Post-Emotional Politics in the Balkans." *Society* 32(2): 69–77.

Nixon, R. (1994). *Beyond Peace*. New York: Random House.

Pavličič, P. (1994). "Lament over Europe." *Most/The Bridge: A Journal of Croatian Literature*, 2: 5–57.

Simmel, G. (1971). "The Stranger" in D. Levine (ed.), *Georg Simmel: On Indivuality and Social Forms*. Chicago: University of Chicago Press: 143–9.

Swidler, A. (1986). "Culture in Action: Symbols and Strategies." *American Journal of Sociology* 51: 273–86.

Tudjman, F. (1989). *Bespuca povijesne zbiljnosti*. Zagreb: Nakladni zavod Matice hrvatske.

Ward, D. (1994). "Antifascisms: Cultural Politics in Italy, 1943–1946." Work in progress.

Weber, M. (1978). *Economy and Society*. Berkeley, Calif.: University of California Press.

8

ISRAEL AND GENOCIDE IN CROATIA

Igor Primoratz

INTRODUCTION

Israel was conceived, and founded, as the state of the Jews, the Jewish State. Although the majority of Jews live in the diaspora, Israel claims a central role in the life of the entire Jewish people. It also claims a special right, indeed a duty, of ensuring that the memory of the Holocaust lives on, of interpreting and transmitting "the lessons of the Holocaust," and of opposing and confuting those who deny that it ever took place.

This might cause one to expect in Israel a certain kind of response to genocide whenever and wherever it might be perpetrated. To be sure, it has been claimed that the genocide of Jews in World War II was in some respects different from all other known cases of genocide. But whatever the Holocaust may have been over and above being the genocide of the Jews, it was the *genocide* of the Jews too, so that its uniqueness should have no bearing on such expectations. These would be primarily expectations of the state of Israel; but one might also expect a certain kind of response to genocide – *any* genocide – from certain Israeli institutions, and from certain prominent individuals involved in researching or commemorating the Holocaust and transmitting its "lessons".

This chapter is a brief review of the Israeli response to a contemporary case of genocide: that perpetrated in the war against Croatia. That war has been called a criminal war. I have elsewhere described its salient traits, and concurred in that characterization: it was not so much a war in the modern sense, i.e., a conflict between two armed forces fighting it out with each other in accordance with certain rules that prohibit some ways and means of fighting as uncivilized and illegal, and require that damage to civilian population be avoided or minimized. It was rather an onslaught of the Serb-led Yugoslav People's Army – the third biggest army in Europe at the time – and Chetniks on the civilian population of Croatia and all that exists on its territory as a witness to its history or part of what makes its continuing existence possible. In this onslaught no discrimination between combatants and non-combatants, military and civilian targets was made. The Serbs refused to be bound by any moral or legal rules, and systematically committed war crimes and crimes against humanity, including genocide. (There has been some debate concerning the definition of genocide, but that is of no concern here, as the Serbs have committed this crime both on the definition contained in the UN Genocide Convention and on any other plausible definition I know of.[1])

ISRAELI MEDIA AND THE WAR AGAINST CROATIA

From the very beginning of the disintegration of Yugoslavia, the Israeli media tended to take a clearly pro-Serbian stand. This was true of reports on what was going on, but was particularly pronounced in attempts to analyze and interpret the developments. There was no trace of sympathy for the attacked as against the aggressor, for the defenseless civilian population on the receiving end of the artillery, navy and air force of the Serbian war machine, which one might have expected and thought natural. Moreover, an invidious policy seemed to be at work in the op. ed. pages: there was no end to letters to the editor and opinion articles that took a pro-Serbian position, while the number of pieces showing sympathy for Serbia's victims was negligible. I have not done research on this, but do know that the *Jerusalem Post* – a leading Israeli daily, particularly important in this context because it is published in English – which has carried numerous pro-Serbian letters to the editor and opinion articles, refused to publish quite a few letters and articles that expressed sympathy for Slovenia, Croatia, or Bosnia-Herzegovina. Thus it was adding insult to injury when a member of the Serbian lobby in Israel, writing in the same paper, found it "remarkable that of the 12,500 to 15,000 Yugoslav Jews and their descendants living in Israel today, many raise their voices on behalf of Serbia, but not a single one has a good word to say about Croatia."[2]

The activity of the Serbian lobby should probably be seen as part of the explanation. The lobby is an informal one, but is very well organized and financed, and includes some well-known media personalities. Enjoying an uncontested monopoly on analyzing, explaining, and interpreting the events in the ex-Yugoslavia well into the summer of 1992, it employed all the main methods the regime in Belgrade has been using in putting across at home and abroad what the Serbs call "the Serbian truth": flatly denying the facts, no matter how obvious; diminishing the dimensions of the devastation the Serbs were wreaking on neighboring republics and the numbers of casualties; explaining away the reports of Serbian atrocities by the "anti-Serbian tendencies" of Western media or, alternatively, as the propaganda of those who stood in the way of Greater Serbia. The Serbian lobby also adopted all the main tenets of Belgrade propaganda, insisting that the current war was to be understood as a direct continuation of World

War II in Yugoslavia, spreading the Serbian revision of its history, and drawing far-reaching moral and political conclusions from these premises.

In a typical article, the author deplored the fact that when World War II was over, Tito did not permit "mass pogroms [of Croats] which would have drenched liberated Yugoslavia in another bloodbath," and "put on trial only those who [had] perpetrated war crimes." The inevitable conclusion was that the current mass pogroms of Croats at the hands of Chetniks and the "Federal" Army were sheer justice, long overdue.[3]

In another article, we were told that any unpleasant connotations of the word Chetnik was due to Croatian propaganda. Conventional Yugoslav history has it that it was the Partisans led by Tito and the Communist Party who fought the German, Italian, and other occupying armies and their local allies, such as Croat Ustashe and Serb Chetniks, and against overwhelming odds achieved what no one else in Europe could: the liberation of their country by themselves, rather than by the Allied forces. Now we learn that it was Chetniks, not the "Partisans" (the quotation marks are the writer's), who were true freedom fighters. The Chetniks of today are freedom fighters too, defending the right of the Serbs "to stay what they are, keeping their heritage . . . unmolested and together," rather than being a minority in any place. "Surely we [the Jews] of all people should feel sympathetic to this sentiment," the writer says in conclusion.[4] This call for Jewish sympathy and support for the Chetniks was published at the time world media were reporting in some detail how Chetniks were rounding up Muslim civilians in the towns and villages of eastern Bosnia, from Foča in the south all the way to Zvornik and further north, massacring them (mostly by cutting their throats with knives), and throwing the bodies into the Drina, thus repeating the same things World War II Chetniks had done throughout the region.

THE WORLD WAR II ARGUMENT

Throughout, a central theme constantly recurs. I propose to call it the World War II argument. It goes like this:

1 The current war in ex-Yugoslavia must be understood as the direct continuation of what happened in Yugoslavia in World War II.
2 In those years, the Croats and Muslims were on the side of the Nazis, and helped them exterminate the Jews. The Serbs, on the other hand, fought against the Nazis, and helped and protected the Jews.

This is offered both as an explanation of the current events meant to be particularly enlightening and significant for us Jews, and as the argument that decides the moral and political issues for us Jews. The Croats and Muslims were Nazis in World War II, and persecuted and exterminated the Jews. The Croats and Muslims *are* Nazis. Accordingly, they richly deserve whatever they are getting today, and there is no reason whatsoever for us

Jews to feel any sympathy for them. The Serbs, on the other hand, were anti-Nazis, freedom fighters, and friends of the Jews. That entails a "historical obligation" on our part to understand their cause and be at their side today. The indignation, revulsion, and hostility the international community has shown in the face of Serbia's wars on its neighbors does not count here, and must not be allowed to blur our sense of the historical debt we Jews have to the Serbs. The clearest and most consistent formulation of this conclusion was given by Mr. Yosef Lapid, one of the most prominent personalities in the Israeli media: we Jews have a clear and irrevocable "historical obligation" to the Serbs to be at their side and give them all the sympathy and support we can, "no matter what they might do."[5] *No matter what they might do*.

This argument has been used by Serbian propaganda in its attempts to win sympathy and support of Jews in Israel and the diaspora.[6] It has been used by every activist of the Serbian lobby in this country on practically every occasion. Some Israeli politicians have made use of it. Moreover, this is the argument I have been hearing since the beginning of the disintegration of Yugoslavia and to this day from innumerable Israeli Jews, secular and religious, of various walks of life and educational and ethnic backgrounds, including many members of this country's intellectual elite (and that means quite a few persons perceived, by themselves and others, as being deeply concerned with the moral aspects of politics and issues of justice, equality, and human rights, and completely free of any tribalistic mentality). I have heard this from Holocaust survivors too.

Faced with this argument, one might want to ask two questions: are the historical claims true and, if so, should they decide the moral and political issue here and now? Anybody who knows anything about the history of Yugoslavia knows that the historical claims are false – or, more accurately, that they amount to a half-truth, which has rightly been called the most dangerous kind of lie. For every Yugoslav nation had both its collaborators and its partisans. In the case of Croatia, the ratio between the two was particularly asymmetrical: while the Ustashe numbered in the tens of thousands, Croat partisans numbered in the hundreds of thousands. But I want to focus on the second question. Let us assume, for the sake of argument, that the factual, historical part of the World War II argument is true – that practically all Croats old enough at the time to do so did opt for Nazi Germany and the puppet Ustasha state set up in Croatia, and took part in the crimes that state committed during the war, or at least supported the commission of those crimes in some way. Would the conclusion of the argument then follow from its premises?

Even after being exposed to it time and again for almost three years now, I still find the World War II argument quite extraordinary. For what it says is that the wholesale slaughter of *Croat civilians* and the devastation of their country taking place *today* is somehow justified, indeed deserved, by the misdeeds the *parents and grandparents* of these Croats committed *half a century ago*. But how? The idea does not begin to make sense – except if one adopts a certain type of moral reasoning that is alien to modern Western civilization, since it contradicts one of its basic notions: that of individual, rather than collective, responsibility. Since the "discovery of the individual" in the Renaissance and the Reformation, our civilization has held, ever more clearly and consistently, that a human being is to be understood and judged in light of his or her free choices and actions, and not on the basis of membership in some objectively defined group, a fact independent of the individual's will and conduct. Ever more clearly and consistently – but, of course, there have been setbacks. In our century, in particular, there was one world outlook that adopted the view that individual human beings, just like animals, are to be seen and judged in terms of the biologically defined groups to which they belong. That was Nazism, and the Jews of Europe were its greatest victims. Actually, without this collective, biological view of humanity and responsibility, the Holocaust becomes utterly incomprehensible.[7]

Of course, it is this same view of collective, biological responsibility that has led the supporters of Greater Serbian ideology to wage the war of devastation, genocide, and "ethnic cleansing" on Croatia and Bosnia-Herzegovina, to engage in "ethnic cleansing" within Serbia itself, and to impose a system of apartheid on the Albanians in Kossova. And it is on account of this crucial tenet of Greater Serbian ideology and the practices it logically leads to that the Belgrade regime has been characterized by so many, including the antiwar circles in Serbia, as neo-Nazi.

What I still find quite remarkable is that today, when we are witnessing the first case of genocide in Europe since the Holocaust, there should be Jews, of all people, in the Jewish State, of all places, showing understanding, sympathy, and support for Greater Serbia, and explaining their understanding, sympathy, and support in terms of the World War II argument.

ISRAEL'S POLITICAL ESTABLISHMENT

For reasons never explained to the public, since the beginning of the disintegration of Yugoslavia, Israel's political establishment has taken a pro-Serbian stand. In the late summer of 1991, when the Serbian onslaught on Croatia was in full swing, and when, as a consequence, Serbia was well on its way to becoming an international pariah, the government of Israel decided to establish diplomatic relations with it. A concerned citizen who at that time rang up the Foreign Ministry would be told that, as a matter of policy, Israel was happy to establish diplomatic relations with any government that was interested in having such relations with us, and that the matter had nothing whatsoever to do with morality.

Serbia duly opened its embassy in Tel Aviv, and in the Spring of 1992 its ambassador arrived in Israel. He turned out to be Dr. Budimir Košutić, who until a few months earlier had served as Vice-Premier of the Belgrade government. He had been prominent in the setting up of Chetnik authorities in the occupied parts of Croatia and the coordination of their work, which for the most part consisted in "cleansing" those areas of their non-Serb inhabitants by physical extermination, terrorism, and organized mass expulsion. He was about to be elected the first president of the Chetnik "republic," comprising all the occupied parts of Croatia when it turned out, as the chairman of the Chetnik "parliament" explained, that although he was indeed the best candidate, enjoying the trust of all the regional warlords assembled, "the Serbian people needs him at another post, and a very, very important one at that. Because of the influence of Jews worldwide, Mr. Košutić has agreed to be our ambassador in the State of Israel. [. . .] This does not mean that he will not be the president of this republic one day."[8] The sanctions imposed on Serbia by the UN Security Council have held up so far Dr. Košutić's submission of credentials to the President of Israel and the opening of an Israeli embassy in Belgrade. But they have not prevented the Serbian ambassador to the Jewish State from assuming a high profile on the local scene and, in concert with the Serbian lobby and the Association of Yugoslav Immigrants in Israel, which has taken a rabidly pro-Serbian stand from the beginning, doing his best to promote "the Serbian truth" in this country.

On the other hand, the Israeli government has repeatedly refused to establish diplomatic relations with Croatia. In the case of Croatia, it turned out, the principle that had been cited to justify the setting up of diplomatic ties with Serbia did not apply. On a couple of occasions, anonymous "sources" in the Foreign Ministry were quoted in the press giving puerile explanations of that.

In October 1991 the Serbian siege and devastation of Vukovar was proceeding apace; the siege of Dubrovnik was getting into full swing. Israel and Serbia were beginning to implement the decision on establishing diplomatic ties between the two countries. The Jewish community of Croatia released an appeal to the whole Jewish world. It opens by noting

> that the Republic of Croatia, whose citizens we are, is attacked by a brutal military force led by the Yugoslav People's Army; that the innocent civilian population is being indiscriminately killed by armed forces from the ground, from the air and from the sea . . . that over two hundred thousand refugees had left their homes and everything they had achieved in their lives; . . . that, contrary to international humanitarian laws, these military forces are indiscriminately destroying hospitals, kindergartens, old age homes, schools and other social care institutions; that hundreds of cultural and historical monuments of the highest

category, including churches, mosques, monasteries, libraries, cemeteries and Jewish monuments of culture are being heavily damaged or
completely destroyed . . . the latest example [being] the city of
Dubrovnik where the second oldest European synagogue stands; that
the Jews in Croatia and their institutions, their communal and private
property are equally suffering from the same threats and that the
destruction of Croatia, its cities and villages may bring to an end the
history of this community living on this soil from ancient times.

The appeal then rebuts the attempts of Serbian propaganda to depict the
government of Croatia as neo-fascist and anti-Semitic, emphasizing that
"the Jewish Community in Croatia enjoys all rights of a religious or national
minority without hindrance or any discrimination," and that the government had "publicly denounced and condemned all neo-fascist and
extremist ideologies and organizations that threaten the democratic system
in Croatia and its citizens and decided to undertake all necessary legal steps
to prevent [their] spread." The appeal also expresses Croatian Jewry's
"fullest support of the efforts and declared policy of the Government . . . to
build a new and democratic society in which human, political, civil,
national and religious rights of every citizen and group will be protected."
It ends with the following words:

We especially call upon all our fraternal Jewish organizations and
individuals around the world and the general public abroad to
impress upon their governments and international organizations the
need for a just and immediate peace in Croatia based on protection
of human life. We will never forget how our Jewish people was
exterminated in the Second World War in front of the eyes of the
whole world which observed our tragedy in silence and indifference.
We do not want this tragic lesson of history to be repeated.[9]

But nobody in Israel seemed to be listening – certainly not the government.
All subsequent inquiries and expressions of concern by members of
Croatia's Jewish community have been ignored, as was the letter the Jewish
community of Zagreb sent to Prime Minister Rabin on 10 December 1992,
voicing the wish and hope of Croatian Jews that Israel would establish full
diplomatic ties with their country. (Incidentally, to date Israel has neither
recognized, nor established diplomatic relations with, Bosnia-Herzegovina
or Macedonia – both internationally recognized sovereign states and
members of the UN.)

Many prominent Jewish personalities and organizations in the diaspora
have joined the rest of the world in condemning the war crimes and crimes
against humanity the Serbs have committed in Croatia and Bosnia-
Herzegovina. Some of these reactions have found their way into the Israeli
media. For instance, in an article entitled "US Jews Call for Action against

Serb Atrocities," published on the front page of *The Jerusalem Post* on 6 August 1992, it was reported that

> American Jewish organizations are taking comparisons of reported Serbian actions to the Holocaust seriously, and have taken a public role in calling for US and international action to stop the atrocities. "As Jews, we are commanded to remember and we have a historical imperative not to remain silent when we hear words such as ethnic cleansing, cattle cars, selections, concentration camps," said Abraham Foxman, national director of the Anti-Defamation League of B'nai B'rith. "These terms evoke chilling memories and send shudders down the spine of every Jew." The ADL, the American Jewish Congress, and the American Jewish Committee sponsored an advertisement published in yesterday's *New York Times*, billed as an open letter to world leaders. Calling on the world to "Stop the Death Camps", the advertisement said, "We must make it clear that we will take every necessary step, including the use of force, to put a stop to this madness and bloodshed." Some 20 Jewish organizations also participated in a rally in Manhattan yesterday calling for intervention in the Bosnian conflict.[10]

However, with the exception of two Knesset members, to this day no Israeli politician has publicly uttered a single word of condemnation of Serbia. Leading Israeli politicians have consistently withstood all attempts by reporters here and abroad to get them to voice the mildest of objections to Serbia's war of genocide and "ethnic cleansing" on its western neighbors. On one occasion, at the time the media were reporting in gory detail about the Serbian concentration camps, Prime Minister Rabin did concede that there was something to be said about the matter. It all goes to show, he said, that Israel must be strong.

YAD VASHEM

With the exception of "Lapid" (an organization for educating the public about the "lessons" of the Holocaust) and the Mapam Party youth movement, no Israeli political, cultural, or religious institution or organization has, to the best of my knowledge, voiced criticism of any sort of Serbia's genocidal assault on its western neighbors or the atrocities the Serbs have been committing in its course. Nor has any individual prominent in Holocaust research in this country or in the various activities whereby Israeli society commemorates it and tries to transmit its "lessons" ever done so.

In this connection, one might have expected that at least Yad Vashem, the Holocaust Martyrs' and Heroes' Remembrance Authority, would not keep silent. According to the Martyrs' and Heroes' Remembrance (Yad Vashem) Law, 5713/1953, its task is to commemorate the Holocaust, but also "to bring home its lesson to the people." But then, it all depends on just what "the lesson" is taken to be. On this, and on the more general subject of how the Israelis have related to the Holocaust, I have found helpful Tom Segev's book *The Seventh Million*. In his chapter on Yad Vashem, Segev writes:

> What, then, is the lesson of the Holocaust according to Yad Vashem? I asked Arad [Dr. Yitzhak Arad, Chairman of the Board] . . . [He] . . . said that he assumed that over the years a national consensus had developed in Israel, largely independent of party affiliation. Everyone agrees that the Holocaust teaches what awaits a nation in exile that has no state of its own; had Israel been established before the Nazis came to power, the murder of the Jews could not have been possible. Everyone agrees that the Holocaust led to the establishment of the state and that its survivors were at the center of the struggle for its independence.[11]

One might think this an overly narrow conception of "the lesson of the Holocaust", both on account of its ethnocentrism and because the "lesson" turns out to be exclusively political. This conception was indeed questioned at the time of the Lebanon War.

> A few weeks after the war began, Begin responded to international criticism of Israel by repeating a premise that his predecessors had shared: after the Holocaust, the international community had lost its right to demand that Israel answer for its actions. "No one, anywhere in the world, can preach morality to our people," Begin declared in the Knesset. A similar statement was included in the resolution adopted by the cabinet after the massacres in Sabra and Shatila, the Palestinian refugee camps on the outskirts of Beirut.[12]

This particular application of the "lesson of the Holocaust" to the war in Lebanon seemed unacceptable to some Israeli intellectuals, and in particular to Professor Yeshayahu Leibowitz.[13] At that stage, Yad Vashem became involved, albeit against its will:

> For the first time since [it] was built, a Holocaust survivor began a hunger strike there: Shlomo Schmelzman, a survivor of the Warsaw ghetto and of Buchenwald, protested both the war and the use of the Holocaust to justify it. His strike prompted more polemics in the press. The Yad Vashem management decided to forbid him to sit on the institution's grounds, and after seven days he gave up.[14]

Later in the same year a military court was trying several soldiers charged with unjustified violence against Arabs in the occupied territories. One of the defendants was alleged to have ordered his soldiers to inscribe numbers on the arms of Palestinians. The board of Yad Vashem was asked to condemn the act. Mr. Gideon Hausner, Chairman of the Board at the time, "squelched the initiative, ruling that it had no relevance to the Holocaust."[15]

If "the lesson of the Holocaust" that Yad Vashem is supposed to "bring home to the people" amounts to nothing more than Jewish statism, that does explain the complete silence it has maintained in the face of genocide in the Balkans. What still remains unexplained is the way the 50th anniversary of the destruction of the Jews of Serbia was commemorated in Yad Vashem on 4 May 1992 – that is, after Vukovar and Dubrovnik, and after the beginning of the Serbian onslaught on Bosnia-Herzegovina. The high point of the commemoration was a lecture by the sole academic member of the Serbian lobby in Israel, a lecturer in history who has been promoting "the Serbian truth" in this country so enthusiastically that he is probably the only academic in these parts certified by his university, black on white, that the rules of professional ethics do not necessarily apply to everything he publishes in his capacity as a university lecturer in history. The lecture consisted, for the most part, in a restatement of some of the main tenets of Greater Serbian propaganda, including an attempt to rewrite the history of Yugoslavia in World War II so as to whitewash the Serbian quislings' role in the extermination of the Jews of Serbia.[16]

IN LIEU OF CONCLUSION

This chapter is a brief review of the Israeli response to genocide in the Balkans, focussing mainly on the response to what has been going on in Croatia. Part of it has to do with the way the political establishment of the Jewish State has responded to the first case of genocide in Europe since the Holocaust. However, an ordinary citizen is not privy to the complex, sophisticated, and sometimes esoteric considerations by which the politicians and diplomats of his or her country make their decisions and shape policies. Thus he or she may not be in a position to pronounce judgment on such matters.

As for the response of ordinary citizens, the crux of the matter is the World War II argument which, as I said, I have been hearing from innumerable compatriots of all backgrounds and walks of life over the last three years. Concerning this argument, let me quote from the book *How Can One Be a Croat?* by the French-Jewish philosopher Alain Finkielkraut:

> Serbia falsifies the past by saying that the Croats were all Nazis and the Serbs all resistance fighters, falsifies the present by saying that the Croats remain a "genocidal people" and, in the shadow of this double falsification, carries out the first racial war in Europe since Hitler. In a word: *the Nazis of this story are trying to pass themselves off as the Jews.*[17]

Being a Jew, says Finkielkraut,

I thought it necessary to deny the Serbian conquerors the blessing of Jewish memory, and to prevent the drafting of the dead, whose guardian I feel myself to be, into the service of those who are perpetrating "ethnic cleansing" today.[18]

I have given this matter much thought. But I still do not have an answer to the question: how is it that so many of my compatriots have managed not to see "the Nazis of this story" for what they are, and have hastened to embrace them as fellow Jews instead?[19]

NOTES

1 See Igor Primoratz, "The War against Croatia: Salient Traits," *Journal of Croatian Studies*, vol. 32/3 (1991/2).
2 Shlomo Tadmor, "Israel's Perplexing Recognition of Croatia," *The Jerusalem Post*, 14 May 1992: 6.
3 Teddy Preuss, "Goebbels Lives – In Zagreb," *The Jerusalem Post*, 6 December 1991: p. 7.
4 Tadmor (see note 2).
5 Nathan Zeev Grossman, "With Whom Do You Have Things in Common?" [in Hebrew], *Yated Hashavua*, 14 August 1992: 9.
6 See Philip J. Cohen, *Serbia at War with History*, College Station, Tx: Texas A&M University Press, 1996.
7 I do not mean to deny that, to the extent an individual conceives of his or her identity, in part, in terms of membership in an ethnic group – and many, if not most of us, do – that self-understanding generates certain moral requirements: to try to understand as fully and objectively as possible the past of the ethnic group one identifies with, to acknowledge the darker chapters of its history, the wrongs and crimes committed by earlier generations, and, most importantly, to help make sure such wrongs and crimes are not perpetrated again (on this see Jerzy Jedlicki, "Heritage and Collective Responsibility," in Ian Maclean, Alan Montefiore, and Peter Winch (eds), *The Political Responsibility of Intellectuals*, Cambridge: Cambridge University Press, 1990). But this, of course, has nothing to do with the conception of collective biological responsibility presupposed by the World War II argument.
8 "Serbs in Croatia: Oath of the New President" [in Croatian], *Danas*, 10 March 1992: 26.
9 The Jewish Community in Zagreb, "Appeal to Our Brothers and Sisters," in Zvonimir Šeparović (ed.), *Documenta Croatica*, 2nd edn, Zagreb: Croatian Society of Victimology, 1992: 227–8.
10 Allison Kaplan and Tom Tugend, "US Jews Call for Action against Serb Atrocities," *The Jerusalem Post*, 6 August 1992: 1.
11 Tom Segev, *The Seventh Million: The Israelis and the Holocaust*, trans. by Haim Watzman, New York: Hill & Wang, 1993: 444.
12 Segev (see note 11), p. 399.
13 See "Prof. Leibowitz Calls Israel's Policy in Lebanon Judeo-Nazi" [in Hebrew], *Yediot Aharonot*, 21 June 1982: 7.
14 Segev (see note 11), p. 401.
15 Segev (see note 11).
16 Dr. Menachem Shelach, "Fifty Years since the Destruction of the Jews in Yugoslavia" [in Serbian] (unpublished MS). A discussion of Serbian World War II revisionism can be found in Cohen (see note 6).

17 Alain Finkielkraut, *Kako se to može biti Hrvat?* [in Croatian, trans. from the French by Šaša Širovec and Višnja Machiedo], Zagreb: Ceres, 1992: 42.
18 Finkielkraut (see note 17), p. 43.
19 Paper read at the International Conference on Responses to Holocausts and Genocide, Jerusalem, 26 December 1993–2 January 1994 (revised in December 1994).

EPILOGUE

Stjepan G. Meštrović

The years 1994 and 1995 witnessed the failure of the United Nations in its mission in the former Yugoslavia; the failure of the so-called "contact group" (the United States of America, France, Britain, Germany, and Russia) to achieve a negotiated settlement between Serbia's Slobodan Milošević and his victims; continued genocide in the former Yugoslavia; and above all, the heightening of a moral climate that made genocide and crimes against humanity more common in areas outside the borders of the former Yugoslavia. All of these, as well as other failures, were obfuscated with rationalizations that deserve to be called postemotional. Humanitarianism became one such postemotional tactic. In the words of Albert Wohlstetter and Gregory S. Jones, Western leaders continued in 1995 to view

> the slaughters and the systematic driving from their homes of the Shia and the Kurds in Iraq, and the similar "cleansing" of non-Serbs in Croatia and Bosnia, of non-Russians in Chechnya and of the democratic opposition in the former Soviet republic of Tajikistan – as solely "humanitarian" problems to be relieved, perhaps, by convoys of food and medical supplies. They see the conflicts themselves as subjects primarily for "impartial" mediation, monitoring and "peacekeeping" by organizations that include the aggressors and their supporters, like the United Nations or the Organization of Security and Cooperation in Europe or the even less plausibly neutral, Russian-dominated Commonwealth (CIS).[1]

Writing in *The Times*, Joel Brand reviewed incidents which "show a pro-Serb bias in statements by the United Nations and raise questions about its credibility" (7 July 1994). In one such incident, in which UN peacekeepers were taken hostage by Serbs, "captors reportedly roasted a pig and played soccer with their captives" (*The New York Times* 1 December 1994: A8). The Prime Minister of Bosnia-Herzegovina, Haris Silajdžić was quoted as saying: "The situation has become so absurd that we believe there are people in high positions in the United Nations who are helping the Serbs to partition Bosnia-Herzegovina" (*The New York Times* 18 November 1994: A5). A particularly noteworthy incident involved the collaboration of UN Major-General Aleksander Perelyakin with Serbs such that

> the general had allowed a thriving trade in UN gasoline with the Serbs and opened the way for a recent shipment of artillery guns and anti-tank vehicles to cross the Danube from Serbia into Serbian-held Croatia. . . . It is now widely known that the porousness of the United Nations trade embargo against Serbia is linked to the corruptibility of some peacekeepers. . . . The incident appeared to underscore the ways in which the Serbian government, led by President Slobodan Milošević, continues to support Serbian territorial ambitions while professing to have nothing to do with the military efforts of Serbs in Croatia and Bosnia. (*The New York Times* 12 April 1995: A8)

Another interesting case of the UN's pro-Serbian leanings occurred after a French UN peacekeeper was killed by a sniper presumed to be Serbian:

> The UN, apparently seeking to avoid confrontation with the Serbs, said today that it was unclear who killed a French soldier here on Saturday. . . . A first bullet fired . . . unquestionably came from a Serbian position. But, he added, a second shot fired just three seconds later might conceivably have come from the Bosnian government side. . . . This possibility would of course require that a Serbian sniper fire at the French soldier and then, immediately afterwards and presumably without any coordination, a Bosnian Government sniper join in the attack. "It's a very slender thread," Colonel Coward conceded . . . the UN account of the incident, which was in line with a policy that has tended to avoid placing blame on either side for sniping and shelling in Sarajevo, appeared in this instance to defy common sense. . . . Francois Leotard, the [French] Defense Minister, suggested that he blamed Bosnian Government forces for the incidents, even as French officers here were saying quite clearly that the second shooting was the work of the Serbs.[2]

Regarding the supposed neutrality of UN Commander, General Michael Rose, Roger Cohen reported that "officials close to the general say he has been pushed toward greater sympathy for the Serbian position" (*The New York Times* 25 September 1994: A6). "Rose's camaraderie with General Ratko Mladić" (the suspected war criminal) was frequently reported, as well as Rose's great reluctance to avoid NATO air strikes against the Serbs (*The New York Times* 27 November 1994: A1). In a television program entitled "The Peacekeepers: How the United Nations Failed in Bosnia," aired in the United States on 24 April 1995, Peter Jennings put some tough questions to General Michael Rose, including: why did the United Nations fail to respond to the Bosnian Serb shelling of civilians in designated "safe havens?" Why was Rose reluctant to request NATO air strikes against active Serbian artillery positions? The program showed former British Colonel Larry Hollingsworth pronouncing, "Sadly, the Serbs proved time and time again that you can mess with the United Nations and get away with it." Peter Jennings pronounced the United Nations peacekeeping mission in Bosnia – the largest and most expensive in the UN's history – a failure.

We should note that this television program did not mention the UN's similar failure in Croatia: as demonstrated by Cigar in this volume, ethnic cleansing by Serbs against Croats continued in areas of Croatia under control by the United Nations. In 1995, Croatia is a largely invisible victim in the current Balkan War with the media focussed almost exclusively on Bosnia-Herzegovina.

> The UN mission in Bosnia costs the West $1 billion per year, but the UN may be sacrificing lives, money and its credibility for nothing . . .
> if UN soldiers at a weapons collection point cannot stop the use of banned weapons, and if NATO cannot exercise its authority to strike against weapons found in an exclusion zone.[3]

The UN's failure in Bosnia became so glaring that Barbara Crossette wrote an article in *The New York Times* entitled, "Why the UN Became the World's Fair," in which she argued that in 1995 the UN was capable only of holding expensive but overall ineffective conferences, not making or keeping peace (12 March 1995: E1). Similarly, the *Wall Street Journal*'s Anne Applebaum wrote in "The UN Offers Summits, Not Solutions," that

> 75% of the World Health Organization's $1 billion budget is spent on staff salaries, and a large chunk of the rest is spent on conferences, office supplies, and printing (in 1994–1995, WHO will spend $14 million on travel alone). Thus do we arrive at the real achievement of the Social Summit: increased payrolls in New York, more spending on rent in Geneva, more money for conferences in Copenhagen.
>
> (8 March 1995: A14)

As for the "peace plan" offered to Belgrade to lift sanctions in exchange for Milošević's diplomatic recognition of Croatia's and Bosnia-Herzegovina's borders – Milošević consistently rejected it.[4] The "contact group" became divided in 1995 on how to deal with Serbian refusals to accept a plan that would essentially reward their aggression.[5] Russia consistently blocked United States' efforts to get tough with Belgrade and to lift the weapons embargo against the victims, the Bosnian Muslims.[6] According to Morton I. Abramowitz, "Despite protestations to the contrary, the West is headed for a policy that would institutionalize the Serbs' gains" (*The New York Times* 21 February 1995: A15). Similarly, United States Senator, Robert Dole, concluded: "We just give the Serbs everything they want and say we've had a victory" (*The New York Times* 5 December 1994: A1).

Despite the sanctions that had been imposed on Serbia by the United Nations, goods continued to roll freely into Serbia through Greece, Macedonia, and Albania (*The New York Times* 31 August 1994: A1).[7] Because of the "leaky embargo" against Serbia, "leverage against Serb-dominated Yugoslavia is weakening," wrote Raymond Bonner in *The New York Times* (11 April 1995: A3). Fuel for the Belgrade war machine flowed particularly easily into Serbia from Italy.[8] Weapons also continued to flow easily to Serbs in 1995:

> It was well known that arms were still being supplied to Bosnian and Croatian Serbs. News reports from the area have been confirming this *almost daily*. Yet United Nations inspectors continue to report that the Serbian Government is meeting its commitment to halt supplies.
>
> (*The New York Times* 20 April 1995: A3)

In 1995, the Serbs fired banned weapons (including cluster bombs) on civilians in both Sarajevo, Bosnia-Herzegovina,[9] and Zagreb, the capital of Croatia, with no UN or NATO response until September 1995.[10]

Against Slobodan Milošević's claim that he had cut off ties with the Bosnian and Croatian Serbs, *The New York Times* reported that "the Bosnian Serbs have received military and economic support from Serbia" (1 August 1994: A5). According to Roger Cohen, "United States military analysts are aware that the Yugoslav Army is already supplying the Bosnian Serbs, and, in a crunch, would not abandon them" (*The New York Times* 25 September 1994: A6). Serbian helicopters were reported flying into Bosnia despite the UN-imposed no-fly zone (*The New York Times* 22 September 1994: A3).

In general, these and other failures by the West continued to be rationalized in 1995 along the lines that we analyzed in this book: Serbs act out of fear, the Croatian Government is an extension of the Ustasha past, and the Bosnian Muslims might establish an Islamic state in Europe. Whereas the West accepted the Serbian victimization thesis early in the war without any criticism, it began to shift in 1994 and 1995 to an allegedly more equidistant position: all the parties in the conflict must share some of the blame. Thus, when Serbs shelled civilians in Sarajevo and Zagreb in 1995, the response of the West consistently blamed the Bosnian Muslims and Croats, respectively, for incidents which allegedly forced the Serbs to retaliate. For example, consider the media coverage of the Serbian shelling of Zagreb, Croatia on 2–3 May 1995. Serbian killing of civilians was depicted as an understandable reaction to the Croatian Government's military operation to secure a highway in the Croatian nation-state, not as an act of terrorism against civilians.[11]

Both the West's information media as well as diplomats avoided bringing up or dwelling on specific facts which we have exposed and documented in this book: First, as argued forcefully by Norman Cigar, Serbian actions throughout the former Yugoslavia in this war are motivated by the ideology of seeking to establish an ethnically pure Greater Serbia. This ideology is openly and defiantly espoused by many Serbian military, political, and spiritual leaders, but despite this documented fact, the West has tried obsessively to maintain the illusion that Croatian Serbs, Bosnian Serbs, and Serbian Serbs are not acting in concert with each other in relation to this ideology.

Second, as Letica points out, Croatian independence was not the cause of this Balkan War, because early on, the Croatian government granted minority Serbs cultural rights that should have eased their fears. Despite this verifiable fact, the media consistently kept to the thesis that the Serbs commit war crimes out of fear. For example, in his coverage of the Serbian shelling of civilians in Zagreb in 1995, Roger Cohen gratuitously invokes the memories that we have analyzed in this book: "The Serbs of Croatia, many of whom live in areas where their forebears were massacred during World War II, remain viscerally opposed to life under Mr. Tudjman's Government" (*The New York Times* 2 May 1995: A6).

Third, Philip Cohen's argument that Greece behaves as an ally of Serbia still holds true in 1995 and is substantiated by consistent documentation of fuel and other goods flowing to Serbia via Greece.[12] In addition, Greece's embargo on Macedonia over its name and emblem (because Greece claims both in its history) is a distinctively postemotional strategy that threatens the stability of the Balkans. As of 1995, the danger that this Balkan War will spread to Macedonia, and involve Greece and Turkey, still holds.

Thomas Cushman's contrast between Italy's and Croatia's efforts to escape the consequences of their past fascisms continues to reverberate in recent developments. The election of neo-fascists to office in Italy in 1994 drew little reaction from the world. And Italy's exports of fuel to Serbia via Albania – in clear violation of UN resolutions, documented above – continue without any appreciable harm to its image as a democratic, civilized nation. On the other hand, Croatia's effort in 1995 to secure a portion of its own territory was rebuked sharply for violating a United Nations cease-fire. The lesson is clear: Certain nations may violate UN resolutions with impunity, and others do so at their peril.

Another illustration of Cushman's thesis has to do with the reaction of the Pope's visit to Croatia on 11 September 1994. Initially, the Pope hoped to visit Serbia, Bosnia-Herzegovina and Croatia, but Belgrade said it could not guarantee his safety in Serbia and the United Nations said it could not guarantee his safety in Sarajevo. Only Zagreb could guarantee his safety, so he visited Croatia, which brought the comment that his visit was a "one-sided visit to Roman Catholic Croatia that played embarrassingly into the political maneuvers of President Franjo Tudjman" (*The New York Times* 11 September 1994: E5). The Pope's visit to Croatia was enveloped by the Western media in memories of the Ustasha, as discussed in several analyses in this volume. Thus, "during airport welcoming ceremonies, the Pope praised the late Cardinal Alojzije Stepinac, who is condemned as a Nazi sympathizer by many Serbs."[13]

C. G. Schoenfeld's observation in this volume that the British and French governments have used their roles in the United Nations peacekeeping missions in Croatia and Bosnia-Herzegovina to pursue their own, perceived foreign policies based on *Realpolitik* still holds true in 1995. Britain and France continue to block every effort by the United States to even suggest lifting the weapons embargo on Bosnia-Herzegovina.

Sadkovich's uncovering of subtle mechanisms by which the American media is biased in its coverage of the current Balkan War is reflected in 1995 in the fact that the Serbian occupation of one-third of Croatia has become practically invisible in the media, as well as the Belgrade-sponsored oppression of human rights in the formerly autonomous provinces of Kosovo and Vojvodina. The Western media in general and the American media in particular discovered Bosnia as a story in 1993, and has remained focussed on it almost exclusively since then. But the result of this one-sided coverage has been that the ideology of Greater Serbia that involves Croatia as well as Bosnia has become obfuscated.

IMPLICATIONS

Historians will someday note that the years 1994 and 1995 witnessed an exponential increase in the number of newspaper and magazine articles as well as books published on the current Balkan War compared with previous years. They will also note that nearly all of these dealt with this war's manifestation in Bosnia. Silence on Serbian aggression in Kosovo, Slovenia, and Croatia will one day seem deafening. The contributing authors to this volume have attempted to offer a more complete analysis of the current Balkan War by connecting Belgrade's actions against all of the above-mentioned victims, and not focussing only on Bosnia-Herzegovina. Croatia was an important case to consider because of the observation made in the introductory chapter, that Serbian aggression against Bosnia is frequently rationalized with reference to the Ustasha regime from World War II Croatian history. Given that this quasi-historical (and illogical) rationalization is frequently found in discourse concerning the current Balkan War, the *actual* manifestations of the War, including the war in Croatia, should not be ignored.

But what is fueling this Balkan War? Various authors cite diverse causes and aims: nationalism, the lust for power, Balkan tribalism, irrationalism, and Western ignorance, while a few refer to the quest for a Greater Serbia. Most of these explanations are *not* compatible with each other. A few authors connect Belgrade-sponsored aggression against Kosovo, Slovenia, Croatia and Bosnia-Herzegovina, but most write as if these are disconnected events. Most authors are willing to lay the blame for the destruction of Bosnia on Belgrade, but even then, they hedge by assuming that Bosnian Serbs are not acting in concert with Serbian Serbs or Croatian Serbs. Croatia, when mentioned in these discussions, is typically blamed alongside Serbia, and the Serbian destruction of Croatian cities such as Vukovar has been almost completely overlooked, remains unexplained, and lies forgotten. The present state of understanding *vis-à-vis* this Balkan War is, at best, fragmented, disjointed, full of prejudices, and incomplete.

When Serbian strongman Slobodan Milošević ended the autonomy of Kosovo in 1989, and began persecuting the Muslims who live there, the world simply did not pay attention. In 1990, Slovenia and Croatia held their first multi-party elections in nearly 50 years – and the communists lost. Western attention was focussed elsewhere, particularly on the Soviet Union. When Milošević attacked Slovenia and Croatia in 1991, following carefully monitored and democratic plebiscites in which their citizens voted for independence from Yugoslavia, the Western world was mesmerized by Francis Fukuyama's inebriated dream of an "end of history," his term for a capitalist paradise that was supposed to replace communism. In 1992, Slovenia, Croatia and Bosnia-Herzegovina became internationally recognized nation-states and members of the United Nations. In that same year, Milošević continued his attack on Croatia, and also attacked Bosnia-Herzegovina. Academics were still silent, while journalists and politicians were lamenting the dissolution of the Soviet Union and Yugoslavia. Federalists, modernists, and seekers of "order" at any cost assumed that any and all nationalism is inherently evil. Thus, the journalist Misha Glenny published *The Fall of Yugoslavia*[14] in which he blamed Croatian and Serbian nationalisms equally for the outbreak of war.

1993 saw journalist Robert Kaplan's *Balkan Ghosts*,[15] journalist Roy Gutman's *A Witness to Genocide*,[16] Lenard Cohen's *Broken Bonds: The Disintegration of Yugoslavia*,[17] the Carnegie Endowment's reissue of the 1914 *The Other Balkan Wars*, and journalist Zlatko Diždarević's *Sarajevo: A War Journal*.[18] No common thread runs through these works. Kaplan nearly equated what he called Croatianism with Nazism. Gutman was among the first to draw a connection between Serb-run concentration camps and Nazi concentration camps, but he notes that many of his colleagues as well as the US State Department shunned his interpretation. Cohen lamented the fall of the alleged federalism that held Yugoslavia together. George Kennan in the Carnegie Endowment reprint connected the contemporary quest for a Greater Serbia to the previous Balkan Wars of 1912–13. Diždarević blasted the West for its broken promises to Bosnia.

By 1994, the war had dragged on for several years, so that one might have logically expected a fair number of books and articles on Serbian history (particularly its Nazi collaboration), the war against Croatia, and the continued suppression in Kosovo. Instead, as stated previously, 1994 was the year of Bosnia in scholarly and journalistic treatment of this Balkan War.

Several themes emerge in these many books and articles that offer a partial explanation for this focus of attention: For some authors, Bosnia is seen as a microcosm of Yugoslavia, for both Bosnia and Yugoslavia were nominally multi-ethnic states. Thus, the federalists who mourned the dissolution of the Soviet Union and Yugoslavia transferred their nostalgia onto the dissolution of Bosnia-Herzegovina. For others, Bosnia represents a veritable Paradise Lost of ethnic tolerance that supposedly can be traced back to the Ottomans. These authors seem to accept the current, postmodernist ethic of tolerance based on the assumption that the previous, modernist "melting-pot" model of ethnic assimilation has given way to the multicultural "salad bowl" model of ethnic coexistence. But despite this chic new ethic, ethnic intolerance and strife have been documented from Los Angeles to Kashmir, so that some authors have projected their longing for tolerance onto an idealized Bosnia of tolerant coexistence among Serbs, Muslims, and Croats. Still another motive seems to stem from the perception that the Cold War has been replaced by an undeclared war by the West against Islam. Bosnia thus foreshadows Chechnya, and Zhirinovsky's promise to rid Russia of Muslims resonates in xenophobia against Muslims in France, Britain, and Germany.

All of these "spins" that are put on the fact of Belgrade-sponsored genocide fit the definition of postemotionalism that was introduced in the opening chapter. With the clear exception of Roy Gutman, most authors did not focus on the contemporary emotions that are appropriate with trying to put an end to genocide, and projected, instead, *postemotional* interpretations onto Bosnia.

For example, Hans Enzensberger's *Civil Wars From L.A. to Bosnia* depicts Bosnia as a metaphor for "violence freed from ideology" and "molecular civil wars" that he believes have been incubating for some time and will dominate the future of the world, but are "wars about nothing at all."[19] Thus, he asks whether one can compare "the Chetnik with the second-hand furniture dealer from Texas who climbs a tower and begins firing into the crowd with a machine gun?"[20] He answers in the affirmative, that both the Chetnik and the Texas sniper are autistic and feel no need to legitimize their actions. But contrary to what Enzensberger asserts, Cigar and others in this volume demonstrate that the Chetnik *does* have an ideology, namely, the quest for an ethnically "pure" Greater Serbia. The Bosnian War is still fueled and exploited by external forces: by the Russians who supply the Serbs with weapons as well as mercenaries, and by the many Islamic nations that supply the Bosnians with weapons through the black market because of the weapons embargo imposed by the West. Great Britain is still playing the nineteenth-century geopolitical strategy of stirring up the Balkans to contain Germany. And neither the Bosnian War nor other current wars are "about nothing at all." Bosnia is definitely about genocide, which is something very specific in the UN Charter.

Against the postemotional strategy of Enzensberger and others who project chaos onto a situation that we have argued is quite clear (namely, Belgrade-sponsored genocide), the Slovenian poet, Ales Debeljak, offers a position that is closer to ours:

> Within the walls of intellectual centers throughout Western Europe and North America, the high priests of enlightenment spread the word of a new philosophy of diversity, tolerance, and multiculturalism. . . . But those of us who watched dumbfounded as the Serbian masses orgiastically observed the six hundredth anniversary of their ancestors' defeat by the Turks on the Plain of Kosovo . . . who looked on in horror as the vengeance of Yugoslavia's flunkies in the school of democracy demolished a real culture of diversity – we were the ones who learned in the hardest way possible that the masses on Europe's periphery, if not in its heart, don't give a damn for reasoned co-existence in a diverse society.[21]

These Western priests of the Enlightenment engaged in Pilate-like washing of their hands as Yugoslavia burned. Unlike many others, Debeljak remembers Vukovar, and is probably correct to predict that "the fate of Vukovar is, or at least is likely to be, the fate of Sarajevo."[22] Sarajevo will soon be forgotten. "We cannot save the Moslems, the sacrificial lambs of the new world disorder."[23]

Perhaps Debeljak's most powerful insight is that the Holocaust never really penetrated into Western moral consciousness despite decades of consciousness raising:

> In spite of all of the trials in Jerusalem, the "banality of evil," the museums and exhibits, the plethora of newspaper and magazine articles, books, university courses, Nazi hunters, and Elie Wiesel's tales of suffering, it is hard to rid oneself of the feeling that the Holocaust does not have a real place in the European conscience. If it did, the Serbian leadership would not be rewarded for its *argumentum baculinum*, big stick, politics with more and more conquered territory.[24]

It would be difficult to argue against this conclusion. And it is difficult to shake Debeljak's prediction that because Europe did not halt Serbian genocidal aggression, "we will have to learn to live with new values and ideals in the coming century, for our century died in Sarajevo."[25]

Breaking ranks with many authors who blame Croatia equally with Serbia for the outbreak of war, Mark Almond concludes that "Tudjman's government acted unwisely but not oppressively when it reintroduced the traditional checkerboard flag of Croatia," and adds: "Knowing that 'nationalism' was a mortal sin in the eyes of the West, Milošević's agents painted a picture of Tudjman as a bogeyman cut just to the West's favorite measure."[26] But Milošević's agents could not have achieved this had they not realized that the West is susceptible to postemotional arguments of this sort. The authors of the present volume agree with Almond that

> since the outbreak of war in Yugoslavia, the idea that Serbs are the victims of a widely spread "Serbophobia" has been invoked by many Serbs to explain their unpopularity in the world, but Milosevic and his supporters had worked hard before hostilities at fostering the notion of Serbia beleaguered in order to cement their hold on society.[27]

Elsewhere he cites "the Serbs' misuse of the suffering of the Second World War to pillory all Croats as enthusiastic collaborators with the Nazis."[28]

Once war broke out in 1991, the West strove to preserve a federal Yugoslavia by siding implicitly with the aggressor, Belgrade. According to Almond, the West favors federalism and dislikes small nations. Postemotionalism helps to explain how the West is suffering from historical lag in this regard, and needs to be related to Almond's analysis of British policy toward the Balkans from 1804 to 1914:

> If they are worried about their own blunderings in the Balkans, then today's Western statesmen may prefer to take some comfort in the fact that they are repeating the errors of more illustrious predecessors. Almost every mistake which marked Western intervention in the Yugoslav crisis after 1991 can find a precedent in the Great Powers' dealings with the Balkans in the nineteenth century. However, unlike the Metternichs and Salisburys, the Christophers and Hurds of the late twentieth century cannot claim to be dealing with an unprecedented situation.[29]

According to Almond, Metternich sought to preserve the Ottoman Empire as much as Bush hoped to salvage the Soviet Union and Yugoslavia. During the Balkan Crisis of 1876, "Whitehall hoped that the Ottomans would act vigorously to put down the rebels."[30] The connection is that in the 1990s, the British were still hoping that the strongest force in the Balkans – this time the Serbs – would quickly crush the rebellious Croats and Muslims. For the West, it does not matter which cause is just, but who holds the big stick. But if true, all this implies that British foreign policy in the 1990s is caught in a postemotional time warp dating back to the 1870s.

Serbia exploited the West's secret desire for an imperialist power to rule the Balkans by attempting to establish a Greater Serbia at every chance. Serbia did not pull the wool over the West's eyes as much as the West collaborated, in some sense of the term, with Serbia. Thus, Milošević exploited the Kosovo myth of Serbian victimhood to fan the flames of resurgent Greater Serbian ideology – but the West did not object! Belgrade's attacks on Slovenia, Croatia, and Bosnia-Herzegovina were the logical consequence of a process ignited by the Kosovo myth. The West responded by making mediation an end itself. It is still true in 1995 that "No matter how much killing went on or how many promises were broken, there was always another last chance for peace."[31] But Russia's position in the former Soviet Union and Serbia's role in Yugoslavia present an ominous parallel. Russian minorities in every other former Soviet republic have recreated a myriad of Serb-like appeals to victimhood as justification for aggression. Many of the contributing authors to this volume agree with Almond that

> Just as the Serbs were able to persuade or bamboozle Westerners into accepting their claim to de facto control over large areas of Croatia and Bosnia-Herzegovina, in which they did not even constitute a majority, so Western governments and media have completely accepted the Russian arguments about persecuted minorities in Moldova, for instance, as well as the Baltic states.[32]

Russia's oppression in Chechnya continues as of this writing, as does the violence elsewhere in the Caucasus.[33] Thus, as most contributing authors to the present volume warn, the danger of not stopping Serbian aggression in the Balkans is that it has created a moral climate in which Russia will plunge the world into a new disorder because Russia will attempt to retrieve the old empire it ruled under the guise of communism. Russia's nuclear arsenal makes this danger all the more horrifying.

NOTES

1 Albert Wohlstetter and Gregory S. Jones, "Alternatives to Negotiating Genocide," *Wall Street Journal* 3 May 1995: A14.
2 Craig Whitney, "Bosnia Peacekeeper's Death Divides French Government," *The New York Times* 18 April 1995: A4.
3 Roger Cohen, "UN and Bosnia: Why Do the Peacekeepers Stay?" *The New York Times* 20 April 1995: A3.
4 Roger Cohen, "Serb Leader Rejects US Backed Plan for Ending Sanctions," *The New York Times* 21 February 1995: A5.
5 Barbara Crossette, "Allies Split on How to Deal With Serbia Curbs," *The New York Times* 20 April 1995: A3.
6 Barbara Crossette, "Russia Balks at a UN Move to Tighten Serbia Border Ban," *The New York Times* 21 April 1995: A4.
7 See also Raymond Bonner, "US Acts to Prevent Oil Rigs From Reaching Yugoslavia" *The New York Times* 8 April 1995: A1.
8 Raymond Bonner, "Embargo Against Belgrade Has a Major Leak," *The New York Times* 15 April 1995: A3.
9 "UN Says Serbs Are Firing Banned Weapons," Associated Press, 10 April 1995.
10 Roger Cohen, "Rebel Serbs Shell Croatian Capital," *The New York Times* 3 May 1995: A1.
11 See Roger Cohen, "Croatia Hits Area Rebel Serbs Hold, Crossing UN Lines: Risk of Full-Scale War," *The New York Times* 2 May 1995: A1; "Croatian Soldiers Push Into Serb Zone," Reuters News Agency, 2 May 1995.
12 Raymond Bonner, "U.S. Asserts Greeks Avoid Yugoslav Ban: Oil Is Smuggled In By Way of Albania," *The New York Times* 30 April 1995: A4.

217

13 "Pontiff is Likely to Infuriate Serbs," *Bryan-College Station Eagle* 11 September 1994: A1.

14 Misha Glenny, *The Fall of Yugoslavia: The Third Balkan War* (London: Penguin, 1992).

15 Robert Kaplan, *Balkan Ghosts: A Journey Through History* (New York: St. Martin's Press, 1993).

16 Roy Gutman, *A Witness to Genocide* (New York: Macmillan, 1993).

17 Lenard Cohen, *Broken Bonds: The Disintegration of Yugoslavia* (Boulder, Colo.: Westview Press, 1993).

18 Zlatko Diždarević, *Sarajevo: A War Journal* (New York: Fromm International, 1993).

19 Hans Magnus Enzensberger, *Civil Wars From L.A. to Bosnia* (New York: The New Press, 1994): 30.

20 Enzensberger (see note 19), p. 20.

21 Ales Debeljak, *Twilight of the Idols: Recollections of a Lost Yugoslavia* (Fredonia, N.Y.: White Pines Press, 1994): 18.

22 Debeljak (see note 21), p. 23.

23 Debeljak (see note 21), p. 24.

24 Debeljak (see note 21), p. 25.

25 Debeljak (see note 21).

26 Mark Almond, *Europe's Backyard War: The War in the Balkans* (London: Heinemann, 1994): 15.

27 Almond (see note 26), p. 22.

28 Almond (see note 26), p. 25.

29 Almond (see note 26), p. 91.

30 Almond (see note 26), p. 99.

31 Almond (see note 26), p. 289.

32 Almond (see note 26), p. 345.

33 See Neela Banerjee, "Russia Combines War and Peace to Reclaim Parts of Its Old Empire," *Wall Street Journal* 2 September 1994: A1.

INDEX

219